THE AUTOBIOGRAPHY OF
LORD ALFRED DOUGLAS

LORD ALFRED DOUGLAS
from a photograph by Georges Malkine, Paris, 1931.

The
Autobiography of
Lord Alfred Douglas

New Edition.

I 9 3 I

London : Martin Secker

First Published *March* 1929
Reprinted *April* 1929
New Edition *October* 1931

LONDON: MARTIN SECKER LTD.
NUMBER FIVE JOHN STREET ADELPHI

TO

WILLIAM SORLEY BROWN

PREFACE TO NEW EDITION

For typographical reasons, connected with stereotype plates and so forth, I am not able to alter the text of this reprint of my *Autobiography*. I therefore take this opportunity of correcting two not very important mistakes: (1) Mr Robert Ross did not die, as stated in this book, in Half Moon Street, but in Georgian House, Bury Street; (2) a relative of the late Mr Wilfrid Blunt has kindly informed me that I was mistaken in saying that Newbuildings Place, the little Jacobean manor-house near Horsham in which he died, was not a family place. It appears that it has been in the family for two hundred years.

There is scarcely a reference in my book to the man who must, I suppose, be described, even by those who consider that he is overrated, as my most distinguished living English contemporary in the world of letters. I refer to Mr George Bernard Shaw.

The only occasion on which I ever met and conversed with Mr Bernard Shaw was the historic one, in the Café Royal, when Mr Frank Harris tried to persuade Oscar Wilde that he ought to abandon his proceedings against my father and go abroad. Attached to Harris's *Oscar Wilde, his Life and Confessions*, to which there are a number of references in this book, there is a letter to Harris about Wilde by Mr Shaw. In the course of this letter Mr Shaw made some not very complimentary remarks about me. He agrees with Harris in putting the blame on me for what subsequently occurred after Oscar Wilde disregarded Harris's advice. Let me therefore note that these remarks were made somewhere about 1914, whereas in 1908, when I was editing *The Academy*, Mr Shaw's views about me did not prevent

him from being quite friendly to me. He wrote me several
amiable letters at that time, and he contributed to *The Academy*
a long article on the Censorship. Even in the letter to Harris he
protested strongly against the "monstrous" injustice to me of
the suppression of part of *De Profundis* during my lifetime. He
described it as "a torpedo launched at me and timed to explode
after my death." And when during the Ransome trial Mr Justice
Darling prejudiced me by parading a pious horror—which I hope
was sincere—at a very harmless Voltairian jape in one of my
youthful letters, Mr Shaw published a caustic comment on this
judicial disregard of the fair play due to me.

When Crosland came on to *The Academy* as my assistant editor
he put me against Mr Shaw, and we fell out over a notice of his
play, *Getting Married*, which I wrote myself, and to which he
replied at great length in my columns.

All this is old history, but it belongs to my *Autobiography*, and
I refer to it now because a few months ago I wrote to Mr Shaw
about his contribution to Harris's book. I pointed out that it
had done me a good deal of harm, not so much because of what
he said about me (which, compared to Frank Harris's vile abuse,
did not amount to anything very serious), but simply because by
contributing to Harris's book he had conveyed the impression
that he was endorsing and countersigning Harris's malicious lies
and misrepresentations (since admitted by Harris himself to be
as I have described them). By way of a peace-offering I sent
him a photograph of myself as I was at the time when the Café
Royal episode took place.

I found that Mr Shaw had already deleted all the references
to myself contained in his letter; and I have his permission to
print his reply to my letter. Though I am far from agreeing
with what Mr Shaw says in his brilliant and entertaining sermon
(nothing will ever cure him of preaching), I do take it to be
kindly meant and pleasantly good-natured, and I am glad to think

that the twenty-year-old feud between us (for which in the main I must admit that I myself was chiefly responsible) is now at an end.

LE GRAND HOTEL, VENISE.
16th April 1931.

DEAR LORD ALFRED DOUGLAS,—It is a pity that Wilde still tempts men to write Lives of him. If ever there was a writer whose prayer to posterity might well have been " Read my works; and let my life alone " it was Oscar.

It is inevitable that you should appear in these biographies as a sort of âme damnée beside him, not in the least because you were a beautiful youth who seduced him into homosexuality (how enormously better it would have been for him if you had : you might have saved him from his wretched debaucheries with guttersnipes !) but because you were a lord and he was a snob. Judging from the suppressed part of De Profundis (Carlos Blacker lent me his copy) I should say that you did one another far more harm socially than you could possibly have wrought by any extremity of sensual affection. You had much better have been at the street corner with me, preaching Socialism.

However, you need not worry. Your autobiography and your book anticipating the publication of De Profundis in full (I have read both of them attentively) have made your position quite clear; and you need not fear that any biographer will be powerful enough to write you down.

Harris threatens me with a biography. I have deleted the allusions to you in the letter which he used as an appendix to his book on Wilde (in case he should republish it). They were not unjust as statements of what we felt at the time. Your hatred of your father may have been very natural, and richly deserved; but you were very young then; and if you had been older, and unblinded by that passion, you would have made Oscar ignore

the card left at the Club as the act of a notorious lunatic lord,
and clear out before the police could be moved to proceed. Consequently we were all rather down on you at the time. Harris's
advice was sound. And I still think his memoir of Wilde, and
incidentally his revelation of himself (which should have appealed
to your sense of humour), much the best intimate portrait that is
likely to be drawn. It may be unjust to you; but you have had
a very full hearing in defence; and anyhow why should you, who
have been so unjust to many good men, expect justice for yourself?
Are you not wise enough yet to pray God to defend you from it?
Does your conscience never reproach you for the reckless way
in which you exploited Crosland's phobia for calumny in *The
Academy*?

I have been forced to leave many hundreds of letters unanswered
by the limits of time and working power; but I have no recollection of your being among the sufferers. They all have to forgive
me; and so must you.

Your picture has not been sent on to me: I shall find it in
London on my return presently. I wonder is there any man alive
except yourself who would take such a step as a defence against
a diagnosis of Narcissism! That flowerlike sort of beauty must
have been a horrible handicap to you: it was probably Nature's
reaction against the ultra-hickory type in your father.

Ross did not get his testimonial for nothing. Only a great deal
of good nature on his part could have won over that distinguished
and very normal list of names to give public support to a man
who began with so very obvious a mark of the beast on him. A
passage in one of my prefaces on the influence of artistically
cultivated men on youths who have been starved in that respect,
and their liability to be imposed on by mere style, was founded
on a conversation I had with Ross one afternoon at Chartres,
in which he described the effect produced on him by Wilde,
who, in the matter of style, always sailed with all his canvas

stretched.   Let Ross alone: the world has had enough of that squabble.

Roman Catholicism was not what you needed: you should have turned Quaker.   I still hold that Creative Evolution is the only religion in all the associations and implications whereof a fully cultivated modern man can really persuade himself to believe. Unless he can content himself with Marxism.

This time you cannot reproach me for leaving you unanswered. Faithfully,   G. BERNARD SHAW.

Some time after receiving and acknowledging, at considerable length, this letter from Mr Shaw I was rash enough to write to him again, asking him to write a Preface for this new edition of my *Autobiography*.   I received a somewhat crushing reply from Mr Shaw, beginning with these words:

"What! *You* among the preface-hunters!   Have you *no* self-respect?"

My reply to this letter is given below.

35 FOURTH AVENUE, HOVE, SUSSEX.
30th May 1931.

DEAR MR BERNARD SHAW,—You have always been a past-master at confusing issues!   Why, if you could write a long screed (not a mere preface but a whole section of a book running to many thousand words) for Frank Harris, in the course of which you said that everybody except your infallible self thought me "a horrid little brat," simply because I did not advise O. W. to run away *after* he had already begun his proceedings against my father, could you not do the same for me (in a very much modified way) without loss of " self-respect " either on my part or yours?   My book has already appeared in four languages. All I did was to ask you to undo some of the harm you had done me by countersigning Harris's malicious lies and distortions of the truth. However, as you say that I am welcome to print your letter, I must make the best I can of that, and I will send you a proof. Your suggestion that it was Harris's Publisher and not he himself who was responsible for printing a large edition of *Oscar Wilde, his Life and Confessions*, with your name alone on the cover, as the Author, will not do. Harris brought out the book himself without a Publisher. When I was with him at Nice in 1925 he boasted to me of his " smartness " in " roping in " a large section of your admirers. Harris is much more of a crook and a confidence-trickster than a man of letters. In the new (American) edition of his book he has published a very private letter of mine about my relations with Wilde, and he added (or forged) a permission to publish the letter, which was not contained in it. Yours very sincerely,

ALFRED DOUGLAS.

P.S.—Have you ever considered what would have happened to O. W. if he had taken your and Harris's advice and run away after starting the proceedings against my father? Where would he have gone? How would he have lived? Would he have even escaped prosecution? All the evidence would have been handed to the Public Prosecutor, and his failure to go on with his proceedings against my father would have been a complete admission of guilt. How would he have benefited?

CHAPTER I

I WAS born on the 22nd of October 1870, in a house called Ham Hill, near Worcester; my father, the eighth Marquis of Queensberry, being at that time Master of the Worcestershire Foxhounds, a position he occupied for only two years.

My father was a fine horseman, and devoted to hunting. He was for a short time Master of the Dumfriesshire (his native county) Hounds, and this hunt was started by my grandfather, the seventh Marquis, who acted as Master for about ten years. My father was also very fond of riding his own or his friends' horses over jumps, and in his time rode quite a lot of winners. On several occasions he rode in the Grand National on his own horses, but never succeeded in winning the race, though he rode " Old Joe," who won in 1886, in a lot of his gallops, and was anxious to ride him in the National itself.

Old Joe belonged to his cousin, Arthur Johnstone Douglas, of Lockerbie, who bought the horse as a hunter for £150, and hunted him for one season. Arthur Douglas put him in training and the horse, after winning a race at Sandown, won the Grand National, starting at 40 to 1. He won " on three legs," and pulled up so lame that he was at first believed to have " broken down.'

My father at that time was past his best in the pigskin, and Arthur Douglas wisely put up a professional jockey, Skelton, in preference to my father, who nevertheless was rather sore about having been " done out of his chance " of riding the winner of the National.

Although in his day my father was very well known as a fine cross-country gentleman-jockey, and a bold and fearless rider to hounds (most of his hunting was done from Melton with the

Quorn and Cottesmore), he is chiefly remembered in the sporting world as the author or compiler of the Queensberry rules of boxing.

I noticed that when he died, in 1899, not a word was written in the sporting papers about his riding record, of which he was far prouder than his boxing. It is astonishing how rapidly memories of that kind disappear. When I was a boy at Winchester one of my favourite occupations was looking up the old numbers of *The Field* newspaper, of which there was a bound set in our house library, for records of the races ridden by my father in the sixties and seventies. As a boy I adored my father, and looked up to him as a wonderful man of almost legendary prowess as a sportsman and a fighter.

My intense admiration of my father was doubtless not at all impaired, but on the contrary greatly increased, by the fact that I hardly ever saw him. I am afraid it would be as impossible to say that he was a good father as to say that he was a good husband. He did nothing for us boys. When he saw us he was generally good-natured and kindly, but he never lifted a finger to teach, admonish or influence us in any direction. It is one of my greatest grievances against him that he never even taught me to ride. I was taught, after a fashion, to ride by coachmen and grooms, and I had a pony given to me by my father when I was six years old. It was called "The Rat," and my father paid £60 for it at Tattersalls'. It was a rattling good pony, and jumped like a stag. I rode a lot, and later hunted with the Cottesmore from the beautiful place, Burley-on-the-Hill, of my uncle, George Finch, M.P. for Rutland. But as a boy I was rather nervous on a horse, and I never really learned to ride properly and with confidence till I did so in a racing stable (my own) at Chantilly, when I was in my thirtieth year.

My father was entirely self-centred—nay, more, he was utterly selfish—and had been from his early youth used to having his own way about everything. He was in the Navy from the age of twelve to about nineteen, when he succeeded to the title through the tragic death of his father, who shot himself in the park at Kinmount, the family place in Dumfriesshire.

Whether my poor grandfather's death was the result of an accident or not is a point which has never been definitely settled. At any rate he died when my father was a boy, and the destinies of our house declined from that moment with great—one almost might say headlong—rapidity. My father came into a property of about 30,000 acres and a rent-roll of at least £20,000 a year. I don't mean that he had that to spend, but at any rate there was plenty of money. He and my brother Percy, the late Marquis, between them got rid of more than £700,000, and there is nothing left—not an acre in Scotland, not a halfpenny-piece from the old property, which was conferred on the elder of his two sons (both illegitimate) by the second Earl of Douglas—himself the head of the male line descended from the original Douglas, " the dark grey man " so often referred to by Walter Scott (he had no legitimate issue of his marriage with the daughter of Robert the Second, King of Scotland)— our direct ancestor, who was killed at the battle of Otterburn (Chevy Chase) in the year 1388. My father sold the whole property, first the Torthorwald Castle property and then the Kinmount property. Owing to the quarrel between him and my late brother, Percy, no settlement was made, and my brother came into about £300,000 in cash, which was " taken off him " in the City in a few years, and he died in South Africa, in 1920, practically penniless. The unfortunate younger children, including myself, naturally came very badly out of this *débâcle*. We were each left a small sum (less than £15,000) when my father died, and, when the main trunk of our ancient house collapsed, we, the branches, went with it.

It is a fairly satisfactory proposition to be the younger son of a marquis who possesses a large landed property, a stable full of horses, a big income, a huge circle of wealthy relatives and friends, and a large crowd of more or less devoted dependents and henchmen. The proposition begins to lose a good deal of its bright colour when the landed property goes ; and when all the money goes, it becomes, what it has been to me any time these last twenty years, a particularly appalling kind of purgatory.

The lot of a younger son with the courtesy title of " Lord " and no money is indeed a miserable one. I have in my life (for my sins) been through every kind of suffering (ranging from mere acute unpleasantness to the most awful mental agony) ; but I believe the most constant cross I have had to bear is precisely that of having been born, and having had to go on all my life being, a lord without money.

From more than a thousand years of ancestors I have inherited all the instincts of the true aristocrat, the chief of which I take to be the instinct to be generous and open-handed, and to be the helper and defender of the poor or oppressed. To see people all round who want helping and not to be able to help them—to be obliged to refuse when appealed to—is a constant and perennial misery. Whenever I have had money I have always given it away to anyone who wanted it or asked for it, and it has generally been a case of " first come first served "—that is to say, whoever happened to ask for it first or most persistently got it.

When I have had no money to give I have given anything else I could produce or be the equivalent for. I have never, as far as I know, refused to " take on " anything to help either an individual or simply the human race or my fellow-countrymen. My motto has always been " Give, give, give." It has been the passion of my life to sacrifice myself for others, to find and fight for " lost causes " (which I never believe to be really lost), to affront unimaginable odds, and never to admit that I was beaten, even when I found myself, as I ultimately did, in prison.

I am now in a sort of backwater of life and I am able to look back and see my own career as if it were the career of someone else. I have analysed myself and the motive-springs of my actions and I have discovered what I have just set down about myself. I certainly do not set it down by way of self-glorification. Probably I might have been much more useful to my family and friends, and to society at large, if I had merely tried to " get on in the world " and to make friends with the mammon of unrighteousness. I am now merely recording facts. Whatever I have done in life has been done in obedience to an overpowering instinct. Anyone who reads my poetry with insight and intelligence will see in it all that I have said here about myself.

While I, necessarily, believe in free-will, I believe also in the influence of heredity. A man cannot help his instincts and the natural tendencies he is born with. But he can control and direct them. I believe I inherited my desire to "help" from my mother, who was, and is, the antithesis of my father in character. My mother has always lived for others, and has reduced herself to poverty by her generosity and her inability to refuse assistance to anyone who appealed to her. It is an interesting fact that my mother, who, on her father's (the late Mr Alfred Montgomery) side, comes from the Scottish Montgomeries of Eglinton (a princely Norman family, nearly as old in Scotland as the Douglas family), on her mother's side can trace her descent back to Jocelyn, the thirteenth and last Earl of Northumberland. Thus, when my father married my mother, the direct descendant in the male line of the Douglas killed at Chevy Chase married a descendant of the Percy who was taken prisoner by the Douglases at the same historic battle. Consequently I combine in my own veins the blood of the two greatest houses of Scotland and England. Obviously, then, I am quite as "well born " as anyone now living in Great Britain, and I must ask my readers to remember this when judging my actions and my methods of looking at life. I have always had the utmost contempt for public opinion. I began by despising it from what one might call, and what my critics (notably Frank Harris, in his *Life and Confessions of Oscar Wilde*) have called, " aristocratic insolence." When I had had the " aristocratic insolence " knocked out of me by a succession of hammer blows from Fate, I still went on despising public opinion from the point of view of religion, which, rightly considered, is in itself the most aristocratic thing in the world. When I became a Catholic (I don't mean an " Anglo-Catholic," but a real Roman Catholic), in my forty-first year, I was uplifted and delighted to find that Catholics are taught to pray to be delivered from " the respect of persons." I have never had the slightest " respect of persons," and it was a great encouragement to find that I had got by nature what numbers of people are not able to attain even by praying for it. "Respect of persons " of course means respecting persons for reasons other than their virtues. For instance, to respect a judge or a duke or a king simply because he is a judge or a duke or a king, and without reference to his character, is quite un-Christian and quite unaristocratic. Conversely, to despise a man simply because he is poor or unfortunate or unpopular is equally un-Christian and equally unaristocratic.

CHAPTER II

IT was, I think, a great misfortune for our family that we lived so little in Scotland on our own place. The happiest days of my childhood were passed at Kinmount, which is about four miles from Annan, and to this day I sometimes dream that we are going back there. We left the place (for ever, as it turned out) when I was about ten years old, and by the time I was seventeen it had passed out of the possession of the family, and the eight hundred years' identification of the Douglases with that part of Scotland which is bounded on the south side by the Solway Firth was finished.

The other part of the property, the Torthorwald estate, had already been sold, and nothing was then left in the way of houses and land but a small place called Glen Stewart and about two thousand acres, which in turn were sold almost immediately after my brother, Percy, succeeded my father. Percy and I were always particular friends, and were, so to speak, paired off together in everything right up to the time when he went into the Navy. We rode about on our ponies together, our favourite objective being the little village of Ecclefechan (the birthplace of Carlyle), where there was a small shop which dealt in such commodities as wooden swords and gold-leaf paper (most of our games being connected with battles and forays). The estate carpenter, Dunkeld, kindest of men, used to make us wooden spears, and shields on which the Douglas Heart was painted; and a thrust directed by Percy from one of these spears on one occasion missed putting out my eldest brother's (Drumlanrig) eye by a fraction of an inch.

Then came the sad day when we moved out of Kinmount and

went up to London, first to 67 Cromwell Road, and afterwards
to 18 Cadogan Place. My father, even in those days, had ceased
to live at home. He had rooms in James Street, Buckingham
Gate, and we hardly ever saw him either in London or at my
mother's country house, The Hut, three miles from Bracknell,
in Berkshire, which we inhabited during the summer months.
The Hut was a picturesque, rambling ranch of a house, larger
than its name might imply (at a pinch it would hold quite
twenty-five people), which had been run up by Lord Downshire
in the pinewoods as a temporary abode while his big place,
Easthampstead, was being built. At the time when we lived there
" Artie " Downshire (the late Marquis) was a boy about the
same age as myself, and he and his mother were our nearest
neighbours, as well as our " landlords." Artie was an amiable
though rather stolid boy, and he had a positive mania for driving
farm-carts. His poor mother's desperate attempts to induce
him to take his proper part in the elaborately organized cricket
matches in the park at Easthampstead, at which my three brothers
and myself were, of course, usually present, were continually
being frustrated. When Artie's turn to go in arrived he had
generally disappeared, and was found later on seated on the shaft
of a manure cart, admonishing the cart-horse to " gee up."

His cousin, Wellington Stapleton Cotton (who would have
become Lord Combermere if he had lived), was a frequent guest
at Easthampstead. There was a tremendous friendship between
him and me. I adored him, and I think he adored me. He was
at school at Wellington College when I was at Winchester ;
and I remember on one occasion, when I had been off in the
summer holidays to Switzerland (Zermatt) in the company of
my house-master, Trant Bramston, and my great school friend,
Encombe (Lord Eldon's eldest son), I returned to The Hut
and developed mumps just a week before the day on which
Wellington and I were due to go back to our respective schools.

It was a bitter blow to us both when he was (of course) for-bidden to come over from Easthampstead to see me. However, I wrote him a note—dispatched by the trusty hand of Harold, the footman—in which I pointed out that if he could only manage to catch the mumps we would no doubt be allowed to be together for the next three weeks, and I begged him to come up to see me in spite of the prohibition of Lady Downshire and my mother. The next morning he turned up before breakfast, and got into my bedroom through the window. We decided that the best way to ensure the desired infection of the mumps was for him to undress and get into bed with me. This he did, and after remaining with me for half-an-hour he departed " as he had come, an undis-cernèd road," by the window. The " cussedness " of things was, however, exemplified in the usual way, for he failed to develop the slightest symptom of the dread disease, whereas Encombe went back to Winchester and infected our House, who in turn passed it on to the rest of the school.

At that time I was fifteen and Wellington a year younger. The last time I saw him was about four years later, when he came over to dine and sleep from Sandhurst. He was killed at Spion Kop in the Boer War. I have never forgotten to pray for him every night since his death, and I look forward to being a boy again with him in Paradise one day not very far off. (When you go to heaven you can be what you like, and I intend to be a child.)

At home, by my brothers and sister, and by all my relatives, I was always called " Bosie," and the name has stuck to me all my life. Its origin is simply that my mother called me so when I was a baby. Obviously it is just a variation of " Boy," and means " little boy."

When I had been about a year at Winchester my brother Percy, who was then a midshipman in the Navy, happened to send me a farewell telegram just as he was starting in his ship for the Pacific. It contained the words " Good-bye darling

Bosie." This telegram was put for me on the table in "hall" in my House. I was not in "hall" when the telegram arrived, and it was opened by inquisitive boys. When I came in I was hailed with derisive shouts of "Hullo, darling Bosie," and from that day forth I was always called Bosie by the boys in my House, and later by my house-master, the Reverend John Trant Bramston, and at Oxford the name stuck to me, as it does to this day.

Searching back in the dim past for memories of childhood one flits past a procession of the ghosts of governesses, nurses and maids. I think all our governesses were more or less beloved. We were very affectionate and sentimental children. To each other we were always "darling," as much as a matter of course as we were to my mother.

My mother was something I despair of describing. She was so beautiful that just after her marriage, when she and her sister (Mrs Finch of Burley-on-the-Hill) went driving in London in the Park, people stood on chairs to see them. My mother was very fair and her sister very dark. There is an angelic picture of the two sisters when they were children, painted by Watts for my grandfather, Alfred Montgomery, and it is now at Burley-on-the-Hill. My mother went on looking like a girl till she was well over forty. She had angels' beauty, a gentle, sad, proud, tiny, flower-like face and head, with a slim figure like a Tanagra statuette. She was, and is. the most unselfish, the most incredibly good and sweet and kind and patient, and also the most valiant and loyal, woman that ever drew the breath of life. Good as she was, she lacked the one thing to make her a perfect mother, which she has obtained since. I mean that she was not definitely religious. Her mother, the Honourable Mrs Alfred Montgomery, who was a daughter of the first Lord Leconfield, became a Catholic (she was a convert of Manning, who at one time was Rector of Pulborough, close to Petworth, her father's house), and she was (most wickedly and cruelly) separated from her children in consequence. My mother was brought up in the Low Church Protestantism, which more or less afflicted my own childhood, and which was the religion of the *crème de la crème* of society in those days.

I suppose my mother (naturally enough) couldn't swallow it, and so she was not religious and never gave us any very definite religious teaching. We went to church regularly, of course (unless we could manage to get out of it), and she gave us an example of a holy, blameless and saintly life. But even all that does not make up for a real religion. My mother became a Catholic in her seventy-eighth year.

My father, on the other hand, was a professed and crude agnostic, and went out of his way to advertise the fact on every occasion. In fact anyone he could get to listen to him he bored to tears about it, and in the end society, which cares very little about religion but which will not stand being bored, turned on him and avoided him.

But to get back to the governesses. The earliest recollection I have of them takes the shape of a somewhat dour and formidable Scotswoman, Miss MacCormick ; but fortunately (or perhaps unfortunately) for me I did not come under her *régime* except for a very short time. She belonged to the old-fashioned school, and went in for " old-fashioned schoolroom discipline " (ranging from the back of a hairbrush to a cane, inflicted " on the raw "). I have distinct recollections of the first-named form of correction, but I was too young during her reign to experience the second My two elder brothers, on the other hand, had the full benefit of her Spartan system for several years (my mother, of course, not being aware of it). It certainly did them no harm, and as they were both quite devoted to Miss MacCormick I don't imagine they would ever have " given her away." Her severities, which were, of course, well known to all the nurses, nursemaids, schoolroom-maids and so forth, eventually produced a rumpus, and Miss MacCormick fell a victim to the advancing tide of humanitarianism, which is undermining the moral character of the rising generation. She went, not unwept by her victims.

Others followed ; and I particularly remember Miss Smelt, whom I adored, and on whose lap I used to sit while she told me the most wonderful fairy stories, which she invented as she went on, and which lasted for days and days. There was also poor Miss Holland, who took a gloomy view of life, and mistakenly took our mischievous pranks for hostility to herself (and in some ways we must have been very trying, for, with all our senti-mentality and our " darlings " and facile tears we were distinctly rough and occasionally violent boys). There was a French governess to whom we were devoted, Mademoiselle de Soubeiran, and I also remember a Miss Humphrey, whom I loved deeply. Then there was dear Lizzie, my mother's maid, the most faithful, loving soul that ever inhabited a mortal body, and who, though she never was our nurse, takes in our family the place of the "Nannie" of tradition. Needless to say she also reposes in my prayers, with her sister Ruthie. One of the advantages of being a Catholic is that when anyone you love dies you " put him into your prayers " and keep him there ever afterwards.

On one occasion, when my younger brother, Sholto, was five years old, he was for some reason left alone in the house with a specially engaged governess for a few weeks. When my mother returned, this governess, whose name I forget, came to see her, and gave formal notice that she wished to leave at once. My mother asked the reason, and the governess gravely replied that it was impossible for her to remain in the house a moment longer, as Lord Sholto had called her a liar !

To about the same period belongs the episode of the " odd man " at Kinmount, whose duties were to clean the boots and knives, and also to wait on the upper servants in the housekeeper's room. When he had been in the house a few days the butler, a most stately person, addressing my mother, said : " If Your Ladyship has no objection, we propose to call the new man ' the Usher of the Hall.' "

As dear old Joe Graham, my grandfather's and father's huntsman, said to me years afterwards (when I turned up to see him in his cottage in Cummertrees one day, and he instantly recognized me, although he had not seen me for ten years, because, as he said, I had my father's smile) : " They was the days."

CHAPTER III

I WENT to a private school, called Lambrook, when I was ten, my brother Drumlanrig (we called him Francie), who was four years older than me, being then in his last term at the same school before going to Harrow. Percy, being destined for the Navy, went to a school at Portsmouth, in preparation for the *Britannia*.

Lambrook was a very "classy" school, in the sense that it was chiefly populated by sprigs of nobility. Two of Queen Victoria's grandsons, Prince Victor and Prince Albert of Schleswig-Holstein, were there, and on more than one occasion the Queen came over from Windsor to see them and spend an hour or two in our cricket field. But after I had been there about a year a "row" took place, the causes of which I did not fathom till many years later, and the school more or less broke up. I was moved to another school, called Wixenford, kept by a Mr Arnold, and my younger brother, Sholto, went with me. My recollections of Wixenford are nothing like so pleasant as those I have of Lambrook, and to this day I feel sore over the fact that I was, as I considered, "done out of" the prize for "classics" (Latin and Greek), which I certainly earned by plurality of marks, but which was diverted from me to Leveson, now Lord Granville.

Not that I had any but the most friendly feelings towards him. His mother, Lady Granville, and my mother were great friends, and I can just remember the celebrated Lord Granville, his father, and a week's visit I paid to Walmer Castle with my mother. Leveson was famed in those days as "the boy who swallowed half-a-crown." He performed this feat accidentally while giving a conjuring performance to a circle of young friends, and the most dire apprehensions were felt about him for several days.

However, he never was any the worse.   He was a flaxen-haired
and waxen-faced child, and looked like a nice doll.   We were
great friends in those days.   But my chief friend at Wixenford was
a boy called Shepherd.   He was an American, and he fascinated
me by, among other things, his way of talking.   He used to call
me "Puppy-dog"; and Mr Arnold, who was of a sarcastic turn
of speech, and fond of exercising his tongue on his pupils,
discovering this fact by chance, said one day : "What sort of
puppy-dog ?   An Italian greyhound, I should think."   After that,
whenever he wanted to annoy me, which was fairly often, he called
me "the Italian greyhound."   This used to fill me with rage and
grief, and often reduced me to tears.   Why I should have objected
so much to being called an Italian greyhound by my schoolmaster
while I gloried in being called "Puppy-dog" by the friend of
my heart is one of the lost mysteries of childhood which I cannot
recapture.

Mr Arnold, though by no means an unkind man, was to my
childish eyes very alarming (he was very tall, with a black beard,
and closely resembled the picture of Agrippa in *Struwwelpeter*),
and it appeared to me that he had a special "down" on me—though
I must add that there was no such thing as ill-treatment at this
school, and the cane was practically unknown.   I remember only
two boys being "licked" (with a birch-rod) all the time I was
there.   What they were supposed to have done I never could find
out, but it must have been considered very serious.   Mr Arnold's
attacks on me were purely verbal, but I suffered agonies from
them, being very sensitive and also (alas that I must say it !)
frightfully spoilt at home by my mother.   I was a very pretty
child and had captivating ways, and my mother could not, or
did not, resist me.   The consequence was, of course, that I suffered
proportionately more at school.

It is a recollection of this fact and kindred consequences that
always makes me gnash my teeth when I see a spoilt child.   I would

rather see a child badly treated than spoilt. Experience shows
that suffering is good for the soul—a theme which I have
elaborated in my poem *In Excelsis*, which I wrote in prison as
the result of the worst possible suffering—namely, the suffering
that comes from the sense of injustice and the ingratitude of
those for whom one has sacrificed oneself.

What was lacking in my home was a father. My mother's
spoiling would not have harmed me if my father had been a real
father, and had ever taken half as much interest in his children
as he did in his dogs and his horses. As it was, I scarcely ever
saw him ; and when, for the first time in his life, he suddenly tried
to exert his authority over me in a very violent way (I am referring to the occasion when he suddenly ordered me to give up
my friendship with Oscar Wilde), I defied him, and he ruthlessly
and deliberately ruined my life. All through my childhood and
youth the shadow of my father lay over me, for though I loved
him, and had indeed a quite absurd admiration for his supposed
heroic qualities, I could not be blind to his infamous treatment
of my mother, even long before she was driven to divorce him,
which took place when I was sixteen.

I must here explain that though my mother divorced my father
she never remarried, or had the slightest intention of doing so.
I mention this because she is now a Catholic, and it is a matter
of common knowledge that the Catholic Church does not recognize divorce, or really, to put it more accurately, does not allow
the remarriage of either party to a divorce. My father, on the
other hand, did marry again, and his marriage was annulled within
six months of its celebration.

When I left Wixenford I went to Winchester, being then just
under fourteen. I wanted to go to Eton (chiefly because my
beloved Shepherd had gone there), and my mother and I had
quite settled that I was to go there, but my father stopped it at
the last moment, and said he would not have any of his sons turned

into " Belgravian loafers," which was his quaint expression for what he imagined to be the typical and representative results of education at that celebrated school! My father was like that. He knew nothing whatever about Eton, or any public school, having been on the *Britannia* and in the Navy himself ; but his prejudices once formed were as utterly insurmountable as they were often unreasonable.

Winchester was in a transitional stage at that time. Just before I got there it was still a very savage place. I came in for the last year of the real savagery, which, really and truly, was very much like that of *Tom Brown's Schooldays.* There was a boy in our House who might have sat for a model of Flashman. I remember thinking that my parents must be quite mad to send me to such an awful place. I don't like abusing my old school, for which I still have a great affection, but, truth to tell, it was a sink of iniquity. My first eighteen months there were pretty much of a nightmare. After that I got used to the conditions, adapted myself to the standard of morality (or rather immorality), and enjoyed the whole thing tremendously. I went up there a sensitive, dreamy child, passionately pure and devoted in my heart to every noble ideal. I had been brought up by my mother to love purity, truth and beauty. I had a natural taste for the best in everything ; at eight years old I preferred *Romeo and Juliet* and *Henry IV.* to any book of fairy tales, not excepting the still beloved Hans Andersen ; I loved music, and I had been accustomed all my life to be in houses where my eyes rested on beautiful pictures, glorious tapestries, and the harmony of everything that is connoted by perfect taste. I left Winchester neither better nor worse than my contemporaries—that is to say, a finished young blackguard, ripe for any kind of wickedness. Of course I don't mean that I, any more than my school friends, had lost all that we had learned (some of us) at home, but we had superadded to it all that our much-vaunted English public schools can teach. I

B

suppose this sort of truth-telling only makes English people angry, so I will say no more. If anyone wants to know what I think about Protestant public schools I refer him to the remarks on the subject of W. G. Ward (" Ideal " Ward) (see *W. G. Ward and the Oxford Movement,* by his son, the late Wilfred Ward). " Ideal " Ward was at Winchester too, and he spoke, as I do, from actual experience. By the time my son Raymond was nine years old I had made up my mind that I would rather see him dead than at a Protestant public school ; and, though it involved a strenuous fight with my father-in-law, Colonel Custance, I kept him from sharing the fate of his father. He went to a Catholic school, with the result that at twenty-five years of age he is as " innocent,". in the true sense of the word, as I was when I first went to Winchester.

My greatest friend at Winchester was Encombe, with whom I afterwards shared rooms at Oxford. Like nearly all the few faithful friends who went on sticking to me after I got into trouble with society, he is dead. Providence has never allowed me to keep a powerful (in the worldly sense) friend. If Encombe had lived, things would have been very different for me ; and the same applies to my cousin, George Wyndham, who became my friend only in the last few months of his life after completely misjudging and misunderstanding me for twenty years before. It shows the sort of man George Wyndham was that we never really became friends till after I had been " smashed " in the Ransome libel case, which I lost, as I shall explain more in detail later on. Just because I was in the world's eyes " down and out " he rushed in to help me, although he didn't really even like me at that time. Once being my friend he would never have left me in the lurch, as so many others did, including many of his and my own family, who had not the excuse of being able to say that they had never cared about me. I have often felt inclined to put the English down as the most cowardly and disloyal people in the world. I have some excuse for thinking so, for English friend after English friend has betrayed me and deserted me and played me false after getting all he could out of me. But when I get to that stage of bitterness, inevitable from time to time, the memory of Encombe and George Wyndham crops up, and for their sake I qualify all I have said about the English.

I have a stack of George Wyndham's letters in my possession. I offered them to those who were compiling a collection of his letters, but they did not appear to want them. It is rather amusing, because in a hundred, or even fifty, years they will be worth more than all his other letters put together, just because they were written to me. If anyone says that this is rank egoism, I reply that a man of my age is entitled to tell what he believes to be the truth about himself in his own autobiography. In fact he is not only entitled to tell the truth, but he is bound to do so.

I cannot leave these recollections of my childhood and boyhood without a word about my great-uncle, the Honourable Percy Wyndham (George's father), and his wife, my great-aunt, Madeline Wyndham. During all that period "Uncle Percy" and "Aunt Madeline" took a place in my affections which enshrines them for ever in my grateful memory. So many people have written about Aunt Madeline and the magic of her personality, her charm, her charity, her kindness, her genius, that I can add nothing to what has already been written. Uncle Percy in his own way was just as entirely delightful. Though generally supposed to be rather formidable, he was, I believe, the softest-hearted and most amiable man in the world. He was also a man of great intellectual acumen and brain power, and had an unfailing eye for shams and humbug. He was very modest and rather shy, and when at Clouds his feelings became too much for him, in the face of any kind of manifestation of "modern" tomfoolery or heresy, he generally, like the young lady of Sweden, "made no observation," but retired to his study and shut the door. He was full of wisdom, and had the perfect taste which always admires the best and is not taken in by mere passing vogues. I am more proud of the fact that he loved *The Academy* when I was editing it, and told me in a letter that it represented "all sorts of, to me, cherished ideals which I had thought had disappeared for ever from modern life," than I am of any other circumstance connected with my "journalistic" career. The approbation of Uncle Percy more than compensated me for the disapprobation of certain degenerate members of his family, one of whom, when I quoted Uncle Percy at her, replied that the "poor darling doesn't know much about literature," and went on to "crush" me by telling me that Mr Asquith didn't at all like *The Academy*! I assured her that I took this as a great tribute, but I doubt whether she believed that I was serious. I was quite serious. I have never sought or desired the countenance or the approbation of the Asquiths. If I had done so, there would not have been the slightest difficulty about obtaining them. When I had edited *The Academy* for about nine months, my cousin, Lady Grey of Fallodon (then Lady Tennant and afterwards Lady Glenconner), asked me to dinner to meet her brother-in-law, Mr Asquith (the late Lord Oxford and Asquith), and she asked me to bring with me and introduce to him all the staff of *The Academy*, who were included in her dinner invitation. Mr Asquith was at that time Prime Minister, and I violently disapproved of his conduct of the affairs of the nation (especially his Education Bill and his Licensing Bill, both of which I had a hand in destroying). I told my cousin that I did not care to meet Mr Asquith, and the projected dinner-party did not come off.

All this, however, belongs to a much later period than that with which I have been dealing, and to which I must return in my next chapter.

CHAPTER IV

LIFE in those days of boyhood at Winchester and Oxford was pretty well rose-coloured all through, once the first two nightmare years of Winchester were over—a wild " rag " at school and the University, and a constant succession of amusement, sport, luxury and pleasure at home. I think I have put it concisely in one of the sonnets in my poem, *In Excelsis*, written more than thirty years later, in my cell at Wormwood Scrubs Prison :

> For I was of the world's top, born to bask
> In its preferment where the augurs sit,
> And where the Devil's grace, to counterfeit,
> Is all the tribute that the augurs ask.

As I am bound to make the attempt to give a true picture of myself to set against the ludicrous caricature that is to be found in such books as Frank Harris's *Life and Confessions of Oscar Wilde*, and the equally idiotic outpourings of Mr Robert Harborough Sherard, I suppose it is necessary to say that I was, until I met Oscar Wilde in my third year at Magdalen, Oxford, very much like other boys of my class and upbringing. I was, I think I may say fairly, without fear of contradiction, very popular, and had a great many " friends " (I put them in inverted commas because, with two or three exceptions, they all, *more anglicano*, left me in the lurch when the time came).

At school and at Oxford I took nothing very seriously. I learned very little at Winchester, and at Oxford I acquired only a certain amount of knowledge more or less by accident and because, although I neglected the work I was supposed to be doing, I did indulge in a great amount of miscellaneous reading. I was never any good as a cricketer, and though I was fairly good at football I never could take games as seriously as the average English boy takes them ; but I was a good runner, and only the bad luck of being ill prevented me from doing well in the sports in my last year at Winchester. I won the school steeplechase (two and a half miles across country) when I was sixteen, in 1887, and I feel pretty sure that I would have won it again from scratch the next year — my last — if I had been able to run ; but unfortunately I was in bed with a bad cold, and unable to compete in that event, and my illness ruined my hopes in the mile, where I would have stood a good chance.

At Oxford I won the two-miles race at the Magdalen College sports, after being second the year before, and I also won the mile handicap. I won these events quite untrained, and if there had been in those days anyone whatever to take interest in me, from a running point of view, I would have undoubtedly made a good show as a three-miler, and might have got my " blue." As it was, I threw away my chances on the only occasion on which I ran in the 'Varsity sports (in the three miles) by running with a plaster bandage round my left knee. Although I was not properly trained I fancied myself to win the three miles, and I had privately tested myself to be, as I thought, good enough to win it. But, as evil fate would have it, on the day before the race a friend of mine who was with me on the running-track pointed out, what I had scarcely noticed before, that I had a slightly swollen vein behind my left knee. I went the next day and showed it to a doctor, and he assured me that it was of no consequence, and did not amount to a varicose vein, but at the same time he said he could " fix me up with a bandage " which would make it perfectly safe to run. He accordingly encased my knee in a stiff plaster. It seems almost incredible that he should have been such a fool, and that I myself should have been such a fool as not to realize that the result of this bandage round my knee was to shorten my stride and put a frightful handicap on me.

I ran in the three miles, and after going just over two miles, and finding that I could scarcely keep my place—about fourth—and that I was twenty-five yards behind the leader, and ultimate winner, I dropped out utterly puzzled and disheartened. At the time I could not understand it, as I knew my form in this race was "too bad to be true." But I was so upset and so disgusted (I had told a few of my friends that I was going to win) that I gave up running from that day forth. It was not till years afterwards that it occurred to me that this wretched bandage was the cause of my discomfiture. I do not, of course, say that I would certainly have won the race without the bandage, but I had run a trial three miles about a week before with a man who had his "blue" for three miles, and I had beaten him very easily by quite a hundred yards; so, obviously, if I had run my true form I should have been "there or thereabouts" at the finish.

I suppose at my age I can talk about my personal appearance in my youth without being denounced for vanity. Frank Harris, in his self-admitted perversion of the truth (as far as I am concerned) entitled, *The Life and Confessions of Oscar Wilde,* says that at the time when he (Harris) first met me, which was in my twenty-fourth year, I was "pretty in a girlish way." This, of course, is the merest malice. There was nothing then, nor has there ever been, anything in the least effeminate about either my appearance or my manners. After all, there is plenty of evidence on this point—the evidence of numerous photographs and pictures, and eye-witnesses by the hundred. There can be no object in pretending that I was not rather exceptionally good-looking as a boy, and it is a fact that I went on preserving my looks and youthful appearance in a truly remarkable way right up till the time I reached the forties. Two years after the Wilde affair, when I was in my twenty-seventh year, I happened to be in Monte Carlo for a few days with my mother. I went to the Casino, and was refused admission on the ground that I was too young to go into the gambling-rooms, the rule being that no one under twenty-one years can be admitted. After arguing vainly for some time with several polite officials, I finally went off and found my mother. She accompanied me back to the Casino, and, producing her card, assured the head official that I was her son, and that I was nearly twenty-seven. The official thereupon gave me a card of admission, with many apologies, saying : " I hope, *milord*, you will excuse me, but I have a son of sixteen, and he looks much older than you do." It is curious that when I went to the Casino two years before, in company with Oscar Wilde, just before his prosecution of my father, I was admitted without question, although I was then only in my twenty-fifth year.

Right up to my fortieth year I could at any time have passed for a boy if I had wished to do so, and in fact I have often done it just for a joke. All I required as a preliminary was a week or ten days' shooting and hard walking in Scotland, or a few gallops or other form of strenuous exercise to clear my eye and get a good colour. With this preparation I would have undertaken to bet that I could go down to Winchester, put on a school straw hat and pass entirely unnoticed as a schoolboy among a group of schoolboys. When I was thirty-one, and owned a racing stable at Chantilly, I was one day playing the piano in the drawing-room of the Hotel Condé, where I was then living, when the old French Baronne de Rothschild came into the room. I stopped my very imperfect execution of Chopin's *First Polonaise*, and got up. Whereupon the dear old lady begged me to go on playing, and, entering into conversation with me, complimented me on my French accent and asked me if I was at school in France !

It was just about that time that I first met my wife, then Miss Olive Custance, and we were married a year later. She can confirm what I have written about my appearance at that time and the fact that it scarcely changed during the next ten years.

I am obliged to go into all this because I am now approaching the most difficult and embarrassing part of my task in writing these memoirs. I mean my association with Oscar Wilde. Anyone who knows anything about life as it really is in England at school, at the University, and later, and who is not a party to the hypocritical wholesale lying and suppression of the truth which up till quite lately was *de rigueur* on this sort of question, will know that, my appearance being what it was, I was exactly the type which attracts boys and men quite as much as it attracts women and girls.

I decline to go on sticking to the convention which has hitherto forced me to suppress the truth. I did it in a former book, because I was then advised by the man who helped me to write it (T. W. H. Crosland, to wit) that to do otherwise would be equal to committing suicide. I have already told the truth about this matter in the witness-box, which is the most public confessional in the world, and I am going to tell it once more in this book, just as I wanted to do when I wrote my book, *Oscar Wilde and Myself*, in 1914. I was persuaded not to tell the whole truth then, but now I am much surer of my ground, and I am convinced that nothing but truth can serve me.

When I was at school, as I have already indicated, I learned, after much initial repugnance and resistance, to do what everybody else did. By the time I was in my last year at Winchester I was neither better nor worse than the other boys in my House. My moral sense had been completely destroyed, and as to religion, it simply did not exist in my day at Winchester. To say that it was treated as a joke would be a euphemism. It was treated with utter contempt, ridicule and blasphemy. There was a picture of

The Last Supper (a reproduction of Da Vinci's picture) hanging over the "high table" in the dining-room of our House. One of the boys who was a prefect, and certainly the most powerful and influential boy in the House (he was in " Commoner Six" at football and in the school eleven), used to make a practice of hurling a piece of bread at this picture every time he came in to tea (there being then no master present), his object being to hit the figure of Our Lord. I give this as a comparatively mild instance of the attitude towards sacred things that existed ; and in this connection I may refer back once more to " Ideal" Ward, whose son, the late Mr Wilfred Ward, quotes his father as saying about the Winchester of his day : " It is impossible to conceive anything more like hell." I am inclined to say ditto.

When I was a boy at Winchester and at Oxford I had many fine friendships, perfectly normal, wholesome, and not in the least sentimental. Such was my friendship with Encombe, which lasted till he died, at the age of twenty-nine. I had other friendships which were sentimental and passionate, but perfectly pure and innocent. Such was my friendship with Wellington Cotton. I had others again which were neither pure nor innocent. But if it is to be assumed from this that I was "abnormal" or "degenerate" or exceptionally wicked, then it must also be assumed that at least ninety per cent. of my contemporaries at Winchester and Oxford were the same. I cannot consent to tell the truth about myself without also telling it about other people, though I shall be careful not to mention names. There is nothing more dangerous and more certain to expose one to violent abuse and hatred than to tell the truth in England, even in the witness-box, when one has sworn on the Bible before God to tell " the truth, the whole truth, and nothing but the truth."

But to get back to my boyhood and youth, I say once for all that I was not at all abnormal or degenerate. I was perfectly healthy and natural, and to quote the words in the witness-box of my family doctor, whom I called as a witness in my libel action against *The Evening News*, " above the average, both mentally and physically." Fifty thousand other boys might have done (and did as a fact do) exactly what I did, but, unlike me, they have not been compelled by a cruel fate to act the lifelong part of a scapegoat, and bear the whole force of all the concentrated hypocrisy and sham virtue which, in these matters, has made England a byword among the nations of the world any time during the last three hundred years.

It is an outrage that I should be obliged at my age, after being married for twenty-six years, and with a son of twenty-five, to put all this into print. If I had been treated, I will not say fairly, but with the remotest approach to humanity and decency, it should never have become necessary. No other living creature has been treated as I have been treated, and has invoked in vain, as I have done, the law of his country to help him against a conspiracy of persecution and blackmail which has gone on for more than thirty years, and is still going on to this day.

CHAPTER V

I HOPE that no reader of what I have just written will imagine that I am defending vice. I am not defending it. I hate and loathe it, and I venture to say that I have more right to stand up in the face of the world and say so than most men. I bitterly resent that I was robbed of my virtue and my innocence in my helpless boyhood, by being put into a community which one of its own most distinguished sons compared to hell. If I had escaped untarnished from Winchester and Oxford it would have been a miracle, and I would have been a saint. On the other hand, if I had been born a Catholic, or had become one in early childhood, it is a thousand to one that I would have passed unscathed through the same period. That is what I mean when I say that I bitterly resent what happened.

The real truth is, of course, that the sort of things boys do at school and college, and that Oscar Wilde and thousands of others go on doing all their lives, are contrary to Christian ethics, but not to pagan ethics. I do not mean that even in classic Greece they were not condemned by the very highest minds, but they were, at the worst, regarded as venial offences, and did not provoke any of that horror and consternation which they are supposed to provoke in this country. But if England is practically to-day a pagan country (and statistics as to the number of church-goers prove that she is), what right has she to pose as aghast at pagan habits? None whatever. When she has returned to the Faith of her fathers, on which for commercial and other ignoble reasons she turned her back at the so-called Reformation, it will be time enough for her to endeavour to get back into the true Catholic attitude towards sin which she has repudiated and denied.

As things are at present, the attitude of the average Englishman on this point is not only hypocritical but absurd. If he really feels such horror at the practices in question, why does he pitchfork his children at the tender age of twelve to fourteen into the very places where they are practically certain to learn them ? Why are boys brought up to read the classic authors, including the *Eclogues of Virgil*, not excepting (as Byron says)

> . . . that horrid 'un
> Beginning with *formosum pastor Corydon* ?

Why were we at Oxford taught to read Plato and to regard the *Symposium* as a magnificent work ? (I am quite aware of course that in the *Symposium* Socrates is on the side of purity, but there is nothing of the "unmentionable" attitude in the dialogue towards what the Englishman pretends to regard with such horror.) One is forced to the conclusion that what England really feels about it is summed up in the one word "Hypocrisy." "Do what you like, it really doesn't matter in the least, we all do it at one time or another of our lives, but we must never admit it, and at all costs we must keep up the attitude of amazed horror at any open manifestation of it in others that comes before us in our official capacity." Well, to paraphrase "Ideal" Ward again, is it possible to conceive anything more like hell than such an attitude ?

When I said at the beginning of this chapter that I had more right than most men to stand up in the face of the world and say that I hate and loathe vice (and particularly this vice) I said something which calls for explanation. Well, here is the explanation.

I take it that no one has a right to condemn others for a vice which he practises himself. Anyone will agree to that proposition, I suppose. I will go a great deal further and say that no one who is not entirely chaste has any right to condemn others for any form of impurity. I would not have dared to write this book, and to tell the truth about myself, if I could not say that I have been absolutely chaste, as I have been, for more than fourteen years, and that I intend to remain in the same condition up till the day of my death. I ceased to have any part or lot in the Oscar Wilde business at least twenty-six years ago, when I married. But that in itself would not give me any right to condemn others. Far from it. Later, when, after my wife had left me, just before the trial of the Ransome action, I was alone in the world, I had the choice of leading an immoral life or conforming to the strict Catholic ideal of absolute purity. For about two months after my wife left me, about fourteen years ago, I lived with a very beautiful girl, who sought me out because she was sorry for me and thought I had been brutally treated. I had already been a Catholic then for about eighteen months, and I knew I was committing and persisting in "mortal sin" by what I did.

My conscience gave me no peace till I finally broke off the affair, and from that day I have lived absolutely chaste (except for two lapses in the first year) and have, as I put it in my poem *In Excelsis*, recaptured my innocence :

> And if, disvouching then my angel's voice,
> I could, by natural spirit, so out-face
> The frowning world and its proclaimed offence
> Against my friend. Shall I not more rejoice
> To hate and brave it now, bestead by Grace
> And my long since recaptured innocence ?

And even this does not give me the right to condemn others. I see that now, though at one time I thought it did. There was a time, when I went after Robert Ross (as I was fully justified in doing in self-defence and to right a great wrong), when I succeeded,

I fear, in " kidding myself " into believing that I was carrying on a sort of purity crusade. The attitude is reflected in some of my *Satires* and in the book, *Oscar Wilde and Myself*, which I wrote with Crosland. I wish to repudiate that attitude here and now. It is not for me to condemn or judge anyone else. But I do repeat that I have now a better right than most men to say that I hate and loathe every form of sexual vice, because it is the literal truth that I would far rather die any day than indulge in any such vice ; and though I do not doubt that there are plenty of virtuous and unmarried men in this country who could say the same (there is, for example, the whole body of the Catholic priesthood) I feel perfectly certain that they are in a very small minority.

It is, I hope, scarcely necessary for me to say that I am not going into all these intimate details about my private life with any idea of holding myself up to admiration as a reformed rake. The fact is that I am forced to do it because of the lies that have been told about me, and because it would be impossible for me to tell what I have set out to tell, at whatever cost to my own feelings, without explaining exactly how I stand. If I refer, as I have done and am going to do again, to " affairs " with women, it is most emphatically not from the complacent point of view adopted by gentlemen like Mr George Moore and Mr Frank Harris. I am so far from being proud of such adventures that I am ashamed of them, and it gives me great pain to have to mention them. But I am trying to show that I was simply just like other young men of my class and education, and not any kind of monster remotely resembling what some of my enemies have tried to make me out.

From a Catholic point of view of course I *was* very wicked. I am quite ready to admit that, provided it is accepted that ninety per cent. of my contemporaries were exactly the same. I will cheerfully submit to be condemned (and afterwards freely pardoned, as I have been years ago) by the Church of Christ, but I utterly decline to do penance before—shall we say?—Mr Justice Darling, or any of the numerous "deadly cross-examiners" who have cross-examined me at various times on the instructions of the late Sir George Lewis.

CHAPTER VI

PERHAPS someone may say : "What is it that you complain of ? Do you suggest that judges and lawyers ought not to adopt an attitude of reprehension towards these vices which you yourself admit to be horrible ?" I reply that I do not complain that judges and advocates should adopt such an attitude, but I do complain most bitterly that a man who is living a perfectly good and proper life with his wife and child, who, in the face of great odds, had established a commanding position in the world of poetry and letters, and who for twelve years has done everything possible to live down youthful indiscretions, for which he has already endured the most frightful punishment, should be denied that protection of the law against malicious libel which is the natural right of any decent citizen.

This is what happened to me in 1913. I had long ceased to have any connection with the Wilde gang or cult. I had been married for more than eleven years, I had recovered my position in society, and I was living a perfectly harmless and reputable life. I had edited a leading literary paper for three and a half years with considerable success and credit, and I had published what even my worst enemies admit to be some of the finest poetry in the English language. Yet when I appealed to the courts for protection against a malicious statement made in a book at the instigation of the late Robert Ross (who hated me and had sworn to revenge himself on me because I declined to go on associating with him) to the effect that I was responsible for the ruin of Oscar Wilde, the courts, instead of protecting me as they should have done, allowed me to be flung to the wolves. Letters written by me to Oscar Wilde, which had been stolen by Robert Ross and kept secretly, although at the time he stole them he professed to be one of my greatest friends, were brought up against me and put to me in court. I was outmatched in the most cruel way by the weight of counsel. I had arrayed against me (appearing, if you please, for Mr Arthur Ransome, the author of the book containing the libel, a young struggling author who, without the assistance of Ross and his gang, would have been hard put to it to find £100) Sir James Campbell, leader of the Irish Bar, Mr McCardie, now Mr Justice McCardie, Mr F. E. Smith, now Lord Birkenhead, and other junior counsel; while I, for my part, was represented by only an inexperienced junior, who had been called to the Bar for only about two years. This junior, my old friend, Mr Cecil Hayes, did his gallant best against hopeless odds, but the attitude of the judge made his already difficult task impossible. There are some judges who, if they see a man in the courts struggling against an overwhelming array of "big counsel," with the assistance of only an inexperienced junior, will make a point of trying their best to help him out, and at any rate see that he gets as good a chance as possible of getting his case before the jury; but Mr Justice Darling is not one of them. Letters written by Oscar Wilde to me, and which had got somehow into the possession of my father (they were stolen by a servant from me and sold to my father), were brought up against me. They were produced by Messrs Charles Russell & Co., my father's solicitors, at the request (doubtless, as they would say, "on subpœna") of Messrs Lewis & Lewis, who were also my father's solicitors in the first place when he had his fight with Oscar Wilde. Thus the two firms of solicitors employed by my father in what he and his counsel, Sir Edward Carson, described over and over again as an effort "to save his son," combined to produce these letters against that son and to ruin him, or endeavour to do so, eighteen years later under the complacent eye of Mr Justice Darling.

In addition to that the judge allowed the whole of the un-published portion of the letter known as *De Profundis,* written to me (but which I never received, as it remained in the hands of Robert Ross) by Oscar Wilde in prison, to be used as evidence against me. For two hours I sat in the witness-box and listened to the poisonous stream of wild lies and grotesque accusations which Wilde, in his rage and despair at the situation he found himself in, had committed to paper in his prison cell, although in the last letter he wrote to me before his conviction he had told me for the hundredth time that his only hope of living through any sentence he might get was that I would stick to him and that he might one day just see me again and touch my hand. I remember this passage from the letter : " Child of all my imagination, little delicate flower, I am going to test the power of love, I am going to see if I cannot make the bitter waters sweet by the intensity of the love I bear you." In another letter of the same period he said : " None of God's created things, and you are the Morning Star of Life, has been so wildly worshipped, so madly adored." In another letter he called me " My darling child, with Christ's own heart in you."

Between the time when he wrote these letters—and at least thirty others in the same strain (all of which, alas ! I destroyed about a year before this Ransome case came on)—and the time when he wrote the *De Profundis* letter nothing whatever had happened between us. He went into prison vowing eternal devotion to me, and imploring me in the most pathetic and heartbreaking terms not to desert him, but to stick to him and wait for him till he came out (all of which and much more I faithfully did), and within a year he was writing this frightful farrago of abuse and vilification. Strange and terrible enigma ! I will return to it later.

Mr Martin Secker, who was the publisher of the book by Mr Arthur Ransome, *Oscar Wilde, a Critical Study,* containing the libel on me, and who withdrew the book from circulation directly I issued writs against him and Mr Ransome, told me some years later the whole story of how the book came to be written, and to contain the reflection on me which goaded me into taking action and thus gave Robert Ross his chance of gratifying his malice.

Mr Secker said to me, in substance, as follows : " I must say that Ransome was perfectly innocent in the matter. He came to me and suggested a book on Wilde, and, after hearing what his idea of the book was, I commissioned him to write it. He then said that it would be a tremendous help to him in writing the book if he could get an introduction to Robert Ross. He subsequently met Ross, who was very friendly and seemed inclined to give him every assistance. Ross told Ransome that if he would be guided by him and do the book on certain lines he would give him access to all sorts of documents and sources of information which had not been available to anyone else. Naturally, Ransome gratefully agreed to all that Ross proposed, and after that it was easy for Ross to get in the attack on you which the book contained and which in itself was only a matter of a few words."

Mr Secker went on to tell me that when his attention was drawn to it he had immediately recognized that the attack on me was unfair and in no way essential to the book, and that he told Ransome that he intended to withdraw the book from circulation and issue a new edition, leaving out the words complained of. He told me that Ransome would have agreed to this ; but, perhaps naturally enough, when Ransome found that the case was to be turned into a *cause célèbre*, and that he was to be provided with all the materials to fight it without any risk to himself, he readily agreed to let Ross arrange the matter in his own way. Ross's way was to make Ransome plead " justification," and by the methods I have described the case was fought and won, and the justification was legally established.

CHAPTER VII

As I have now got on to the subject of the Ransome libel suit, which was tried in the King's Bench Division in 1913, I will here reproduce a portion of the letter I wrote to Frank Harris in Nice at his request in 1925, and which is incorporated in the " New Preface " to Harris's *Life and Confessions of Oscar Wilde*. The " New Preface " was published by the Fortune Press in London in the same year, and a second edition of it has recently appeared. I quote here all that part of my letter which relates to Robert Ross and the Ransome case ; I shall then go back to the period I had reached in these memoirs when I was at Oxford and first met Oscar Wilde :

" Now to come to the question of Robert Ross. When I start to write about him, I am reminded of that phrase of St Paul, ' the mystery of iniquity.' Why he behaved in the dreadful way he did, and what made him hate me and use diabolical skill and cunning in his efforts to destroy my character, I have not the slightest idea. The trouble about Ross has always been that what he did was so bad as to be, on the face of it, incredible. Most people simply will not believe that any man could be such a villain and such a hypocrite. All I can do is to give as briefly as possible the main facts as they exist and can be proved, not by my own statements, but by the irrefutable evidence of publicly recorded events. When Oscar Wilde died in Paris I was in Scotland, and I did not reach Paris till two days after his death, just in time to attend the funeral, the cost of which I paid. Ross, with whom I was then, as I supposed, on terms of great friendship, was there when Wilde died, and it was he who telegraphed informing me of Wilde's death. While Wilde lay dead, and before I arrived in Paris, Ross went through the papers and manuscripts he found in Wilde's rooms. Among them he found a quantity of my letters to Wilde. These letters he appropriated without a word to me. I naturally had not the slightest idea that he had found and stolen letters written by me to Wilde, and I suppose that even those queerly misguided persons who profess to admire Ross as a model of 'faithful friendship,' and who gave him a public testimonial after I had exposed him in 1914, at the Old Bailey, will admit that to steal or appropriate letters written by one of one's friends to another friend, and to keep them secretly and finally use them against their writer in a law court, is a wicked, disgraceful and dishonourable action. The facts as to this business cannot be denied. Ross took my letters, and his executors or heirs have got them to this day. How many letters he found and kept I have no idea. When the Ransome case (in which I sued Ransome for a libel, which he had been inspired by Ross to write against me in his *Oscar Wilde, A Critical Study*) came on, some of these letters were produced by Ross and put to me in court during my cross-examination by Sir James Campbell, Ransome's counsel. The letters produced were letters of which, as I said then and have frequently said since, in the witness-box, I am ashamed. Their production when I was quite unaware of their existence, and their being 'sprung upon' me in the witness-box, fifteen years after they were written, caused me to lose my case against Ransome. Mr Comyns Carr, K.C., who was subsequently my counsel in four other lawsuits, in all of which I was successful, told me some years later that he could not understand how I lost the Ransome case. He said to me : ' If your case had been put to the jury you could not have lost it.' My case was not put to the jury partly because my counsel and old friend, Mr Cecil Hayes, was (as he would be the first to admit) outmatched and overwhelmed by the array of counsel against him—Sir James Campbell, Mr F. E. Smith (now Lord Birkenhead) and Mr McCardie (now Mr Justice

McCardie). Mr Hayes was at that time an inexperienced junior, and had not the skill and power as an advocate which he has since acquired. The judge who tried the case, Mr Justice Darling, was bitterly hostile to me throughout, and I was, unfortunately for me, bound by a promise that I had given to Cecil Hayes, on my word of honour, that I would not attack the judge however great provocation he gave me. So I was simply a dumb lamb for the slaughter ! Although I produced my pass-books and proved that I had given Wilde £390 in cheques (in addition to a lot of ready money) in the one year between the death of my father and the death of Wilde, and although I proved that when I left Wilde at my villa in Naples I gave him £200, paid to him by my mother through Mr More Adey, whom I called as a witness, and that at the very moment when he was writing his disgraceful letter to Ross, printed (at Ross's instigation) in your book on p. 406, in which he says that I left him penniless at Naples, he had £200 of my money in his pocket, a fact perfectly well known to Ross, who was sharing rooms with More Adey at the time the payment of the £200 was made—in spite of all this, I say, I lost my case on the prejudice caused against me by the production of these letters stolen by Ross and secretly kept for all those years.

" At the same Ransome trial, the unpublished part of *De Profundis* was brought out against me. For the history of this manuscript I can best refer you to Ross's own preface to the first edition of *De Profundis*, published in 1905 (which I reviewed for you in that year in your paper, *The Candid Friend*, without having the slightest idea that it was a letter addressed by Wilde to me). Ross, in his preface, says that the manuscript was given to him by Wilde on the day he left prison. Neither he nor Wilde ever said a word about it to me. I had no knowledge of its existence till the year 1912, when a copy of the whole manuscript, including the hitherto unpublished part, was sent to me as part of Ransome's ' particulars of justification ' by the solicitors, Lewis & Lewis.

" I have little to say about this dreadful piece of cold-blooded, malignant malice, hypocrisy and lying. It passes my comprehension that any reasonable being can be taken in by such stuff. As I have already convinced you that almost every word it contains is a lie or distortion of the truth, and as moreover you always thought very meanly of it and would never, as you now tell me, have 'swallowed' any of it if Ross had not bolstered it up by his own lies and misrepresentation, I need not now waste much more ink over it. The letters of Wilde to me, written at Berneval, after he left prison, which have been published in America, in a privately printed edition issued by Mr William Andrews Clark, are in themselves quite sufficient to demonstrate the falsity and wickedness of his attack on me in *De Profundis*. I have, moreover, answered his (mostly absurd) allegations fully in my book, *Oscar Wilde and Myself*.

" Just take this as an example of Wilde's reckless perversion of truth. He says in *De Profundis* (p. 555 of your book, Appendix) :

" ' I am not speaking in phrases of rhetorical exaggeration, but in terms of absolute truth, when I remind you that during the whole time we were together I never wrote one single line. Whether at Torquay, Goring, London, Florence, or elsewhere, my life, as long as you were by my side, was entirely sterile and uncreative. And with few intervals you were, I regret to say, by my side always.'

"Well, as stated in my book, *Oscar Wilde and Myself* (p. 137), the fact is that Wilde planned and wrote the whole of *A Woman of No Importance* while we were together at Lady Mount Temple's house, at Babbacombe, Torquay (Lady Mount Temple lent him the house, and I stayed there with him, accompanied by a tutor, Mr Dodgson Campbell, now of the British Museum, for about two months) ; that he wrote the whole of *The Importance of Being Earnest* while I was with him at Worthing, and *An Ideal Husband* partly at Goring and partly in London, in rooms he took in St James's Place, where I saw him every day. He also did the final version of *The Ballad of Reading Gaol* in my villa at Naples. Even *De Profundis* is a letter written to me ! In his letter to me from Berneval, beginning 'My own darling Boy,' written just before he joined me in Naples, he says : ' I feel that my only hope of doing beautiful work in art is being with you—it was not so in old days (*sic*) but now it is different. . . . I feel that only with you can I do anything at all.'

" It is the same right through the *De Profundis* letter. Lie, lie, lie. Oscar Wilde told you himself that in prison he suffered from ' wild delusions.' He appears to have committed the record of these delusions to paper. Most of his letter is simply incomprehensible to me. He invents the maddest fictions. ' An eleven page telegram,' supposed to have been sent by me to him. Purely imaginary scenes at Voisin's and Paillard's. The grotesque nonsense of his account of a quarrel we had at Brighton, which both of us had (as I supposed) forgotten all about a week after it happened. My alleged threats of suicide and wild despair while I was separated from him and staying in Egypt (where, as a matter of fact, I stayed for three months as the guest of Lord and Lady Cromer, at the British Agency, and had a most lively and cheerful time, as Reggie Turner and E. F. Benson, who met me out there and went up the Nile with me, could testify). His monstrous lies about the money he alleged I got from him, lies which he could not support by one single cheque or entry in his pass-book. The whole letter is the raving of a lunatic, a man driven mad by impotent rage and malice and malevolent desire to injure at all costs the friend he professed to love and with whom he at once resumed friendly relations when he got out of prison.

" I pass to what happened after the Ransome case had gone against me. My wife left me, my only child was taken away from me, my home was broken up, and I was left penniless and ruined, socially as well as financially. I recognized that the author of all this havoc was Robert Ross. I knew of my own knowledge, as did literally thousands of others in London, that Ross was exactly the same sort of man in his private life as Wilde had been. The difference between Ross and me was that while I, as a boy of twenty, had come under Wilde's influence and had got myself mixed up in the awful gang that surrounded him, I had long since (more than twelve years then) escaped out of it all. I had married within a little more than a year of Wilde's death, and I was living a happy, healthy and normal life with my wife and child. Ross, on the other hand, had become more and more obsessed with the dreadful vice which had been the bane of Oscar Wilde. The mantle of Wilde in this respect had fallen on him. He was the High Priest of all the sodomites in London, and it was he who was held up to the world as the faithful friend of Wilde (out of the exploitation of whose cult he had made a fortune), the noble disinterested friend, the pure, the holy person, in contrast to the wicked and depraved Alfred Douglas who had ' ruined ' Oscar Wilde and ' deserted ' him. Flesh and blood couldn't stand it, and I swore the day after the Ransome trial that I would never rest till I had publicly exposed Ross in his true colours.

" I don't want to prolong this letter unduly, and I must endeavour to stick to essentials and to be as brief as possible. It took me two years to bring Ross to book. How I did it without money and with scarcely a friend in the world, apart from my mother, is something of a miracle.

" I adopted the same method as that employed by my father. That is to say, I libelled Ross and at last forced him to take criminal proceedings against me. It took a good deal more libelling to bring Ross to the fighting point than it did to bring Wilde. I began by libelling him to Mr Justice Darling, the judge who had tried the Ransome case. Mr Justice Darling made a public reference to my letter from the Bench, read it aloud in court and handed it to counsel representing Ross. No doubt he thought that immediate criminal proceedings against me would follow. But Ross took what I had said 'lying down.' It was not till I had several times repeated the libel in writing to his friends, Mr and Mrs Asquith, and till I had printed and broadcasted two pamphlets containing the same libel, that I goaded him into action. My father had accused Wilde of ' posing as a sodomite.' I applied the following flowers of speech to Ross : ' An unspeakable skunk,' a ' filthy b——,' a ' notorious sodomite,' an ' habitual debaucher and corrupter of young boys right down to the present day,' and last, but not least, a ' blackmailer.'

" I was arrested and kept five days without bail at Brixton Prison. I pleaded justification, and when I finally got out of Brixton, on bail, I had about five weeks in which to find enough evidence to justify my libels, with the alternative of getting anything between six months' and two years' imprisonment ! I had not a scrap of evidence beyond my own private knowledge, which was based on the fact that Ross never made the slightest attempt to conceal his proclivities. He boasted openly of what he did and had done all his life.

" This, however, was no good, or very little good, for my plea of justification. I cannot tell you now (it would take too long) all about how I got the evidence. I firmly believe that my getting it was a supernatural business and was due to the fact that, having by this time become a devout Catholic, I cast myself wholly on Providence and prayed for help in my desperate need. Just about a week before my trial, and when I had almost given up hope, I stumbled right into the evidence. In two days thereafter, with the assistance of my solicitor, Mr Edward Bell, I had an array of thirteen or fourteen witnesses, and the plea was drawn up by my counsel, Mr Comyns Carr.

" The trial lasted eight days at the Old Bailey. It went my way from the first. After Sir Ernest Wild, K.C. (now Recorder of London), had ' opened ' for Ross in a speech in which he painted me as blackly as possible to the jury, he put his client into the box. Ross's cross-examination by Comyns Carr was quite as sensational as that of Wilde by Carson. By the time it was half over I had the case won. The foreman of the jury told me, after the case was over, that he and most of the jury wanted to stop the case and give me a verdict immediately after Ross's cross-examination, but that one man (the same who ultimately caused the disagreement of the jury) refused to listen to such a proposition. So the case went on. I went into the box myself and was cross-examined for many hours by Wild, and my stolen letters were again put to me. But, ' this time round,' they produced little effect. (They have been produced twice since, once at the Pemberton-Billing trial, when I scored heavily and helped to win the verdict, and finally at the hearing of my action against *The Evening News*, in 1921, for libelling me by saying that I had ' shown marked signs of degeneracy,' when I was cross-examined by Sir Douglas Hogg, the Attorney-General, for six hours and got a verdict and a thousand pounds damages, and a rider from the jury expressing an opinion that the constant bringing up of these letters was disgraceful and that they ought to be returned to me or destroyed.)

"Witness after witness gave the most damning evidence against Ross, and the judge (Mr Justice Coleridge) summed up against him in a very deadly, though perfectly fair, way.

" In fact, the charges I brought against Ross, which were specific charges giving names of victims, dates and full particulars, were proved up to the hilt. The evidence of Inspector West, with twenty-five years' service at Scotland Yard and Vine Street, would alone have been enough to justify my charges. The inspector, who came of his own accord and volunteered evidence, swore that in his professional capacity as a detective, who had for fifteen years patrolled the neighbourhood of Vine Street

(Piccadilly, etc.) at night, he had known Ross during all those years as an habitual associate of sodomites and male prostitutes.

"However, the jury, after being out about three hours, came back and said they could not agree on a verdict, and I was released again on bail and bound over to come up for trial at the next sessions. When I left the court I found nine members of the jury, including the foreman, waiting for me outside. They expressed their deep regret at the result and told me that it was due to one man who absolutely refused to give a verdict against Ross. They all shook hands with me and congratulated me. They told me they were all against me at first, and amazed to find how right I was and what a different person I was from what they had always imagined.

"Meanwhile the papers in London had almost entirely suppressed all mention of this sensational case. Instead of the columns and columns which they had given to the Ransome case when I lost, now there was day by day a meagre half column or a mere paragraph. The public was left quite in the dark as to what had happened, and Mr Blumenfeld, the editor of *The Daily Express*, when I complained to him of the shameful way I had been treated in the reports in his paper, naïvely told me that the bad reports were not due to any prejudice or unfair feeling against me, 'because,' said he, 'to tell you the truth, I haven't the least idea how or why you were acquitted or what happened!'

"Yet the *verbatim* report of this, probably the most sensational case that has ever been tried at the Old Bailey, was available to all the newspapers. The treatment I received at this time destroyed the last vestige of a belief in 'British fair play' which had survived my former experience. However, even the Press couldn't save Ross. His counsel first proposed to enter a *nolle prosequi* with my consent, each side paying its own costs. I declined to agree to this, and expressed my firm determination to come up at the next sessions and be tried again, and I added a little more evidence to my plea of justification. That settled Ross. He 'climbed down' completely. His counsel, Wild, now came forward with the proposal that if I would agree to allow a *nolle prosequi* to be entered (that is, allow the prosecution to be withdrawn), Lewis & Lewis, on behalf of Ross, would pay my costs and out-of-pocket expenses (about six hundred pounds). This was a godsend to me, as I was practically without a penny, and I accepted the offer with joy, my plea of justification remaining on record as established at the Central Criminal Court, where anyone is at liberty to go and inspect it.

"On the other hand, the 'disagreement' probably saved Ross from a criminal prosecution, which would almost certainly have followed unavoidably if the jury had brought in a verdict against him.

"It was, by the way, Mr Forrest Fulton, junior counsel for Ross, and the son of the late Recorder of London, who pointed out to Mr Bell, my solicitor, that the entering of a *nolle prosequi* on Ross's behalf was an even greater victory for me than a verdict would have been, for the obvious reason that a *nolle prosequi* entered under such circumstances is an acknowledgment of guilt and is equal to a plea of 'guilty' on the part of the prosecutor.

"I have only to add, to be finished once for all with the odious subject of Ross, that about three months after the result of my trial at the Old Bailey had been reported in the papers a public testimonial and a gift of £700 were presented to Robert Ross. The testimonial, which expressed the greatest love, friendship and admiration for Ross as a 'faithful friend' and 'distinguished man of letters,' was got up by Mr, now Sir, Edmund Gosse, who, together with Mr H. G. Wells, gave evidence as to character for Ross at my trial. (They both declared, to the bewilderment of the judge and jury, that they had known and loved Ross for years, and that he was 'the most pure-minded man' they had ever known !)

"The testimonial was signed by about three hundred and fifty people, including the Prime Minister and Mrs Asquith, a dozen peers, an Anglican bishop, and a number of more or less distinguished persons in the social, literary and artistic world.

"After the trial Ross had to resign the lucrative post of 'assessor of picture valuations to the Board of Trade,' at £1500 a year, which had been bestowed on him by Mr Asquith ; but he was neither ostracized nor seriously affected in his social position. The Asquiths continued to receive him, another Government appointment was given to him a year later, and when he died *The Times* devoted a whole column to his praise as a type of all that is noblest and best in an English gentleman.

"Comment is needless. I have never been able to understand the attitude of the curious people who make a hero of Ross, any more than I could ever understand Ross's own villainies and unspeakable meannesses. It is well to remember that when I 'justified' against Ross I had to prove that, in addition to being a votary of Wilde's vices, he was also a blackmailer. I proved the one thing just as much as I proved the other. If the Asquiths and Messrs Gosse, Wells, and the rest like that sort of thing it is, of course, no affair of mine, but surely there is something very queer about the whole business. I have long given up bothering about it myself, and I must leave the further discussion and examination of it to you and to your readers if you decide to incorporate this letter in your revised *Life of Oscar Wilde*."

CHAPTER VIII

I LEFT Winchester at Christmas 1888; I had then just passed my eighteenth birthday. Early in 1889 I was sent abroad with a tutor, Mr Gerald Campbell, younger brother of Sir Guy Campbell, Baronet, a nephew of my great-aunt Madeline (the Honourable Mrs Percy Wyndham), to whom I have already referred, and in that way a connection of my own. Mr Campbell is, and has been for years, a member of the staff of *The Times*. While I was with him in the south of France I had my first "affair" with a woman. She was a lady of celebrated beauty, at least twelve years older than myself, the divorced wife of an earl. She had run away with a lover, but at this time they were definitely separated. I stayed in the same hotel with her and she was a cousin of my tutor, Gerald Campbell. The affair proceeded on classic lines, and except that there was no outraged husband (and to do myself justice I must say that I have never, even in the days when I had no morals to speak of, so much as contemplated the possibility of making love to another man's wife) it worked out very much on the lines of the first episode of Byron's Don Juan and Julia.

It culminated in a terrible moment when my tutor (very indiscreetly as I thought then and still maintain) knocked at the door of the lady's bedroom one night and demanded in stern tones the restitution of his ravished ewe-lamb. The ewe-lamb, reduced to tears and dressed in one of the lady's much-beribboned nightgowns, was duly handed out after a painful scene, and to the accompaniment of loud barks from the lady's pet dog. Thereafter the poor lady was mercilessly attacked and blamed by whole juries of matrons for her wickedness in "seducing an innocent boy."

48

I am glad to remember that I had sufficient chivalry to protest loudly, and without regard to my own interests, that after four years at Winchester I was no more an innocent boy than I was an angel out of heaven. I don't believe my protestations were taken seriously, and in any case I was of course separated for ever from my lovely lady and sent back to England in disgrace. This was some months before I first went up to Oxford.

I don't want to be frivolous on the one hand or hypocritical on the other. In the then existing conditions, in which it was utterly impossible and out of the reach of dreams that I should preserve my already damaged purity, I cannot but think that I might have done a good deal worse, and it is probable that, if we had been left alone, my lady love would at any rate have kept me away from baser promiscuities. As it was I gravitated inevitably, exactly like every other boy of my age and upbringing in those days, to the promenade at the Empire (for which, when its existence was threatened by Mrs Ormiston Chant, Winston Churchill put up his first " great fight "), and later to the slightly more aristocratic Corinthian Club, in both cases with what might be described as " the usual trimmings." If I laugh at all this dismal business it is, I assure you, my gentle readers, only, like Figaro, *de peur d'être obligé d'en pleurer*.

I am obliged to tell all this about myself because it is an answer (though not the one I should like to be able to give) to the accusation which has been made against me of being what is called abnormal and degenerate from a sexual point of view. (By the way, the last time this accusation of being " degenerate " was made against me was by *The Evening News* in 1921, and it cost that enterprising journal £1000 in damages to me and a good many more thousands in costs.)

I went up to Magdalen College, Oxford, in October 1889, just about the time of my nineteenth birthday. My outlook in life

D

at that time was largely sporting and convivial, though I had my intellectual and artistic side. I had hunted quite a lot as a boy with the Cottesmore from the glorious house, Burley-on-the-Hill, of my uncle, the late George Finch; I was fond of shooting (though I did not become, what I can claim to have been afterwards, a good shot till many years later); I played games, went a lot on the river, though I did not take up rowing seriously, and was fond of cross-country runs with parties of friends—the rule being that if anyone jumped anything all the others were obliged to follow. This engaging pastime very nearly cost me my life on one occasion. I was with a party of seven or eight friends, running and jumping across country. It was just after the historic great frost (in 1890, I think) when the Thames at Oxford was frozen solid and a coach-and-four was frequently driven down the river right past the row of college barges. The frost had broken up, but the river was still jammed with ice. I suddenly conceived the idea of crossing the river by jumping or stepping from block to block of ice and, calling on the rest to follow, I got across, followed by all the others. We all got across safely by something like a miracle. Whereupon I started to cross back again. I jumped on a large floating block of ice, and to my horror it dipped and pitched me right into the swirling, icy water, the block of ice on which I had stepped going clean over my head. When I tried to come up my head bumped against the ice, and meanwhile my companions on the bank were splitting themselves with laughter at my mishap. I was very nearly drowned before one of them, my old and dear friend " Tyler " Reid (dead, alas ! many years ago), tumbled to the fact that it was no laughing matter, and waded in up to his waist to pull me out, which he did after a struggle. A minute or two's gasping on the bank and I was all right again, and able to run home and get warm (I was clad only in a " zephyr " and running shorts with bare legs) without suffering any ill results.

Intellectually at that time I was (as I always had been) a lover of the best in literature. I began to love Shakespeare when I was a mere child (my mother used to read him aloud to me), and I was fond of and had read most of the best English poetry and all the standard novels by the time I had finished my second year at Oxford. Mr Frank Harris, in one of his periodical spiteful attacks on me, reproaches me because he says that in my book, *Oscar Wilde and Myself,* I give no credit to Wilde for the intellectual stimulus I got from him. The accusation is, like nearly all Mr Harris's accusations against me, quite unfounded. Anyone who reads that book will see for himself that I do give Wilde every credit in that direction that is due to him. At the same time, it was certainly not Wilde that taught me to love or to write poetry, and as Harris himself (to do him justice for the only honest thing he has ever said about me) has emphasized over and over again his opinion that I was always a far better poet than Wilde it is rather difficult to guess what it is that he thinks I ought to have said about Wilde's "intellectual stimulus" that I have not said over and over again.

I began to write poetry in my first year at Oxford. I had before, in my schooldays, written verse, chiefly humorous, but none of it was good enough to survive. The only extant examples of it can be found in a paper called *The Pentagram,* which, in conjunction with two friends of mine, "Sal" Phipps of my own House and Lidderdale of Morsehead's, I brought out at Winchester during the summer term of 1888. I have a bound copy of this paper, of which a dozen weekly numbers appeared. It had a tremendous success at the time, and the circulation, at the end, worked out at a good deal more than one copy a head for every boy in the school. Lots of "old Wykehamists" took it in. There used to be a bound copy of it in our House library, and I expect it is still there.

In my second year at Oxford I wrote my first serious poem

It was called " Autumn Days " and appeared in *The Oxford Magazine.* Mr (now Sir Herbert) Warren, the President of Magdalen, wrote me a letter of congratulation on it. I have not kept his letter, but I remember these words from it : " I thought it really passionate and really fine. I must confess I had no idea you could do anything so good." I happen to remember these words from his letter because, seven or eight years afterwards, when my volume of poetry, *The City of the Soul,* was brought out anonymously, I sent Sir Herbert Warren a copy of it, which he sent back to me by return of post with a letter in which he said : " I regret that I cannot accept this book from you." It struck me at the time as being rather a brutal and unnecessarily unkind thing to do, and I remember looking up and finding his letter about " Autumn Days," which I had preserved, and reading it again before tearing it up. The phrase I have quoted stuck in my memory. I give this story as a typical example of the sort of thing I have had to put up with all my life as the result of my friendship with Oscar Wilde (who, by the way, was also an old friend of Sir Herbert Warren's and used to make a point of calling on him every time he came to see me at Oxford).

In addition to a real love of literature, and especially of poetry, I had also a passion for music. Although I had, by the time I got to Oxford, lost all belief in religion, I scarcely missed a day in attending the evening service in Magdalen Chapel. The celebrated choir, which was and is, I believe, the finest in the world (it ought to be, for it is a separate foundation and has about £5000 a year to spend), was a lure which I could not resist. I got by this means a real knowledge of some of the finest Church music. It also led to my great friendship, which I am glad to say still continues, with Frank Marshall, one of the " Academical Clerks," who was and is a splendid musician and pianist. I had another great friend in the choir, by name Tapsfield (now a Canon of St Paul's), who had a magnificent bass voice and was an accomplished musician. I was also on terms of great friendship with dear old Dr Roberts, the organist, kindest-hearted and most loyal of men, and had the free run of his organ loft.

CHAPTER IX

THIS kind of life went on for two years, varied in the vacations with shooting and hunting and a certain amount of racing. My mother's country house was about four miles from Ascot, and we had a party for the races every year, which always included my uncle, Percy Wyndham, and my Aunt Madeline. It is interesting to recall that in those days (when Lord Coventry was Master of the Buckhounds) the price for a ticket to the Royal Enclosure for the whole week (four days' racing) was one pound ; now it is five guineas. Quite half the people who get into the enclosure nowadays would have had "no earthly" at that period. My brother, Drumlanrig, being in the Coldstream Guards, supplied us all lavishly with tickets by the dozen for lunch and so forth in the Guards' tent.

Later, when I had horses of my own in France (for two short years only, alas !), I had the opportunity of comparing French and English racing methods. I consider that the French system is far the better. There is a mania in England for special "reserved enclosures," which is very snobbish, and also gives an opening to all sorts of undesirable, and what the English (with beautiful unawareness of their own characteristic failings) are wont to describe as un-English, differentiations. In the year 1910 I was refused admission by the late Duke of Richmond to the Private Stand at Goodwood, though I had no difficulty in getting into the Jockey Club Stand at Doncaster, the County Stand at York, and similar enclosures all over the country. Of course as long as the Duke of Richmond has a Private Stand he is at liberty to refuse admission to persons of better birth than himself, while admitting any kind of *nouveau riche* or dubious profiteer. But the point is that racing is a national institution, and depends for support on those who pay for it, the public ; and no private individual ought to be in a position to exercise the power of ostracism at his own private whim. At the time when the Duke refused to let me into the Private Stand at Goodwood I was a member of White's Club (I had to leave it automatically when I was driven into the bankruptcy court by Ross and Lewis & Lewis in 1913), and to keep me out of a place to which I had a perfectly clear, natural right of entry can only be described as ill-natured, to put it as mildly as possible. The fact that the Duke of Richmond happened to be a friend and partisan of my father-in-law, Colonel Custance (they had been in the Grenadiers together), with whom at the time I had a feud about my only son, Raymond, did not make his attitude any more chivalrous.

At the beautiful racecourses round Paris, where one can go racing (fifteen minutes in a taxi) day after day all the year round, except during the time when the *venue* is changed to the south of France and during the Deauville fortnight, there are only two enclosures. When I was racing, the *Pesage* (grand stand and paddock, consisting of spacious lawns, gay with flowers and capable of holding a huge crowd without discomfort) was priced at twenty francs, which was then equivalent to sixteen shillings, while the *Pelouse* was three francs, about half-a-crown. Anyone who chose to pay could go into the one or the other, according to his or her own fancy ; the price for ladies was half that for men. The racing in France was and is just as good as it was and is in England, and, from the point of view of breeding stayers, the French are rapidly getting the better of the English —have, in fact, definitely established their superiority. I never go near a racecourse in England now, chiefly because I consider the prices of admission to be exorbitant, and the crowd and discomfort of the incessant railway journeys which are necessary if one wants to race regularly make the game hardly worth the candle, except either for the very rich or those who go racing professionally or semi-professionally.

During my school holidays and vacations, between the years 1886 up to the outbreak of the Oscar Wilde scandal in 1895, I frequently met and consorted with the late King Edward (then Prince of Wales), the Duke of Cambridge, and other royalties. I spent two seasons at Homburg, while I was an undergraduate, with my mother and my grandfather, Alfred Montgomery, who was on very intimate terms with the Prince, and we dined with the Prince (*à la belle franquette* in the then prevailing fashion at Homburg) at least half-a-dozen times. My grandfather also introduced me to the Duke of Cambridge at Homburg, and afterwards used to take me to his house in Piccadilly.

I have recollections of a dinner given to the Duke by my grandfather at the Travellers' Club, when the Duke (who was a very amiable old gentleman and most kind to me) fell asleep after dinner and snored, just at the moment when urgent reasons for leaving the table had manifested themselves in me. After a whispered and agonized appeal to my grandfather I was given leave to slip out quietly, but, as luck would have it, I knocked over a knife or a fork and the noise restored His Royal Highness to consciousness, to the great relief of his equerry and the rest of the party, which numbered about eight guests.

It was just about this time that I had what I can only (*pace* Mr Frank Harris) describe as the great misfortune to meet Oscar Wilde. I was taken to his house, 16 Tite Street, by Lionel Johnson, the Wykehamist poet, who was one of my greatest friends at Oxford. He was two years at Winchester with me, but, as he was a scholar in College and I was in a House, and was moreover three years younger than he, I never had any acquaintance with him at school. He himself used to tell with great gusto the story that, when, in my second year at Winchester, I was told by one of the masters (or "dons," as we

called them at Winchester), Mr Toye, to "order my name"
—that is to say, report to the "Prefect of Hall," who in turn
reported to the Head Master, who sometimes thereupon ad-
ministered a "licking" with a birch-rod—it was he, Lionel
Johnson, who, as Prefect of Hall at the time, officiated by
holding up my shirt on the only occasion when I was "licked."
My executioner was Dr Fearon ("the Bear"), for whom, by
the way, I retain a feeling of great affection, and who, for
several years at Winchester, persisted in regarding me, in the
face of all evidence to the contrary, as a sort of budding saint or
angel child, and who let me off in consequence at least half-a-
dozen other "lickings," which I fully merited to receive. Lionel
told this story, as I have said, but I can only say that I have no
recollection at all of seeing him on that painful occasion, as I did
not get to know him to speak to till two or more years later. He
contributed a very charming, half-whimsical, half-pathetic poem
to the last number of *The Pentagram*, and a magnificent one, as
well as several contributions in prose, to my Oxford paper, *The
Spirit Lamp*, of which more anon.

Lionel was a delightful fellow, though exceedingly eccentric,
and, alas ! in his later years greatly addicted to potations, which
his small and childlike frame could not withstand. He was not
much over thirty when he died. He had a mania for not going to
bed, and if he could get anyone to sit up with him he would dis-
course in the most brilliant way up till five o'clock in the morning.
At other times of the day he was rather noticeably silent. He was
a great scholar, and undoubtedly a great poet, but the austerity
and profundity of his best work makes him one who is never likely
to appeal to any but a very eclectic audience. It was one of the
griefs of his later years that he had introduced me to Wilde
(though, of course, his doing so could not possibly have had any
bearing on the events that followed), and Mr Frank Harris
may be interested to hear that his terrible and celebrated sonnet,

beginning " I hate you with a necessary hate," was, as Lionel told me himself long after it was written, meant for Wilde, and that the "friend" to whom it referred was myself, which indicates that he did not share Lord Darling's view as to the apportioning of the responsibility for the " ruin " which overtook us both more or less. This sonnet was written quite a year before the final catastrophe, and Lionel Johnson's natural kindness of heart constrained him, in his sorrow for Wilde's terrible punishment, to deny the reference to Wilde of his sonnet to many people, though he admitted to me that he had meant it for Wilde at a time when he considered that he was ruining me, his junior by eighteen years. I deeply regret that Lionel did not live to have the satisfaction of seeing me in his beloved Catholic Church, which he joined almost immediately after he went down from Oxford ; but as I knew he always prayed hard for my conversion he no doubt had something to do with it, though I was almost anti-Catholic in the days of our association. After all, there is no reason to regret that he did not live to see his prayers answered, for of course he knows all about it now.

CHAPTER X

LIONEL JOHNSON, as I say, called for me one day during the vacation at my mother's house, 18 Cadogan Place, and took me on to see Oscar Wilde, in Tite Street. We had tea in his little writing-room facing the street on the ground floor, and, before I left, Oscar took me upstairs to the drawing-room and introduced me to his wife. I was always on the best of terms with Mrs Wilde. I liked her and she liked me. She told me, about a year after I first met her, that she liked me better than any of Oscar's other friends. She frequently came to my mother's house and was present at a dance which my mother gave during the first year of my acquaintance with her husband. After the *débâcle* I never saw her again, and I do not doubt that Ross and others succeeded in poisoning her mind against me, but up to the very last day of our acquaintance we were the best of friends. The last time I saw her was two nights before the proceedings taken by Oscar Wilde against my father at the Old Bailey, when we all three had dinner in a restaurant and went on to a box at the St James's Theatre, where Oscar's play, *The Importance of Being Earnest*, was running to crowded houses. She was very much agitated, and when I said good-night to her at the door of the theatre she had tears in her eyes. I felt dreadfully sorry for her, for though I then believed that Oscar would beat my father, and had not the slightest anticipation of the frightful catastrophe that was imminent, I knew that at the very best the whole business must be a terrible ordeal for her. Honesty compels me to say that Oscar during the time I knew him was not very kind to his wife. He certainly had been (as he often told me) very much in love with her, and the

59

marriage was purely a love match. At the time when I first met him he was still fond of her, but he was often impatient with her, and sometimes snubbed her, and he resented, and showed that he resented, the attitude of slight disapproval which she often adopted towards him. Towards the end of the time before the catastrophe (and they never met again after he came out of prison) the relations between them were distinctly strained. To try to make out that this had anything whatever to do with me is simply dishonest and untruthful. Those who know the facts (and there are many now living who do know them) will, if they tell the truth, bear witness that I was never " a bone of contention " between Oscar and his wife, although I once used that very phrase in a jocular way in a letter to Ross, which was used against me at the Ransome trial. The evidence as to the sort of thing Oscar was doing, and the kind of people he met and associated with, which came out at his trial, is surely enough to account for the by no means complete estrangement that had arisen between his wife and himself, without trying to drag me into it.

The real truth is, as Harris and Ross and the rest of my detractors always knew perfectly well, that if Oscar had confined himself to his extravagant devotion to me (even admitting, as I do, that there was, for a time, an element of perverseness about it) he could have laughed at all his enemies, not excepting my father. The letters he wrote me, which were used by my father (not, as was expressly and carefully explained by Sir Edward Carson to the jury at the Old Bailey, with any idea of suggesting that there had been anything actually wrong between us, but as a father's justification for his action in intervening to end a " dangerous friendship "), have been printed over and over again in the newspapers. There were only two of them. Anyone can read them for himself, and I will defy anyone to say that they contain any evidence whatsoever of misconduct. They proved, what neither Wilde nor I ever denied, that Wilde had an ex-aggerated devotion to me and an unbounded admiration for my personal appearance. He compared me to Hylas and Hyacinthus, and the language he used was of course extravagant and unusual. But there is nothing whatever in his letters which could not be matched in Shakespeare's *Sonnets* (also written to a boy), and though I believe it is the fashion nowadays to accuse Shakespeare of having had the same vices as Wilde, this merely shows the ignorance and baseness and stupidity of those who make such accusations on such grounds. Shakespeare, as I have pointed out before, refuted his detractors, by anticipation, in the last six lines of the very sonnet which is generally quoted as the strongest evidence against him. I refer to the sonnet beginning :

> A woman's face, with Nature's own hand painted,
> Hast thou, the master-mistress of my passion.

The lines enumerated above clearly show, not only that Shakespeare's passion for "Mr W. H." was perfectly innocent, but that Shakespeare himself had never envisaged the possibility of its being anything else. "Nature," says he, "who intended thee for a woman, ' fell a-doting ' and, ' by addition, thee of me defeated.' " Could anything be clearer ? "If you had been a woman . . . but unfortunately you were a boy, so that I was defeated." To rub it in still more strongly he goes on to say :

> But since she pricked thee out for woman's pleasure,
> Mine be thy love, and thy love's use their treasure.

The effect of the lines referred to is even stronger because they are so obviously not deliberately made in answer to, or in anticipation of, any adverse suggestion. Shakespeare exculpates himself, in the eyes of any reasonable being, quite definitely and quite unconsciously. Obviously it never occurred to him that anyone would put a bad interpretation on his love and adoration for " Master W. H."

In the same way, I repeat, I will challenge anyone who is not prejudiced to find anything in any letter of Wilde's to me that exists, or ever has existed, that is not consistent with a perfectly pure devotion. The two letters produced by my father were the two "worst" from Wilde's point of view and from mine, chiefly because they were artificial and therefore not moving. But there is really nothing wrong or incriminating in them. If Wilde had not been proved up to the hilt to have been what he was, on the evidence of a whole troop of male gutter-snipes, for frequenting whose society he could not produce any other possible explanation, he would certainly have been in no danger from anything connected with his friendship with me. The gentle Harris and others who are so ready, for reasons best known to themselves, to fling at me the accusation of having " ruined " Wilde and " sacrificed " him to gratify my " hatred of my father," overlook the fact that the numerous boys in respect of whom he was accused and convicted one and all became his accusers. It was they that " gave him away," and gave evidence against him in the witness-box. All I did was to stick to him through thick and thin and to offer, and indeed beg to be allowed, to go into the witness-box to defend him.

While I am on the subject of the two letters of Wilde's to me, produced by my father (and brought up against me several times since without causing me to " turn a hair "), I may give an example of the methods which commend themselves to Mr Frank Harris in what he wishes us to believe is a noble and disinterested effort to " defend the memory of his friend." One of the letters to which I have just referred contains the following words :

" I am sure Hyacinthus, whom Apollo loved so madly, was you in Greek days."

This is what Mr Harris thinks it fair to the memory of his dead friend to turn the words into, in his book, *The Life and Confessions of Oscar Wilde* :

"No Apollo followed love so madly as you in Greek days."

In his anxiety to get in a foul blow at me he deliberately makes out his " beloved friend " to be the author of the vile phrase quoted, concerning which it might well be said that Oscar Wilde would turn in his grave if he knew that he had been accused of writing such an appalling and disgusting vulgarism.

If, as I say, there was nothing whatever in Wilde's letters to me which could have caused him the slightest serious trouble, it is equally true that there was not, and never has been, any other serious evidence against us. Harris, in his "New Preface" to *The Life and Confessions of Oscar Wilde,* refers to my relations with Wilde in the following words : "Little can be laid to the charge of Douglas in his relations with Wilde but intense admiration for an older and very brilliant man, and for having permitted, against the grain, such familiarities as are common among boy friends at English public schools. . . . The graver accusation was simply invented from beginning to end." Quite so ; invented by Frank Harris. No one else has ever made the accusation.

Harris wrote the words quoted above after I had, of my own free will, told him exactly and in detail what my relations with Wilde were for a comparatively short period of time. There was nothing whatever to make me confess to him to the extent I did except a regard for truth. If I had sworn that there never had been even what there was (for a short time) in our relations, Harris would not have had it in his power to produce a tittle of evidence to the contrary. As a matter of fact, no such suggestion (even to the extent of imputing what I have voluntarily confessed) was made against me either at the trial of my father, when the suggestion was formally repudiated by my father's counsel, Carson, or later at Wilde's trials. Apart from malicious and lying gossip, no such charge has ever been made against me in such a way that I could take steps to refute it. Harris, in his book, invents a deliberately lying account of my first meeting with Wilde. Remembering that Lionel Johnson was present at this meeting, and that Mrs Wilde was in the next room, it does not require any more than the most elementary common sense for anyone to decide that Harris's story is a wicked, malicious and grotesquely preposterous lie. How could Harris possibly know what took place or what was said at my first interview with Wilde? He does not in his book pretend that his information came from Wilde, and the only two other persons who could know were myself and Lionel Johnson. What really happened, of course, at that interview was just the ordinary interchange of courtesies. Wilde was very agreeable and talked a great deal, I was very much impressed (much more so than I have admitted in my book, *Oscar Wilde and Myself*, which I wrote with Crosland), and, before I left, Wilde had asked me to lunch or to dinner at his club, and I had accepted his invitation.

Of course if Harris's book, *The Life and Confessions of Oscar Wilde*, had been published in England, I would long ago have taken criminal proceedings against Harris and his publisher, and he would, without the shadow of doubt have, been sent to prison, probably for the maximum two years. But as the book was published in America by Harris himself, without a publisher, I was powerless to do anything. Want of money prevented me from going to America, and even if I had gone there, what chance would I have had of obtaining in that country the justice which I have only barely succeeded in obtaining in my own country after a long and bitter fight against frightful odds?

CHAPTER XI

IT has been pointed out to me that to the present or rising generation of those who may read this book the names of Frank Harris and Robert Ross convey little or nothing. Frank Harris had certainly, before he left England for good—about three or four years before the war—established a reputation as a considerable man of letters and a " great talker." His name and reputation are perfectly familiar to most of the elder men of letters in London to-day, but outside this circle he is now unknown. His books are not read in England and his name is almost forgotten. When I first met him, in 1894 or thereabouts, he occupied a commanding position in contemporary letters and journalism. He was editor of *The Fortnightly Review*, and had published a volume of short stories, called *Elder Conklin*, which was highly praised by competent critics.

As editor of *The Fortnightly Review* he had the discrimination to print (and pay highly for) Oscar Wilde's brilliant essays, "The Decay of the Art of Lying" and "The Critic as Artist."

He married a wealthy lady, who had a house in Park Lane next door to that occupied by George Wyndham and his wife, Lady Grosvenor. While Frank Harris remained with his first wife he came into considerable prominence in the social and literary world as the giver of dinner-parties, where the conversation was supposed to soar to unusual heights of " brilliance."

His origin was "wropped in mystery," and those who wish to examine his own account of his youth, parentage and early adventures can, unfortunately, only do so by reading his latest book, *My Life and Loves*, which is a work of almost pure pornography. Copies coming into England by post are seized and

destroyed by the postal authorities, and anyone found selling it
would be liable to be sent to prison.

During the short period already alluded to in this book when
I was on friendly terms with Harris again—after an interval of
fifteen years' estrangement—when he was writing the "New
Preface" to *The Life and Confessions of Oscar Wilde*, he sent
me a copy of *My Life and Loves* to the hotel where I was staying
in Nice. I read about thirty or forty pages of it and then wrapped
it up in paper and sent it back to Harris by special messenger
with a note in which I told him that it was quite impossible for
me to keep such a book in my possession, and begging him, if he
wished to continue on good terms with me and not once more
to break up our newly re-established *entente*, not to mention it
or discuss it with me. Beyond a jocular remark about my
"prudery" he never referred to the subject again.

From what I saw of Harris's book, I think that if all the filth
were cut out of it, it would make a very interesting biography.
Harris's life, apart from his sordid and depressing "amatory"
adventures, was, according to his own account, dramatic and
adventurous. His father, if I remember right, was a skipper in
the Merchant Service. Harris ran away from home at the age
of about sixteen and went to America, where he was in turn a
"bell-boy," a cowboy, an advertising canvasser and a journalist.
He seems to have had a thirst for knowledge and a real love of
literature, and some rich man paid for him to go to a university.
I believe he is a good scholar. You cannot be in his company
more than an hour without hearing him quote a long passage in
Greek from the *Odyssey*. He does it with great gusto and in a
sonorous voice. It is true that it is always the same passage,
but, on the strength of it, I am quite prepared to accept his
word that he is or was a good Greek scholar.

I myself knew Greek quite well when I was at Oxford.
The other day I came across two volumes of Herodotus which I

used when I was reading for " Greats." They were interleaved and had copious notes in my handwriting, including long passages in Greek. I am, I regret to say, utterly unable to read or understand a word of Greek to-day. So I should be the last to deny Harris's title to have been the scholar he claims to have been. I know that he was for a time a master at Brighton Grammar School, but what he taught the boys there I have no idea.

His chief asset at the time when I first met him in London was (as it is to-day) his deep and impressive voice—his " sucking-dove roar," as Crosland in Shakespearian phrase called it. He and Wilde met at a dinner-party and Harris told the company an epic story about some prize-fight where Slavin the Australian fighter was attacked by the crowd, and how he fought the whole lot with his back to the wall. Oscar, who up till then had disliked and avoided Harris, was fascinated by the splendid way Harris told the story. He complimented Harris, and they immediately became friends.

Harris was afterwards owner and editor of *The Saturday Review* and, later, of *Vanity Fair*. When he had the last-named paper I occasionally wrote for him, and he published in its columns a quantity of my light verse, as well as one or two of my sonnets.

Harris has written a lot about Shakespeare. His book, *Shakespeare the Man*, is interesting, and shows that he has a profound knowledge of Shakespeare's text, but the conclusions he arrives at seem to me to be fantastic and demonstrably false. As I pointed out in an article in *Plain English*, Harris's main idea was to " prove " that Shakespeare was very much the same sort of man as Harris. This is not a view that I can accept.

Quite apart from anything he has written about me in his book, *The Life and Confessions of Oscar Wilde*, it is very easy to demonstrate that Frank Harris is a monumental liar and worthy in that respect to rank with Robert Ross and Wilde himself.

When I was his guest at Nice in 1925 he was rash enough to present me with a copy of his book, *Contemporary Portraits— Fourth Series*. The first pen " portraits " in the book are those of Wilfrid Scawen Blunt and George Wyndham, both of whom were my cousins, and with both of whom I was on very intimate terms. I quote the first paragraph of the chapter, more as an example of ignorance than lying :

" The other day Wilfrid Blunt died, when over eighty years old, and left everything he possessed to his secretary. . . . Those who knew the man and the chief circumstances were not surprised, but most people, and particularly those who knew a little, were dumbfounded.   Surely Blunt had a daughter ? Why had he not left his property, and especially Crabbet Park, to her ? "

Anyone who knows anything at all about the matter knows that Mr Blunt's daughter, my cousin Judith, formerly the Honourable Mrs Neville Lytton and now Lady Wentworth (she is a peeress in her own right), is in possession of Crabbet Park, which her father made over to her in his lifetime. When he died he left the little Jacobean manor-house, Newbuildings Place, and a few hundred acres to his cousin, Miss Dorothy Carleton, who had kept house for him during the last few years of his life. This house was not a family place, and he was, of course, free to leave it away from his daughter, who in addition to the entailed property had all her mother Lady Anne's money, and will also ultimately inherit a large part of Lord Lovelace's property.

Harris goes on to talk of " when I knew Blunt, in the eighties," and, following his usual custom in dealing with dead celebrities, he pretends to an intimacy which is purely imaginary, and reports long and equally imaginary conversations.

Wilfrid Blunt told me that he had seen Harris only once, when he came to interview him for a paper, and that after a conversation lasting about five minutes he rang the bell and told the servant to show Harris out !

Harris in the same chapter of his book gives a long account of the meeting of the Crabbet Club when Oscar Wilde was " attacked " (in a chaffing way, in an after-dinner speech) by the late Lord Curzon of Kedleston, and Oscar's reply. He represents that he (Harris) was present on this occasion. He goes on to give an account of what happened the year after that at the annual meeting of the Crabbet Club (when, as it happens, I, the youngest and most recently elected member, was present). Again he describes the scene throughout as if he had been present, and he says plainly that he was a member of the club.

This is an almost incredible piece of impudence. Harris never belonged to the Crabbet Club, and was never present at any meeting of that club. There are at least a dozen members of the club now living who would bear me out in this—for instance, Lord Crewe and Mr Laurence Currie.

Harris describes the whole scene from the description which I gave to him and Wilde at the time. He goes on to give conversations with George Wyndham which bear the plainest evidence of their utter falsity on their surface. Wyndham, it is true, did know Harris slightly, and, I believe, once dined with him and his wife in Park Lane, but he disliked and mistrusted Harris intensely, and when I became very friendly with Harris, at the time of the South African War, when George was Under-Secretary for War, he wrote me a letter warning me against having anything to do with Harris, of whom he expressed a very low opinion.

The rest of Harris's book consists of portraits of persons with most of whom I have never had any personal acquaintance. But *ex pede Herculem.*

As to Robert Ross, when I first met him he was a rather pathetic-looking little creature, in appearance something like a kitten. He was the son of a Canadian lawyer who, I believe, at one time, occupied a prominent position in Canadian politics, but who was ruined financially by the Grand Trunk Railway smash. Robert Ross (called by his friends Bobbie or Robbie) lived with his mother, Mrs Ross, a charming old lady, who had a house in Onslow Gardens. He went up to Cambridge, but after he had been a year there he was " ragged " by the undergraduates of his college (King's) and ducked in the fountain. The reason of his unpopularity I do not know, but anyhow, he left Cambridge abruptly. At the time I first met him, about eighteen months later, he had known Oscar Wilde for about a year. He had by that time moved into rooms of his own in Church Street, Kensington (No. 39, I think). He had a tiny bedroom and sitting-room there, and an allowance from his mother of £200 a year. He earned a little more by writing for *The Saturday Review*, under the editorship of the late Mr Pollock.

He also knew Henley, and introduced me to him in Henley's favourite resort, the Solferino Café (now extinct), in Rupert Street. Henley liked Ross in those days, and, I believe, also gave him work. Afterwards Henley's hatred of Oscar Wilde caused a breach between them. The same cause prevented Henley from printing in his monthly review, *The New Review*, my " Ballad of Perkin Warbeck," which he greatly admired, and which was shown to him on my behalf by George Street, at that time a great friend of mine.

Ross was by way of being devoted to me in those days. If I had followed his example, and kept the letters he wrote to me, I could have showed that he professed devotion and admiration for me in as extravagant terms as those used by Wilde. It was I that made Ross socially, for but for me he would never have got to know the people in " Society " whose countenance he so skilfully exploited in later years. I brought him to my mother's house in Cadogan Place, where he met a lot of people whom (without any desire to be snobbish) I can only describe as being in a much higher class than himself. I also, later, introduced him to the Glenconners, through whom he became very friendly with Mrs Asquith, who was his principal stand-by after his *débâcle* in 1914, and who also signed the celebrated "Testimonial" which was given to him after his exposure at the Old Bailey.

In the early days I was very fond of Ross, and it is difficult for me to realize, even now, that he was the same man who afterwards treated me in so cruel and abominable a fashion. I cannot recall another instance of such a complete change of character as that which took place in this nervous, affectionate, sentimental and emotional little man, between the time when I first met him and the last twelve years of his life. The last time I set eyes on him in 1914 at the Old Bailey he was, I must say, not a pleasant object to behold. It would have been impossible to recognize the slender, attractive, impulsive boy I had once known in that sinister-looking, bloated and bald-headed person, with his snaky eyes, his round bulging face and body, and his nigger-like mouth and teeth.

Ross left about £40,000 when he died. How he got it I do not know, though I can make a guess. When I first knew him he had only a small allowance from his mother, and was always desperately "hard up." At her death he got a small income (certainly not more than £500 a year). He then ran a little picture-shop in Ryder Street, and it afterwards blossomed into a bigger establishment, known as " Carfax," in Bury Street. According to what he told me himself, this business was never a great financial success. But he became friendly with the Asquiths, and the late Lord Oxford, when he was Prime

Minister, gave him a government appointment as " Assessor of Picture Valuations to the Board of Trade."

After the collapse of his prosecution of me at the Old Bailey, to which I have already alluded, he, of course, lost this job. He was given another job later, during the Premiership of Mr. Lloyd George, but he died suddenly one night just after he had got his appointment, and before he had had time to enjoy any of its fruits. His great friend, when I knew him, was Mr More Adey, also at one time a great friend of my own, and after Ross left Church Street, Kensington, he and Adey shared rooms for years in Hornton Street, and afterwards again in another house in Church Street. Ross died in rooms in Half Moon Street, which he had occupied then for several years. I am informed that his death took place on the night after he had given a dinner at Prince's Restaurant to a company of his friends to " celebrate " his new appointment. He was found dead in the morning by his servant.

He was undoubtedly a man of brains and ability, and a good talker. After Wilde's death he seemed to make a fairly successful effort to model himself on Wilde as a conversationalist. His writings consisted of only a few odd " papers." I myself published a story by him in my Oxford magazine, *The Spirit Lamp.* It was called " How We Lost the Book of Jasher." It was quite a good story, but Ross never had any real pretensions to outstanding literary talent, and would never have come into prominence apart from his association with Wilde and the fact that he became Wilde's literary executor.

He played this up for all he was worth, and he made numerous friends in more or less prominent positions in society. His method was flattery " laid on with a trowel."

He could, when he liked, make himself very agreeable, and he always contrived to convey to the particular person with whom he wished to ingratiate himself that he or she was the object of his profound and respectful admiration. When you had had ten minutes' conversation with him you went away with a pleasing feeling that you were really an important person, and that Ross appreciated it, and would never be likely to forget it. The resultant glow of satisfaction, multiplied in hundreds of different cases, produced the atmosphere which enabled Ross to climb into a position which was far beyond the wildest dreams of his youth.

Max Beerbohm was my contemporary at Oxford and we were on intimate terms. I met him through his chief friend there, Reggie Turner, also a contemporary and a great friend of mine. They were both friends of Ross's and Adey's. I published in my undergraduate paper, *The Spirit Lamp*, the first article of Max's that ever appeared in print. It was an essay on "The Incomparable Beauty of Modern Dress." It was an entirely characteristic piece of cleverness and artificiality, and caused intense annoyance to the " Philistines " of the period. I do not think it has ever been reprinted. It was signed " H. M. Beerbohm."

When I quarrelled with Ross I lost touch with both Turner and Beerbohm. This I regretted very much, especially in the case of Turner, of whom I was very fond, and who was at one time quite devoted to me. When I was in Cairo, as the guest of the Cromers, Reggie Turner was staying with his half-brother, Frank Lawson, on a dahabeeyah which was the last word in comfort and luxury. I was a frequent guest on the boat. Reggie Turner is the author of a number of novels, but I believe the only poem he ever wrote in his life was addressed to me. It was a "sonnet," and was produced after terrific wrestlings of the spirit on board the dahabeeyah. I remember only the first two lines :

> More fair than any flower is thy face,
> Thy limbs from all comparison are free.

Reggie Turner, Robert Hichens and E. F. Benson were all at Luxor, staying in the same hotel as myself, and we went up the Nile in a " Post Boat."   I saw a lot of Hichens at Luxor, and he wrote his book, *The Green Carnation*, entirely on the strength and as the result of his association with me, for he had at that time never met Oscar Wilde. The book did me a lot of harm, and the writing of it (and the appropriation without acknowledgment of a large number of my " good things " and jokes) constituted a piece of perfidy for which I refrain from reproaching its author because he has publicly expressed his contrition for it.

Freddie Benson, on the other hand, was a real friend, who tried to influence me in the right direction, and who also endeavoured to get his publisher, Methuen, to publish my poems. Methuen declined them after being kind enough to say that they " showed a certain amount of promise," and they were afterwards " turned down " by, among others, Heinemann. As already related, they were first published in 1896 by the *Mercure de France*, and in London in 1899 by Grant Richards. I afterwards, when I became a Catholic, was a great friend of Hugh Benson (Monsignor Benson), and stayed with him on several occasions in his house near Buntingford.

¶ I knew Aubrey Beardsley, and met him often, in London, with Wilde and Ross ; but truth compels me to say that I did not like him, although I greatly admired some of his drawings. I liked poor Dowson, and regret that in the last two years of his life, when he was living on a small pittance from Smithers, the publisher, I did not do what I might have done to help him. I also used to meet Arthur Symons pretty frequently, but I was never on anything like terms of friendship or intimacy with him. I recognize his great talents now more than I did in those days. But from the poetical point of view he belongs to a school which I cannot truthfully profess to admire.

CHAPTER XII

FROM the day when I first met Oscar Wilde, as I have described, he "made up to me" in every possible way. He was continually asking me to dine or lunch with him, and sending me letters, notes and telegrams. He flattered me, gave me presents, and made much of me in every way. He gave me copies of all his books, with inscriptions in them. He wrote a sonnet to me, and gave it to me at dinner one night in a restaurant. That was after I had known him about six months. It is in the Methuen complete edition, and it begins : " The sin was mine, I did not understand." Anyone who takes the trouble to read it carefully will see that it shows clearly that the " familiarities " (to use Harris's word) had not then begun. I wish to get over this odious subject once for all as quickly as possible. These familiarities were rare, but they did occur spasmodically. They began about nine months after I first met Oscar Wilde as the result of a long, patient and strenuous siege on his part. They were completely discontinued about six months before the final catastrophe, and were never resumed after he came out of prison. Wilde always claimed that his love for me was ideal and spiritual. I once, after he came out of prison, in the course of a somewhat acrimonious discussion, brought up against him that this was not strictly the case, and that there had been another side to it. He said : " Oh, it was so little that, and then only by accident, essentially it was always a reaching up towards the ideal, and in the end it became utterly ideal." Honestly, I believe he thought this to be true and meant what he said. In any case I am perfectly certain that his love for me, such as it really was before he went to prison, was the nearest he ever got to a pure and spiritual love. I have here, at great cost to myself, given a

true account of our relations. Anyone is at liberty to believe me
or not, but I wish to say solemnly that I have not tried to gloss
them over or make them appear less guilty than they were. Of
the sin which takes its name from one of the Cities of the Plain
there never was the slightest question. I give this as my solemn
word before God, as I hope to be saved. What there was, was
quite bad enough. But, as I have already remarked, when all this
happened I had been six years at school and at Oxford, and I had
lost my moral sense and had no religion. Years afterwards, when
I became a Catholic, in the course of the " general confession "
which every convert has to make as a preliminary to being
received into the Church, I confessed all this, but I said then
to the priest who heard my confession (Monsignor Bickerstaffe
Drew) : " At the time when I did these things I did not consider them wrong. If I had thought them wrong I would not
have done them."

Even before I met Wilde I had persuaded myself that " sins
of the flesh " were not wrong, and my opinion was of course
vastly strengthened and confirmed by his brilliantly reasoned
defence of them, which may be said almost to have been the
gospel of his life. He went through life preaching the gospel
which he puts into the mouth of Lord Henry Wotton in *Dorian
Gray*. Wilde was, in fact, a most powerful and convincing
heresiarch. He preached that it was the duty of every man to
" live his own life to the utmost," to " be always seeking for
new sensations," and to have what he called " the courage " to
commit " what are called sins." I am trying to be fair to Wilde
and not to make him responsible for " corrupting " me more
than he did. All the same, I must say that it strikes me now
that the difference between us was this : that I was at that
time a frank and natural pagan, and that he was a man who
believed in sin and yet deliberately committed it, thereby
obtaining a doubly perverse pleasure. I was a boy and he

was a *blasé* and very intellectual and brilliant man who had immense experience of life. Inevitably I assimilated his views to a great extent. In fact, I was so completely obsessed by them that they exercised over me the same kind of subconscious tyranny which the Darwinian theory of man's evolution from apes exercises over the minds of millions of men at this day. I really thought Wilde's arguments were unanswerable, just as otherwise reasonable people are hypnotized by the Darwinian theory, which as a matter of fact is only a theory, and likely to remain one.

Long after Wilde was dead, and after I was married and had utterly got away from the Wilde cult and tradition, I went on subconsciously believing that he was, more or less, a prophet and that his views about morals, whether one liked them or not, were based on abstract truth and were unanswerable and irrefutable. It was not till after Wilde had been dead at least eight years, and while (being then of course quite ignorant of the way he had turned and rent me in the unpublished part of *De Profundis*) I was still devoted to his memory, that it first occurred to me that he really was a very wicked man, quite apart from his sexual aberrations. I was then gradually getting towards a comprehension of the Christian system of ethics which I had so long scorned. I passed through about two years of High Church Anglicanism while I was editing *The Academy*, and then, in 1911, I became a Catholic.

It is a consideration of all these facts and abstractions which makes it impossible for me to pretend, as I would really like to be able to do (if only for the sake of obliging Mr Frank Harris), that Wilde's friendship was ever any kind of a blessing to me, or that I owe him anything which I would not willingly part with, if I have not done so already. As I have already stated, it was certainly not he who taught me to love poetry or to write it. In the articles I wrote in my undergraduate magazine, *The Spirit*

Lamp, and even in some of my first articles in *The Academy* (about 1907–1908), it is easy to trace a certain amount of his influence on my style and point of view ; but I will defy anyone to find it in the stuff I wrote in prose in the last two years of my editorship of *The Academy* or in that which I wrote in *Plain English* (1920–1921). While as far as poetry (which is my long suit) is concerned I can say without much fear of contradiction that (fortunately for me) he had no influence on me at all.

His views on poetry, and on literature generally, were on the whole much sounder than one might suppose would be likely to be the case. He liked the best among dead authors, and was not above admitting that Dickens was a man of great genius ; and he had a very fair critical faculty. On the whole I would, even as I am now, have trusted him to pick out good new stuff when he saw it for the first time. He was quite capable of admiring the work of persons whom he personally disliked (a feat which appears to be beyond the compassing of a good many of our present-day critics)—Henley, for example—and he always spoke generously about his contemporaries, provided, of course, that his artistic conscience (which was much more potent than his moral conscience) would permit him to do so. He greatly admired Pater, and he told me he would rather have written Swinburne's *Poems and Ballads : First Series* than anything that had appeared in the English language in his lifetime. He thought highly of Meredith, even more so of Tennyson, and he admired Frank Harris's short stories, *Elder Conklin,* and so forth—more than I have been able to do myself. He had at one time a considerable cult for Robert Louis Stevenson, and he was even sometimes enthusiastic about Kipling. His taste was sufficiently catholic to include Anatole France, Paul Bourget and Huysmans.

He always professed to admire my poetry very much, though in the unpublished part of *De Profundis* (I am obliged to call it "the unpublished part " to differentiate it from the well-known book, though actually the "unpublished part" has been published broadcast in our own newspapers and in book form in America, Germany and France) he refers to it contemptuously as my "undergraduate verse." However, as in the same intemperate outburst of spite and malice he makes slighting remarks about my personal appearance, and refers sneeringly to my "low stature" (I am five feet nine inches, which for a man of my originally very slight build and weight, nine stone seven in those days, was just about the right height), I do not take what he says very seriously. What I mean is that if he had worked himself up in *De Profundis* into the incredible state of mind in which he could run down the personal appearance of "Hylas" and "Hyacinthus" (not to insist on "the Rose of all the World," as he once called me in a letter) there can be no difficulty in supposing that his detraction of my poetry (which he had professed greatly to admire) was on the same level of sincerity or insincerity.

To sum up what I want to convey, I mean that while he certainly did not corrupt my taste in literature, or do me any harm from a literary point of view, I am not conscious of being under any debt to him in that direction; while on the moral side he did exercise a most frightful influence on me, which it took me many years to outgrow.

How then can I pretend to feel gratitude to him for what he did? All I can truly say is that I was at one time absolutely devoted to him, as he undoubtedly was to me, and that in those days my greatest pleasure was to be with him. He had delightful gifts as a talker and as a friend. He was (before prison had smashed him and demoralized him) most kind and hospitable, and generally sweet-tempered. The appalling bad taste of his references in the unpublished part of *De Profundis* to the money he spent on entertaining the darling of his heart and soul would have been utterly impossible to the old Oscar

Wilde as I first knew him, even if his always exuberant
imagination had been equal to the task of inflating that sum
into the good round one of five thousand pounds, which is the
figure he arrived at in gaol, apparently by the simple process of
adding together nearly all the money he had during all the
time that he had known me, and lumping it together as the
amount he had spent on me !

I have expressed in one of the sonnets I wrote about him
after he was dead, *The Dead Poet,* the magical quality of his
conversation :

> And as of old, in music measureless,
> I heard his golden voice, and marked him trace
> Under the common thing the hidden grace,
> And conjure wonder out of emptiness,
> Till mean things put on Beauty like a dress
> And all the world was an enchanted place. . .

He did succeed in weaving spells. One sat and listened to him
enthralled. It all appeared to be Wisdom and Power and Beauty
and Enchantment. It was indeed enchantment and nothing else.
But a man who has broken loose from a spell cannot look back
on the enchantment again and recapture the illusion of the
shattered spell. He can only, as I do, remember that it was so,
and wonder, and perhaps shudder a little.

CHAPTER XIII

I MUST beg to point out that if in this book I go into the odious question of finance it is only because Wilde has forced me to do it by the deliberate lies and misrepresentations he was guilty of in the unpublished part of *De Profundis*, and again, afterwards, by word of mouth to numerous persons between the time of his release from prison and his death. As I have already remarked in my last chapter, this meanness and bad taste were quite alien to Oscar Wilde as I first knew him. Up to the time of his imprisonment he was exceedingly generous, hospitable and open-handed. It was surely natural enough that a man of nearly forty, who takes a violent fancy to an undergraduate of twenty-one and constantly invites him to lunch and dinner at the best restaurants, should incur a certain amount of expense without expecting that his young friend should make a point of keeping the account balanced by an equal return of hospitality.

When I first met Oscar he had an income of at least £2000 a year (quite a lot of money, I can assure you, in the eighteen-nineties, and equal to at least £4000 in the present day), and I had an allowance from my father of £350 a year. I lived with my mother, of course, and had practically everything paid for me, besides having the run of a large number of country houses, and so many invitations to balls, parties and dinners that it would have been impossible for me to keep pace with them all, even if I had tried to do so. Obviously, at my age, and with my amount of pocket-money, I was more often a guest than a host. But as Oscar Wilde has set down, in his unpublished *De Profundis* letter, the grossly untrue statement that he had spent more than £5000 in entertaining me during the time that elapsed between our first meeting and his conviction and imprisonment (just about three years), I am constrained to say that £500 or £600 would be much nearer the mark. On the other side of the balance sheet there is to be considered that, about a year after I first met Wilde, my father wrote to me and said that unless I dropped his acquaintance, and gave my word of honour that I would have no more to do with him, my allowance would cease. I refused to drop Wilde, and told my father that if he was mean enough to stop my allowance he must do so. My allowance was stopped in the year 1893, nor did I ever receive another penny from my father till his death in December 1899, when I came automatically into my share of the money provided for the younger children of his marriage. So that my friendship with Wilde and my refusal to give him up cost me £2450 in those seven years. What I lost in other ways, such as social position, the natural and unquestioned right of entry into the inner circle of what was probably at that time the most exclusive and aristocratic set in the world, is not to be gauged in terms of money. But to stick solely to the money side, I may say, as I said in *Oscar Wilde and Myself*, that I really actually spent far more on him than he did on me. When he started to fight with my father I gave him £360 to pay the expenses of the action (of course I had to get the money from my mother, but practically all the money I had at all after my father cut off my allowance came from my mother), and later, when I left him in my villa at Naples, I gave him £200. Not much, you may say, but it was all I could manage to get, and represented a lot to me at the time.

During the five years that elapsed between Wilde's imprisonment and the death of my father, when I came into a certain amount of money, I was always very "hard up." My average income during those years, most of which I spent abroad and living "on my own," was certainly not more than £400 a year. In fact I had barely enough to keep myself going, but even so I was continually helping Wilde to the utmost extent that I could manage. In the year that elapsed between the death of my father and that of Wilde himself I gave the latter quite £1000. As long as he lived I would have gone on giving him money whenever I had it to give. The last cheque I sent him (for £10) reached him—as (marvellous to relate) is actually recorded by Robert Ross in his account of Oscar's death, which appears in Harris's *Life and Confessions of Oscar Wilde*—only a few days before he died.

Frank Harris, in that book, affirms that after Oscar's release from prison what he is pleased to describe as the "Queensberry family" undertook to provide Wilde with money, and he bitterly reproaches me, by implication, because this money was not forthcoming. Like almost everything else in Harris's book which concerns me, directly or indirectly, this story is utterly untrue. Who were the "Queensberry family" at that time? The term in this connection could apply only to my father, who had deliberately smashed Wilde, and would be as likely to give him money or any other assistance as he would have been to give it to the devil himself; my mother, who looked upon Wilde as a villain and a scoundrel, and bitterly lamented my association with him; and my brother, Percy (afterwards ninth Marquis of Queensberry), who disliked and despised Wilde, and did what he did for him (that is to say, went bail for him after he had been committed for trial) only at my urgent request, because he loved me and was prepared to back me up against my father, or against anyone else, to the last limit of his capacity.

The only glimmering of a foundation for this preposterous story of promised assistance for Wilde from "the Queensberry family" lies in the fact that I myself told Wilde on one occasion that I would endeavour to get my brother Percy to help him. I was as good as my word, and I did implore my brother to "do something for him." My brother was the most good-natured and kind-hearted man who ever lived, and he was also devoted to me. His answer to my appeal was the answer he almost invariably made to any appeal for assistance that I ever made to him. He was, as everyone who knew him could testify, a man who always imagined that he was just on the brink of making an enormous fortune. He replied to my request by telling me that he was " for the moment very pushed for money," but that in a few months he expected to bring off a very big *coup*, and that as soon as the *coup* materialized I could have all the money I wanted, to give to Wilde or for any other purpose. " Don't worry, my dearest boy," he wrote ; " in a short time I shall be a very rich man, and if I am a rich man you, of course, will be the same." Naturally, being in those days nothing if not an optimist, I passed on the glad tidings to Oscar ; and it is on this slender foundation that Harris's bunkum about the " Queensberry family's undertaking to provide for Oscar Wilde " is based. To do my dear brother justice, I do not doubt for a moment that if he had brought off a " big *coup* " at that time, or at any time afterwards, he would have immediately made me a large participator in his good fortune ; but the *coup* never materialized, and, on the contrary, my brother, instead of making a fortune, lost practically every penny he had in the world, including about £300,000 which he inherited at the death of my father.

The time when he came into this money synchronized with my own inheritance of my modest younger son's portion, so that there was, naturally, no call on him to provide anything for Wilde, whom, as I have already stated, I immediately made a participator in my improved fortunes. Oscar Wilde lived only a year after my father's death, and during that year he had enough money from me and from other sources (including Frank Harris, who claims to have given him £1000) to have lived in the greatest comfort and luxury. I commend these facts—which, as far as my share is concerned at any rate, can be proved by documentary [1] and legal evidence—to Mr Robert Harborough Sherard, who is chiefly responsible for the legend that Wilde was " left by his friends to starve in Paris." I also commend them to Messrs André Gide and Davray, who have added their quota to the heavy load of unprovoked and reckless abuse, calumny and vilification which has been heaped on me in return for the constant sacrifice of my own interests which I made on Wilde's behalf from the day of his downfall to the hour of his death.

[1] *See* Appendix, p. 319.

CHAPTER XIV

During the three years which elapsed between my first meeting with Oscar and his conviction in 1895 I stayed with him, as his guest, in Lady Mount Temple's house at Babbacombe (the house was lent to him and Mrs Wilde), where he wrote *A Woman of No Importance*, at a farmhouse which he took near Cromer, at a house in Goring, where he wrote *An Ideal Husband*, and at Worthing, where he wrote *The Importance of Being Earnest*. In every single case Mrs Wilde was with him, though at Goring she was absent for some weeks. He stayed with me as my guest on two occasions at Oxford in the rooms (34 High Street, over the Loders Club) which I shared with my great friend, Lord Encombe. He also stayed at my mother's house near Bracknell. On several occasions we went abroad together. We went to Paris, to Algiers and to Florence. At the last-named place I was by myself for some time, my mother having sent me there chiefly with the idea of getting me away from Oscar. But after I had been there about a month he followed me. While at Florence he began *A Florentine Tragedy*, but whether he finished it there or not I cannot now remember. During the time I was with him I wrote some of my own best poetry.

I was away from him altogether for quite three months when I went to stay at Cairo as the guest of Lord and Lady Cromer, at the British Agency. Lady Cromer (Lord Cromer's first wife and the mother of the present Lord Cromer) was one of my mother's greatest friends. (I have already referred to the wildly untrue statements Oscar makes in the unpublished part of *De Profundis* referring to this time, during which there was a slight coolness between us.) My devotion to Oscar was at this time again a serious handicap to my material and social interest. In this way. After I had been with the Cromers for three months I was, partly through the influence of my grandfather, Alfred Montgomery, and partly through the good offices of Lord Cromer himself, appointed honorary attaché to the Ambassador at Constantinople, Lord Currie.

The news of the appointment was given to me by Lord Cromer, and I must say, in explanation of subsequent events, that I did not get the impression that I was bound to take it up immediately. I told Lord Cromer that before going to Constantinople I wanted to go back to London, or at any rate as far as Paris. He did not raise the slightest objection, nor did he give me any hint whatever that such a proceeding on my part would be construed (as it actually was) into a piece of rudeness or impertinence to Lord Currie.

My longing to see Oscar Wilde again was what made me go back to Paris. I wrote and told him I was coming and asked him to meet me there. In the "unpublished *De Profundis*" he represents that he, at that time, had determined to break away from me, and that he came to meet me again with reluctance. This is deliberately untrue. As soon as I suggested meeting him in Paris he telegraphed his delight at the prospect. I left Cairo and went with "Dodo" Benson, the novelist, with whom I was at that time on terms of great friendship, to Athens, where I stayed as his guest at some rooms he had there. I spent about a week there in perfect weather and passed most of my time sitting in the Acropolis and delighting in the Greek sculpture and its contrast to what I have always regarded as the ugly and unattractive Egyptian monuments. I greatly enjoyed my visit, and Reggie Lister, who was there at the Legation as second secretary, made himself very agreeable, as he always did.

I then went on to Paris, where I spent a week with Oscar,

and so back to London to my mother's house. I fully intended to go on to Constantinople after spending a few days with my mother. But directly I got back I was told that Lord Currie was in a frightful rage because I had not come straight on to Constantinople, that he regarded my conduct as a piece of insolence, and that he now declined to have me as honorary attaché. I was amazed to hear all this, but not particularly perturbed. The disapproval of Lord Currie left me quite unaffected. I had never had the honour of meeting him, though I knew his brother, Bertram Currie (the head of the family), very well, and he (Bertram Currie) was a friend of my mother's and had always been charming to me. I am afraid that I simply regarded and stigmatized Lord Currie's indignation as an unreasonable display of "middle-class fussiness." I failed to understand what it was all about, and secretly I was delighted to escape from the necessity of going to Constantinople, and to be able to get back to London. Looking back at the whole thing now, I still do not understand why Lord Currie should have been angry. The only possible explanation of his attitude, which has since occurred to me, is that someone may have made mischief by deliberately misrepresenting the facts, and by representing my attitude towards my appointment as one of what Frank Harris is fond of describing as "aristocratic insolence."

All I can say is that I had not the slightest intention of being rude to Lord Currie, that I was gratified at getting the appointment, that I liked what I had seen of diplomatic life (I spent most of my time in the "Chancery" at Cairo and was good friends with all the secretaries and attachés, particularly with Mitchell-Innes), and that if I had known that it was expected of me I would have gone straight off to Constantinople without a murmur. As it was, and considering that I went back to Paris and London with the knowledge and approval of Lord Cromer, and after consulting him, I cannot see that I was in the least to blame. I regard the whole incident as one of those numerous cases in which my most simple and harmless acts have been misconstrued and misrepresented, and when I have been blamed and abused without the slightest regard to kindness or charity or good feeling. If Lord Currie—who, to quote Wilde, did not "rise from the ranks of the aristocracy but was born in the purple of commerce"—had been a little more *grand seigneur* than he was he would not have made such a ridiculous fuss, and it would not have occurred to him (he was a newly created peer) that any assault on his dignity had been so much as dreamed of. However, there was the end of my "diplomatic career," and I was in disgrace with my grandfather, Alfred Montgomery, and once more exposed to the risks of the mad-dog threats of my father, who had then already for some time past been threatening Oscar Wilde and me because of our association and our being constantly in each other's company in public places.

The miserable story of how my father deliberately set about ruining his son under the hypocritical pretence of "saving" him has been told often enough, with more or less accuracy. In the letter I wrote to Frank Harris at Nice in 1925 (which is incorporated in the "New Preface" to *The Life and Confessions of Oscar Wilde*, which Harris undertook to print as a Preface to all future editions of his book, while at the same time deleting or annotating and stigmatizing as deliberately false practically everything he says about me in that book) I have given my final and official account of the matter. I am very reluctant to rewrite the story once more. The simplest thing is to reproduce that portion of my letter to Harris which relates to the action of my father, and my own action in advising Oscar Wilde to fight him, and supporting him, as I did, with money and with my offer to go into the witness-box for him. This I do in the next chapter.

CHAPTER XV

"MY DEAR FRANK,—I do not dispute the substantial accuracy of your account in your book of the meeting between Oscar Wilde and myself on the one hand and Bernard Shaw and yourself on the other, at the Café Royal, just before the proceedings against my father were started. Your complaint against me as expressed in your book is that, having heard all you had to say about the strength of the case against Oscar, I still persisted in egging him on to fight, and declared that anyone who advised him to the contrary was not playing the part of a true friend. It is true that you presented my father's case quite correctly. At the time both Oscar and I already knew what that case was. My father had declared, from the first moment that the proceedings against him were started in the police court, that he intended to plead 'justification,' that is to say, prove that what he had written was true and written 'in the public interest.' Whether or not Oscar and I had actually seen my father's 'plea of justification' at the time when the Café Royal incident took place I can't say for certain, but in any case we saw the plea and went through it, with all its names and allegations, and particulars, with Sir Edward Clarke and his junior, Mr (now Sir) Travers Humphreys, and the solicitor, Mr C. O. Humphreys, in Clarke's chambers, at least a week before the case opened at the Old Bailey.

" It follows that what you said to Oscar about my father's plea was no news to us ; and we both knew all about it, and knowing all about it had resolved to fight. Neither you nor Shaw had the slightest idea (because we did not tell you) what our case against my father was. In the event, this case was never brought before the jury at all, but at the time when the Café Royal interview took place, Sir Edward Clarke was pledged to fight the case according to my ideas and to put me into the witness-box immediately after his opening speech. If you want to know why he didn't do this, I can only say that you had better ask him. I have never seen him or spoken to him since the catastrophe, for which he, in my opinion, was largely responsible, though I don't for a moment suggest that he acted otherwise than in what he considered to be the best interests of his client.

"To understand what our case against my father was, it is necessary to understand what his relations had been at that time for at least twenty years with my mother and us children, his sons. I don't like dragging things up against my father, and in my own book, *Oscar Wilde and Myself*, I have allowed him to keep the *beau rôle* which public opinion gave him at that time, but to which he was, in truth, very far from being entitled. It seems that the time has come when the whole truth, and the real truth, *must* be told. The case against my father, which Sir Edward Clarke undertook and solemnly promised to bring before the Court in his opening speech, and to support with my evidence in the witness-box, was simply that he was an inhuman brute, that he had bullied and persecuted and outraged my mother for years (long even before she divorced him in 1887, seven years before the case between Wilde and him came on), and that he had for twenty years neglected and ill-treated his children and had forfeited all claim to a father's authority over them.

" I am not going into a lot of details. The memory of the whole business is sickening to me, and it is hateful to have to write about it, but I will give you one or two instances of the sort of man he was. For years before my mother at last divorced him (the final straw that broke the back of my

mother's angelic patience was that my father wanted to bring
his mistress to my mother's house, and proposed that they
should all three live together under one roof) he had made a
practice of going away for months and years at a time. We
children scarcely ever saw him. Between the time when I was
five years old and the time when the Wilde-Queensberry con-
flict began I can truthfully say that I could count on the
fingers of both hands the number of the occasions when I had
been under the same roof with him. He did not live with us.
He had rooms in London, and he hardly ever turned up at
our house in London or the country except for one or two
nights at the most. I have been as much as two or three years
when I was a boy without seeing him at all.

"After my mother divorced him, the Scottish courts fixed a
certain annual sum of money which he was to pay to my mother
for herself and the education of the children. Although he had
no legal right to do so, he retained in his own hands the payment
of this jointure, which was really a first charge on the whole of
his property and estate. This enabled him to torture my mother
by refusing, as he regularly did, to pay her the allowance when it
came due twice a year. Over and over again he refused to pay
it, and it was necessary for my mother to resort to lawyers and
to go to the first stages of legal proceedings to induce him to pay
her the money necessary to keep up her establishment and to
feed and educate her children. Under threat of legal proceedings he paid a month or so after the right date, but when the
next half-yearly payment came due he would repeat his tactics.

"As I have implied, he practically ceased living with my
mother nearly twenty years before the Wilde-Queensberry case
came on, and seven years before it came on she had divorced him.
During the whole of those years he made a practice of writing
her brutally abusive letters. I have read some of these letters,
and they are the letters of an unmanly brute or a crazy lunatic.

"On one occasion, before the divorce, he suddenly turned up at my mother's house near Ascot, and turned her and all us children out of the house at twenty-four hours' notice, because he wanted to come there for Ascot with a party of his friends, including a certain lady whom it was impossible for my mother to meet. My mother had herself invited a party of a dozen friends for the race week, and my little sister and three of us boys were also in the house. We all had to clear out, bag and baggage, the next day and go up to London, and my mother had to telegraph to all her guests to put them off.

"My father was a madman, and his mania was to persecute my mother. My mother was and is an angel and a saint, who has never done a wrong thing or thought a wrong thought in her life. When my father was dying she went to him, and in the lucid interval that came to him before death he expressed his contrition, but right up to the time of his final illness he continued to persecute her.

"My eldest brother, Drumlanrig, was, just before his early and tragic death, private secretary to Lord Rosebery, who was then Minister for Foreign Affairs under Mr Gladstone. Lord Rosebery suggested that an English peerage should be bestowed upon Drumlanrig, which would enable him to be a Lord-in-Waiting to the Queen. There is no English peerage at present in our family. My father had a Marquisate, Earldom, Viscounty and Barony, but they were all in the peerage of Scotland, and, by an absurd anomaly and injustice to Scotland, a Scottish peerage does not carry with it a seat in the House of Lords. Sixteen Scottish peers are elected by their fellow-peers to sit in the House of Lords as representative peers. The head of our family had always been elected as a representative peer almost as a matter of course. My nephew, the present Marquis, is a representative peer, and my father sat as a representative peer until he made a scene one year by declaring that he was not a Christian and refusing to take the oath, which he characterized as ' Christian tomfoolery.' Thereafter, his fellow-peers refused to elect him again, and he went about raging against them and heaping abuse on them all in consequence. Accordingly, when the proposal to make Drumlanrig a peer of the United Kingdom in the lifetime of his father was mooted, my brother, knowing full well the sort of man my father was, declined it on the grounds that his father would be sure to be furious if he (Drumlanrig) were to have a seat in the House of Lords when Queensberry had none. Gladstone and Rosebery then suggested that my brother should approach my father and ask him if he had any objection or if he would consent to the peerage being given to Drumlanrig. Queensberry, on being approached, was all smiles. He raised no objection at all and declared he was delighted at the honour paid to his son. But Drumlanrig, wishing to bind him down and commit him irrevocably to this consent, begged him to write directly to Gladstone to the effect indicated. This my father did. He wrote to Gladstone thanking him and expressing his great satisfaction at the honour done by Her Majesty to his son.

" Drumlanrig was made a peer of the United Kingdom as Lord Kelhead (the title is now extinct as he died without ' heirs of his body '), and within a month my father was writing abusive and insulting letters to him, to the Queen, to Mr Gladstone, and chiefly to poor Lord Rosebery. He actually threatened to horsewhip the last-named and followed him for that purpose to Homburg, where he used to walk up and down outside Rosebery's hotel with a dog-whip in his hand. The late King Edward (then Prince of Wales) at last interfered, and by the exercise of much tact and conciliation induced my father to give up the idea of thrashing Rosebery and to leave Homburg.

"My father's treatment of my second brother, Percy, late Marquis of Queensberry, and at the time of the Wilde affair

Lord Douglas of Hawick, was just as bad. When Percy married his wife, the charming daughter of a Cornish rector, the off-shoot of an ancient and gentle family, he abused and insulted him without rhyme or reason, and made foul aspersions on his girl-wife and her family, who were utterly unknown to him ; he always refused even to see my brother's beautiful children (two boys and a girl), and he died without ever having set eyes on any of them. Simply because my brother Percy, who loved me dearly, stuck up for me when my father attacked me with brutal abuse and insult after ignoring and neglecting me for years, my father exhausted his vocabulary in abuse of him, and, not content with that, showered obscene and insulting letters and postcards on his young wife. Driven nearly frantic by this treatment, my brother, who simply because I had asked him to help me had gone bail for Wilde after he was committed for trial, meeting his father by chance one day in Piccadilly, went up and asked Queensberry to desist from writing obscene letters to his wife ; my father thereupon (to quote from the report in the papers) 'made a vulgar noise with his lips,' and Percy hit him. My father hit back, and several blows were exchanged before the police came up and took them both in charge. They were both 'bound over to keep the peace.' My father never spoke to Percy again, deprived him of all allowances and financial assistance (thereby compelling Percy to borrow money on his expectations as heir to the entailed property), and per-sisted to the last in ignoring the existence of Percy's wife and children. When he was dying Percy went to see him, and my father spat at him. My brother Percy was the kindest-hearted and sweetest-tempered man I ever met, and such faults as he had were never able to obscure the essential goodness of his character, as an innumerable host of friends of all classes, ranks and con-ditions would testify. My father's treatment of him was brutal. In fact, it was as bad as his treatment of me and Drumlanrig.

"Well, to cut a long story short, this was the Queensberry who was to be presented, with all the forensic skill of Sir Edward Clarke, to the jury and to the public. I attended the consultations with Clarke and told him all the story I have told here and a great deal more beside, and I gave a written 'proof' of it to Humphreys, the solicitor, as a basis of the brief he prepared for Sir Edward Clarke. I told Sir Edward that if he would call me as a witness at the beginning of the case, *before* Wilde, we could create so much feeling and prejudice against my father that no jury would give him a verdict.

"The main point was to show that his pretended solicitude for his son and his alleged desire to 'save' him were nothing but a hypocritical pretence, and that his real object was to do, what in effect he succeeded in doing, ruin his son and finally break the heart of his martyred wife.

"I knew then, instinctively, that if I got into the witness-box I could carry a jury with me. I have proved it since over and over again. I told Clarke that if he did not put me in the witness-box we might as well throw up the case at once. He said, 'Make your mind at rest, Lord Alfred, I agree with everything you say. My idea of the way to conduct this case is to launch out at the outset with a deadly attack on Lord Queensberry for his conduct to his family, of which we have ample proof in his letters to you and to your grandfather, Mr Alfred Montgomery, supplemented by your own evidence.' I said, 'Yes, but will you promise faithfully to put me in the box?' He replied, 'I promise you I will ; you shall go into the box immediately after my opening speech.'

"On that, I went away content. I knew we were in for a hell of a fight ; I knew that Oscar was guilty of what my father had accused him of (though I denied this, on Crosland's advice, in my book *Oscar Wilde and Myself*). I thought we should win, and think so now. I attribute the breakdown of Wilde's case entirely to Sir Edward Clarke's abandonment of his declared intention to conduct the case on the lines indicated. What induced him to change his mind and his tactics I have never had the slightest idea. All I know is that if I had gone into the box I would have won the case for Wilde (who was himself the worst witness I have ever heard give evidence), just as I have won case after case in later years, out of the witness-box, for myself and others (*e.g.* Pemberton-Billing and Crosland).

" At the very worst, even if he had lost the case, there would have been no subsequent criminal prosecution of Wilde. All the sympathy and all the feeling would have been on our side instead of on Queensberry's. This is what I knew and what I was thinking when I met you and Shaw at the Café Royal. I had screwed Oscar up to the ' sticking place,' and I had all my family (leaving out Queensberry) behind me, and I had paid out of my own pocket all the expenses of the case. (This fact, that I paid £360 for the cost of Wilde's case, is always ignored by the Ross-inspired biographers, though in the Ransome trial it was used against me as an example of my unfilial conduct !) When, therefore, you and Shaw gave your advice, based on a one-sided knowledge of the facts, I resented it, and I was terribly afraid that Oscar would weaken and throw up the sponge. I knew he was an awful coward. I did not dare tell you our case for fear that I might not convince you and that you and Shaw might, even after hearing it, argue Wilde out of the state of mind I had got him into. My one object was to get him out of the café as soon as possible. Hence my rudeness. I was rude I quite admit. But then, at that time, I hardly knew you, and I had never even seen Shaw before, and I was then, as I am now, very diffident until aroused by opposition, as, for example, when I am cross-examined, when I become ' a terror,' and more than able to hold my own with any counsel at the Bar."

G

CHAPTER XVI

I SUPPOSE, after all, it is necessary to a complete comprehension of the case that I should fill in the gaps in the narrative contained in the last chapter. The story has been told so often that I am apt to forget that many of my readers may not know it. What happened was that, after I had known Wilde a few months and had been about a great deal with him, my father suddenly one day spoke to me about it, and told me that Wilde was not a fit man for me to associate with. I must do my father the justice to say that at this stage he was not unkind or offensive, as he became afterwards. He light-heartedly told me that I must give up knowing Wilde, and seemed to think that this would be quite enough. Naturally, considering that in the first place I was of age and free to choose my own friends, and in the second place that my father had neglected me for years (in fact, all my life), and had never shown more than the very slightest and most perfunctory interest in my doings, I ignored my father's instructions. I wrote to him and told him that I did not see any reason why I should give up my friend, and that I really could not think of such a thing. I wrote my father a perfectly respectful and affectionate letter and begged him not to interfere. He replied, telling me that I was a fool and a " baby," and that I did not understand what I was doing.

The controversy began to get acrimonious, and my father had already begun to make threats of cutting off my allowance when, one day, while I was lunching with Oscar at the Café Royal (upstairs), my father came in and sat at another table. I immediately went over to my father and asked him to come and join Wilde and me for lunch. He refused at first, but I pressed him and he said, "Very well," and came rather sulkily over to our table. I introduced them to each other. Oscar exerted himself to be agreeable. He was in good form, and in about ten minutes he had my father laughing and listening eagerly to his conversation. The lunch was such a success that when they got on to Christianity (which was my father's bugbear and therefore his favourite topic—he actually, a little while before this time, gave public lectures against Christianity, and he always described himself as an Agnostic) lunch was over and they had got to the cigar and liqueur and coffee stage. In the end I got bored and left them, at about three o'clock, still talking to each other and leaving me out. When I saw Oscar that evening he informed me, with pardonable pride, that he had completely "got round" my father, that they were now great friends and had arranged to meet again, and that the luncheon at the Café Royal had been prolonged till past four o'clock.

I was of course delighted to hear this, and still more so when, two days later, I got a letter from my father saying that he wished to take back all he had said about Oscar Wilde, that he considered him a charming fellow and very clever, and that he did not wonder I was so fond of him. He went on to say that he had been told by his old friend, Lord de Grey (afterwards Lord Ripon), that Wilde was a friend of his and Lady de Grey's, and that he was "perfectly all right" in every way, besides being a man of genius and a most delightful and amusing talker. This pleasant state of affairs lasted, however, only about two months.

One day I got another letter from my father repeating his old accusations against Wilde, and requiring me, once for all, to give an undertaking, on my word of honour, not to see him or associate with him again. Failing this my father told me that he would stop my allowance. I wrote back an angry letter, in which I said that I declined to do anything of the kind. I

reminded my father of his neglect, and said that I did not consider that he had any right to interfere in my life, and I told him
that if he was "mean enough" to stop my allowance he could go
ahead and do it, which he promptly did. I am not justifying my
conduct ; I am merely relating the facts. No doubt it would
have been far better for me if I had obeyed my father. On the
other hand I am entitled to say (and in this I am supported by
my mother and also by my uncle, my father's now sole surviving
brother, the Very Reverend Canon Lord Archibald Douglas,
who is a Catholic priest) that the main responsibility for the
trouble must rest with my father. His brutal treatment of my
mother, his noisy repudiation of Christianity, which had resulted
in his being practically turned out of the House of Lords, and
the fact that he was himself living a notoriously immoral life,
deprived him of what in other circumstances would have been
his legitimate authority. Moreover, considering that such a
short time before he had met and liked Wilde, and had actually
written telling me that he withdrew his aspersions and giving me
full authority to go on with my friendship, I felt that he had at
any rate no right whatever to adopt the threatening and bullying
attitude which he had now taken up. I am the last person in
the world who can be bullied or threatened into doing anything.
In that respect I very much resemble my father. Neither of us
would give way. My father wrote to me in insulting terms, I
replied in the same vein, and when he wrote to me his most
outrageous letter of all, in which he made a perfectly untrue
statement as to something which he alleged he had "seen
with his own eyes" (need I say that his letters have been used
against me in the law courts over and over again ?), I sent him
my celebrated telegram : "What a funny little man you are ! "
I did this deliberately, as being what I considered the most
effective way of hitting back at him.

Harris, in his *Life and Confessions of Oscar Wilde*, says that

I showed "feminine ingenuity" in devising such a telegram. That is exactly typical of Harris's spiteful methods, which, as a matter of fact, are far more feminine, in the bad sense, than mine have ever been. My father at that time, and indeed all his life, was a formidable person. He was a man who had established a reputation as a dangerous man, and one who would stick at nothing if he was roused. He was, at one time, amateur lightweight champion boxer. He had repeatedly threatened to thrash me if he found me in Wilde's company, and he went round to all the restaurants we frequented and "warned" the managers and *maîtres d'hôtel* that he intended to assault both Wilde and myself if he "caught us together" on their premises. When I heard this I made a point of going regularly with Wilde to these very restaurants. I wrote more than once to my father and told him that on such-and-such a day, at such-and-such an hour, he would find us in such-and-such a restaurant, and I invited him to come round and "see what happened" to him if he started any of his "ruffianly tricks." I see nothing "feminine" in this conduct. No doubt it was wrong of me to defy my father, but at any rate I question whether Harris himself, for all his Ancient Pistol truculence, would have had the pluck to do as much. Everyone in London was apparently afraid of my father, with the solitary exception of myself. For he was allowed to do things which would have been tolerated in no one else, and no one ever had the courage to tackle him. To do Oscar Wilde justice he showed plenty of spirit, and was not unduly intimidated by my father's threats. He was nervous, but he did not "climb down" or show the white feather. All through life I have found that persons who make threats of the "thrashings" they are going to give, and who "warn" other people about the terrible things they are going to do, are very unlikely to be really dangerous. If my father had really meant to assault me or Wilde in a restaurant he would have done it first and talked about it afterwards. I sent him the telegram I have quoted precisely to show him that I treated his threats with utter contempt. No doubt it filled him with rage, but it had the result of convincing him that I was not disposed to be bluffed, and we heard no more about "thrashings" and "chucking out" of restaurants.

In the various letters that my father sent me he of course libelled Oscar Wilde quite sufficiently for Wilde to have taken proceedings against him long before he actually did. I am not and never have been at all ashamed of the fact that I urged Oscar from the very first to take proceedings. According to what were then my lights, I did right in doing so. I told him that he should go for my father at once. If he had done this my father would not have had a leg to stand on. The evidence which my father got later took a long time to collect, and could not have been available at the time when he first started his attack. Curiously enough, in this as in other ways, history repeated itself when I "went for" Ross. If Ross had started proceedings against me directly after I first began libelling him he would almost certainly have succeeded in squashing me.

The climax came soon after the first night of Oscar's play, *The Importance of Being Earnest*, at the St James's Theatre. My father went to the box-office with a bunch of carrots in his hand, which he proposed to throw at Wilde when he appeared before the curtain at the end of the play. He was refused admission to the theatre. I was absent in Biskra when this happened, but on getting a letter from Oscar, relating the incident as well as an account of the great success of the play, I rushed back to London. Shortly afterwards my father left one of his cards at one of Oscar's clubs, the Albemarle, on which he had written the words : "Oscar Wilde posing as sodomite." On this Oscar Wilde took action. In the book, *Oscar Wilde and Myself*, which I wrote in collaboration with Crosland, there is (written by Crosland) an account of this episode which gives an entirely false account of my own actions at this moment. I am, of course, myself responsible for this mistake, because I asked Crosland to write this part of the book, feeling at the time so shaken and unnerved by the experiences I had been through at the Ransome trial that I felt I could not bring myself to write about it. Crosland wrote the story, and I read it and passed it. Not till after the book was published did I realize that what was written contained a grave blunder. It is stated in *Oscar Wilde and Myself* that I went with Wilde to Bow Street when he applied for a warrant for my father's arrest. This is not the case. I did not go with him, and what is more I did not know, till the day after it was done, that he had at last actually started proceedings against my father.

As a matter of fact, Robert Ross was at the time Wilde's adviser in the matter. It was Ross who induced Wilde to go to his (Ross's) solicitor, Mr Humphreys, a charming man and an able solicitor, but the last solicitor in the world who could be useful to Wilde in such a juncture. Humphreys was a "high-class family solicitor," and had, I believe, no experience in criminal matters. He knew nothing whatever about Oscar Wilde, of course. I mention all this not because I wish to evade responsibility for advising Oscar to proceed against my father—as I have already explained, I had advised him to do it long before —but it is important to record the fact that directly Oscar told me that he had got a warrant for my father's arrest, and that his solicitor was Humphreys, I said : "Why on earth didn't you go to George Lewis ? " That, of course, was during the lifetime of the original George Lewis, the father of the late Sir George, Ross's great friend, who pursued me for so many years in the law courts.

CHAPTER XVII

OLD Sir George Lewis was a personal friend of Oscar Wilde. He knew a great deal about him, and he was at that time the one solicitor in London (except perhaps Mr Arthur Newton) who was really competent to deal with the situation that had arisen. After the failure of Oscar's prosecution of my father, when Sir Edward Clarke had thrown up the sponge and my father had been acquitted, I drove with Oscar to George Lewis's office. It was then too late. George Lewis had actually appeared for my father at the police court, but owing to his friendship for Oscar and his wife he told my father that it would be impossible for him to go on with the case, and he passed the case and all the documents, including the letters stolen from me, to Charles Russell & Company.

When Oscar and I saw old George Lewis directly after the collapse of the case against my father he said to Wilde : "What's the use of coming to me now ? I am powerless to do anything. If you had had the sense to bring Lord Queensberry's card to me in the first place I would have torn it up and thrown it in the fire, and told you not to make a fool of yourself." Of course this was being wise after the event, but all the same I think it is highly probable that if Oscar had gone to Lewis, as I always took it for granted he would in case he contemplated proceeding against my father, Lewis would have settled the matter, in one way or another, without letting it get into court. Unlike his son, the late Sir George (who always appeared anxious to thrust his clients into the law courts), the old George Lewis (he was not made a baronet till many years later) was a past master at settling awkward cases out of court and without public scandal.

It was precisely this faculty of his that made him so celebrated, and enabled him to build up his great business and obtain the confidence of so many prominent persons.

I certainly had always advised Oscar to fight my father, but I was not impervious to reason, and if old George Lewis had assured Wilde that he had no chance, and was cutting his own throat and playing into my father's hands, I would probably have been convinced ; and in any case I had no power (though both Harris and his friend, Bernard Shaw, the supreme *farceur* of his age, seem to assume that at the age of twenty-four I was entirely responsible for everything that Wilde did or did not do) to make Oscar Wilde disregard the advice of his solicitors.

As it was, the case was hopeless from the moment it reached the Old Bailey. Sir Edward Clarke " opened " in much the sort of way he would have done if his client had been the Archbishop of Canterbury, and then left him to be torn to pieces by Carson. Poor Oscar scintillated brilliantly in the witness-box. His answers in cross-examination bristled with polished wit, and from the point of view of mere verbal repartee he " scored off " Carson again and again. But from the point of view of winning his case or getting the jury on his side (which ought to be the aim of every witness) he was hopeless. Carson happens to be one of the extremely few " eminent counsel " who really are eminent. Most of the " great counsel " (I speak from a lot of personal experience) who are supposed to be " deadly cross-examiners " are men whom I would look upon it as a real treat to take on from the witness-box. But Carson is the one and only counsel I have come across who really is formidable to a man with brains. He is even clever enough not to mind being made to look like a fool.

Quite apart from his cleverness he had the most wonderful material for cross-examination in the case of Oscar Wilde that any counsel at the Bar was ever blessed with. Sir Edward Clarke made no attempt, as he should have done, to take the wind out of Carson's sails by asking Wilde in his examination-in-chief the questions in a modified form which were to be expected in cross-examination (which is the supreme art of examining in chief). He left everything to Carson and to his unfortunate client. The more brilliant and amusing and witty Oscar became, the more the jury hated him and totted up the points against him. When Carson had finished, Clarke re-examined without repairing any of the damage, and the next day chucked up the case and left his client to the tender mercies of the police and the Public Prosecutor! My father walked out "triumphant and elate." Thanks to Sir Edward Clarke nothing of any consequence had been brought up that might even have caused him a moment's slight uneasiness. He had assumed the mantle of the heart-broken, loving father, fighting nobly to "save his son," and Sir Edward Clarke did not lift a finger to disturb the classic folds of the mantle.

That same evening Oscar Wilde was arrested in my rooms at the Cadogan Hotel in Sloane Street. I was with him from the moment when the case against my father was abandoned by Clarke right up to about an hour before his arrest. At the moment when he was arrested I was away (having gone to the House of Commons to see my cousin, George Wyndham, and find out for certain whether there was to be a prosecution). When I got back to the hotel, Oscar had been gone, with the detectives who arrested him, for about half-an-hour. I immediately followed him in a cab to Bow Street and tried to bail him out, which of course was quite absurd; only I did not know anything about these things in those days. I was in a frightful state of despair and consternation, but I never for a moment thought of "clearing out," as Ross and all the other immediate *entourage* of Wilde (I will not give their names) did. All these "faithful friends" went out of the country and remained abroad till Wilde was convicted.

I do not imagine that I was ever in the slightest danger of being arrested myself as the result of my father's noble efforts to "save" me, but it is the fact that I was "warned" that I was "in great danger" both by my friends and my enemies, who agreed in hoping that I would leave the country. I stayed on in the Cadogan Hotel. My brother Percy turned up the day after Oscar's arrest and gave me £250 (I was "cleaned out," all my money having gone to Oscar's solicitors and counsel). He also told me that he would stick to me through thick and thin, and that if Oscar could get bail later on he would stand for any amount up to £10,000, which was at that time about all the money he had in the world. His indignation against my father was extreme, and I have already related what it led to.

I went to see Oscar at Holloway Prison every day up till the time he was committed for trial, except on the day when I went to see him at Bow Street Police Station. The police were very friendly (as they always are, God bless 'em !), and in the intervals of Oscar's appearance in court I spent several hours with him in a comfortable room upstairs, cigarettes and whiskies-and-sodas being distinctly not barred. Sir Edward Clarke " put the lid on " his performance at the Old Bailey by failing to cross-examine the witnesses at the police court, and Oscar and Alfred Taylor were committed for trial. At that time, of course, I knew nothing about the law courts, neither did Oscar. We were really in the state (generally described as an ideal one by judges) of being " entirely in the hands of our legal advisers." A more terrible position for a man it is difficult to imagine this side of hell. If I had known about the law courts what I know now (and learnt to know very quickly once I went into the matter) I would have urged Oscar to say that if Sir Edward Clarke would not cross-examine the witnesses at the police court he must request him to retire from the case, and let someone else (even any smart

junior) do it instead. At that time we were both such simpletons
in legal matters that it never even occurred to either of us that
Sir Edward Clarke was not performing prodigies of skill and
courage in his conduct of the case ! I have even recollections
of writing Sir Edward a long and pathetic letter of thanks for
what he had done, after poor Oscar's conviction. It does not
bear thinking of.

I used to see Oscar every day at Holloway in the ghastly way
that " visits " are arranged in prisons. The visitor goes into a
box rather like the box in a pawnshop (if my gentle readers will
forgive an allusion to such a low place). There is a whole row
of these boxes, each occupied by a visitor, and opposite, facing
each visitor, is the prisoner whom he is visiting. The two sides
of visitors and prisoners are separated by a corridor about a yard
in width, and a warder paces up and down the corridor. The
" visit " lasts, as far as I remember, a quarter of an hour. The
visitor and the prisoner have to shout to make their voices heard
above the voices of the other prisoners and visitors. Nothing
more revolting and cruel and deliberately malignant could be
devised by human ingenuity. And it is to be remembered that
I am speaking of a remand prison, where the prisoners are waiting trial, and possibly quite innocent of any offence whatever.
Poor Oscar was rather deaf. He could hardly hear what I
said in the babel. He looked at me with tears running down
his cheeks and I looked at him. Such as it was, as he told me
in nearly every letter he wrote (and he wrote every day with
clockwork regularity), this interview was the only bright spot
in the day. He looked forward to it with pathetic eagerness.
There was literally nothing else I could do for him. The world
outside the prison, as represented by the newspapers, was howling
for his blood like a pack of wolves. One of the evening papers
had an article describing (of course from imagination) his first
night in the cell at Bow Street, where he was locked up on the

night of his arrest. With ferocious glee it described how he paced up and down all night. I do not remember ever before or since reading such a revolting article, so full of devilish malice and bestial cruelty. Certainly, whatever poor Oscar had done, from the moment the prison gates closed upon him he began to redeem himself by suffering, and even to shine in contrast to the conduct of his enemies. At the noble game of hitting a man when he is down the English can give points to any other nation on earth.

CHAPTER XVIII

JUST after finishing the writing of the last chapter I happened to have a conversation with Mr Arthur Newton, the solicitor who defended Alfred Taylor, who was charged at the same time as Oscar Wilde. I had not seen Mr Newton for at least sixteen years. He reminded me of what I had completely forgotten, that I sent him £50 to defend Alfred Taylor. Taylor was never a friend of mine — indeed I scarcely knew him; and in the course of the evidence given against Wilde it was established (more or less accidentally, and, as I imagine, to the chagrin of the counsel who was prosecuting Wilde) that I had never been in his rooms in Great College Street. I felt sorry (not being English) that Taylor should be left as he was: in prison, quite penniless, unfriended and undefended. So I sent Mr Newton a cheque and asked him to do the best he could for Taylor with such a small sum. No doubt if this fact had been within the knowledge of Robert Ross it would have been brought up against me at the time of the trial of the Ransome libel action as an example of my innate depravity, when it would, doubtless, have furnished Lord Darling with another convenient stick to beat me with, in the interests of impartial justice. But as it happens, this dark deed has remained in obscurity to this day, when I make a present of it to those whom it may concern.

Oscar was about three weeks in prison at Holloway before he came up for trial at the Old Bailey before Mr Justice Charles. The day before the trial came on I left the country, because I was asked to do so by Sir Edward Clarke, who said that my presence in London was prejudicial to his client. (As a matter of fact, if he had called me as a witness, as I implored him to do even at this late hour, he would in all probability have saved Oscar.) I declined to leave except at the direct request of Oscar himself, and he, poor man, being "entirely in the hands of his legal advisers," urgently begged me, both by letter and by word of mouth, to go. He thus, without knowing it, of course, threw away his last chance of acquittal. I went to Calais and stayed at the Terminus Hotel of the Gare Maritime. From there, on or about the third day of the trial, I telegraphed to Sir Edward Clarke, giving him certain information which I implored him to use, although it was compromising to myself, and again offering to give evidence. In reply I got a "stern rebuke" from Wilde's solicitors, who informed me that my telegram was "most improper," and that Sir Edward Clarke had been greatly upset by receiving it. I was solemnly adjured not to attempt any further interference, "which can only have the effect of rendering Sir Edward's task still harder than it is already." In my own mind I have not the slightest doubt that if I had given evidence Oscar would have got off. As it was, the jury disagreed, and he was sent back to prison to await another trial.

An application was then made to a judge in chambers for bail, which in common justice ought to have been granted by the magistrate in the first place. This time bail was granted, and my brother Percy (then Lord Douglas of Hawick and afterwards ninth Marquis of Queensberry) went bail for Oscar. The other bail was a clergyman of the Church of England, Mr Stewart Headlam. There can be no harm in mentioning now that my brother had to guarantee Mr Headlam against loss, as, if Oscar had "bolted," as he might have done, Headlam would have been completely ruined. So my brother made himself responsible for the whole sum—£3000. I immediately wrote to my brother and begged him to tell Oscar that he was at liberty to go if he would and could. My brother replied that he sincerely hoped that Wilde would go and that he was quite prepared to "stand the racket." Frank Harris made elaborate arrangements to get Oscar out of the country : he borrowed a yacht (from a Member of Parliament) and had it lying at a port ready ; he got Oscar one night into a carriage with a pair of fast-trotting horses and started to drive him to the port, but Oscar absolutely refused to go.

He wrote me a very touching letter giving his reasons for not going. It made me weep at the time, and even now I don't like to think of it, but I have thought since, a hundred times, that it was an insane thing not to go, and that it would really have been a braver thing to do. Oscar said in his letter that he could not "run away" and "hide" and "let down" his bails (but my brother wanted him to go on my account, and Mr Headlam would not have been affected in the least). He wrote : "A dishonoured name, a hunted life are not for me to whom you have been revealed on that high hill where beautiful things are transfigured." He also, pathetically, thought that he had a "good chance of being acquitted" at the second trial. If he had scrapped Sir Edward Clarke, defended himself, and called me as a witness he might even then have had a sporting chance ; but as things were there was not the slightest hope for him. To the very last I urged him to go ; and at the time when I wrote to him from Paris a letter which Harris gives in his book as an example of my heartlessness, chiefly, apparently, because I mentioned in the letter that I had with me young Charlie Hickey (a charming boy about a couple of years younger than myself and well known to Oscar, a son of Colonel Hickey), I was expecting him to arrive in Paris to join me at any minute. (Harris, in the "New Preface" to *The Life and Confessions of Oscar Wilde*, explains that it was Ross who misrepresented the Hickey incident to him, and he expresses great regret for the injustice he did me.)

When Oscar got out on bail he went with my brother to a

hotel and took rooms. But my father (I blush to have to tell it of him, though his friend, Sir Claude de Crespigny, evidently thinks it is something to be proud of!) went to the hotel and denounced Oscar to the manager, who promptly turned him out. He then went to his mother's house in Oakley Street, where his brother, Willie Wilde, took him in for the night. At this point two Jews (not English, please observe), Mr and Mrs Ernest Leverson, offered to take him into their comfortable house in Courtfield Gardens. He remained in their house till his conviction. Mrs Leverson (the "Sphinx," as Oscar called her, and the name has stuck to her) is of course well known as a brilliant and witty writer. Both she and her husband showed on this occasion great courage and chivalry, and, I might add, Christian charity. People who live in this more tolerant (or at any rate less fiercely hypocritical) age can have no conception of the courage required in those days to be seen even speaking to Oscar Wilde or having any association with him.

Oscar wrote to me every day while he was out on bail (about three weeks) and I wrote every day to him. Where are the letters I wrote to him? I know that Ross, as I shall relate, stole or "conveyed" (if you prefer the Falstaffian word) a large number of my letters. Any that were or could be made to appear detrimental to me or to reflect on my character he used against me. But there must have been a great many others that would at any rate have shown how utterly devoted I was at that time to Oscar Wilde, and how completely I was ready to sacrifice my own interests, my safety, and even my honour, to help him. As at the Ransome trial Ross's object was to show that I had "abandoned Wilde" and "deserted" him and "ruined" him, these letters were of course suppressed. Where are they now? I ask. When I won my action for libel against *The Evening News*, in 1922, the jury added a rider to their verdict, expressing a strong opinion that my letters

H

should be returned to me or at least destroyed. My solicitors, Messrs Carter & Bell, wrote to Messrs Lewis & Lewis and asked them if they intended to carry out the recommendation of the jury. Lewis & Lewis replied that the letters were "not in their possession." Mr Comyns Carr, K.C., who was my counsel in this case, advised me that it would be possible for me to apply to the Chancery Court for an order, or injunction, enforcing the jury's recommendation ; but my experience of Chancery Court judges gave me no kind of encouragement to expect anything at all from them except cynical injustice. Moreover, Mr Carr pointed out to me that it really did not matter who had the letters, as, in view of the verdict I had obtained and the jury's rider, they could never be used against me again without disastrous results to those who used them. Consequently, I have never taken any steps to try to recover these letters. May I suggest now that it would be a graceful action on the part of someone (whoever he may be) to return them to me ? Nothing could more serve to rehabilitate Wilde, from a moral point of view, than (if it were only possible) the publication of every single letter he ever wrote to me and every single letter that I ever wrote to him. As it is, just those few selected as damaging to us (first by my father and then by Robert Ross) have been produced. Those published would not amount to more than five per cent. of the whole lot we wrote to each other. I myself destroyed at least one hundred and fifty letters of his to me, keeping only those which were comparatively colourless (all published in America, by Mr Andrews Clark). Of those I wrote to Wilde, which must be quite as numerous, only the few produced at the Ransome trial by Ross have been given publicity. Ross had too strong a commercial instinct, unless I am very much mistaken, to have destroyed the rest. Again I ask, where are they, and what prevents the person (whoever he may be) who now holds them from returning them to me or making them public ?

The whole of this question regarding the property in letters might be held up as an example of what the English call "un-English," but which I call typically English. The letters which Oscar Wilde wrote and those which my father wrote to me can be with impunity stolen and kept openly in the possession of persons and firms who make no secret of the fact that they keep them on purpose to use against me whenever occasion may arise or it may suit their convenience. Messrs Charles Russell & Co., my father's solicitors, have several times brought Oscar Wilde's two letters to me, to which I have referred previously, into court against me, and they have had them framed and covered with glass. Why should these letters, which are my property, be in the possession of anyone but myself? The same applies to the whole MS. of *De Profundis* (including the "unpublished part"). This is a letter to me written by Wilde in prison. It begins "Dear Bosie" and is signed "Your affectionate friend Oscar Wilde." Ross obtained possession of it and kept it, concealing all knowledge of it for twelve years. He says in one of his Prefaces that Wilde gave it to him on the day he left prison, but he has never attempted to explain why he did not send it on to me, or even send me a copy. In any case the MS. (which now reposes in the British Museum, and which is of course enormously valuable) really belongs to me. Why should the British Museum retain possession of my property? On the other hand, letters I wrote myself to my father, to Wilde, to Ross and to others can be, and have been at different times, brought up against me in court and can remain indefinitely in the hands of my enemies. Apparently Wilde's letters to me and my father's letters to me belong to anyone who can manage to get hold of them, and the same applies to the letters I wrote with my own hand!

CHAPTER XIX

To return to Oscar's trial. He was convicted and sentenced to two years' hard labour by Mr Justice Wills. He was very unlucky, because I knew for a fact that if the jury had not disagreed at his first trial, and if he had then been convicted, Mr Justice Charles would have given him six months. When Mr Frank Harris, in his *Life and Confessions of Oscar Wilde*, is not inventing fairy tales about me he often says things that I cordially agree with and endorse. I do entirely agree with him that the sentence of two years' hard labour passed on Oscar Wilde by Mr Justice Wills was cruel and outrageous. I invite anyone who disagrees, or pretends to disagree, with me to look up the records of sentences passed for similar offences any time during the last thirty-five years. I doubt if he will find a single instance of a man getting so terrible a sentence unless there were greatly aggravating circumstances (*dètournement de mineurs*, or brutalization, or cases of master and pupil, for example). As Harris points out, it was never even suggested by a peculiarly fierce and vindictive Prosecution that Oscar had corrupted any single one of his "victims." In fact they were not victims at all. One and all were accomplices, and should have been in the dock with him if there were any prosecution at all. As a matter of fact all the evidence was obtained by giving the "victims" the choice between giving evidence or being prosecuted themselves.

The choice was also offered to Alfred Taylor. He was visited by the late Inspector Littlechild, of Scotland Yard, who assured him that if he would give evidence against Wilde he would be safe. I had this information at the time, and it was recently confirmed to me by Mr Newton, the solicitor who appeared for

Taylor. To his lasting credit, Taylor refused to give evidence against Oscar Wilde, and preferred to go, as he did, to two years' hard labour rather than, by betraying his friend, to sully his honour, which to my mind remains, from this very fact, far brighter than that of many of those who helped to hound Oscar Wilde to his doom.

All the other witnesses (with one exception, of whom more anon) gave evidence to save their skins. Of course if they had all refused to give evidence (as this one did) the case would have collapsed. I mean that this case differed from most others of the kind, in which there is an injured prosecutor (a father or guardian) and at least one real victim. All this is very important, because after all there is such a thing as justice and fair-play even in the case of Oscar Wilde. That sounds a commonplace now, when he has been turned by his misguided admirers into a martyr and a hero. But at the time when these things happened I was the one and only man in England who openly and publicly stuck up for him, and declined to back down or yield an inch to popular clamour. It is perhaps hardly necessary for me to say that the idea of acting otherwise than I did never even occurred to me for a moment. Perhaps if I had been able to guess that years later I was to lose a case for libel in which I was accused of "abandoning" Wilde and "ruining" him and "deserting" him, and that my accusers were to be Wilde's most intimate *soi-disant* friends, who would produce Wilde's own posthumous abuse of me (penned at the very time when I was suffering exile, obloquy, poverty and disgrace on his behalf and out of my loyalty to him), I might have been tempted to think twice before committing myself so completely as I did to his cause.

But at the time I had no thought but to carry out the solemn promise I had given him that I would stick to him through thick and thin, and that neither bribes nor threats would move me an inch from my determination that when he came out of prison he should find me exactly the same as I was when he last saw me a few weeks before his conviction. From this determination I never moved. As I have already explained, at that time I had no religion at all, and very little moral sense. It never occurred to me as conceivable that it would be right for me to give up Wilde. To do so, on the contrary, would have appeared to me dishonourable, cowardly, mean and disgraceful. The idea that it would have been a moral act to disown him and make terms with his enemies (chief of whom was my father) never presented itself to my mind. Nor do I, even now, consider that it would have been anything but dishonourable and cowardly on my part to abandon him.

I had of course the opportunity for a very good "get out," if I had cared to avail myself of it, when, after he had been about nine months in prison, I was told by Ross that Oscar had "turned against" me, that he now spoke of me with bitterness and dislike, that he did not want to have any letter from me, and in fact stated categorically that I was on no account to write to him and that I was to hand over any letters of his I had to Ross. Instead of doing what I might have done, and saying "Oh, very well, of course if he does not desire my friendship there is no object in going on making myself into a martyr and a pariah on his account," I determined all the more to stick to him. I said to Ross in effect : " I don't care what you say, it may be true that Oscar has turned against me, but that is probably only because he is half mad as a result of his sufferings in prison, and in any case, whether he has turned against me or not, I have not turned against him. I promised him on my most sacred word that I would stick to him, and I shall go on doing it. When he comes out of prison, if he chooses to say he does not want my friendship, and that he wants his letters back, he can do so with his own mouth ; but in the meanwhile I am not taking any advice or any messages from you, nor shall I give you any of

Oscar's letters, and you can mind your own d——d business and leave me to mind mine." I believe Ross's hatred of me and a subconscious determination to "get even with" me, although he went on pretending to be my friend, began from the moment when I gave him this answer to his attempt to interfere between Wilde and me and to obtain possession of Wilde's letters. I have no doubt now at all, though I never dreamed of such a thing at the time, that he deliberately poisoned Wilde against me at this time by misrepresenting my attitude and my actions, and I have no doubt that he acted out of jealousy.

Before I leave the subject of Oscar's trial and conviction I will explain my allusion, a few pages back, to the one witness who, after giving a "proof" of his evidence to the Prosecution, declined to bear it out in the witness-box. This youth was a gentleman by birth and of an entirely different character and class to the other witnesses. He was terrorized into making a statement against Wilde (I am not suggesting that what he alleged may not have been true) by the same means as the other "victims."

I happened to see him in the corridor at Bow Street Police Court while he was waiting to give evidence. I went up and shook hands with him, and said: "Surely you are not going to give evidence against Oscar?" He looked round in a frightened way, and then whispered: "Well, what can I do? I daren't refuse to give evidence now, they got a statement out of me." I said: "For God's sake, remember you are a gentleman and a Public School boy. Don't put yourself on a level with scum like —— and —— [two of the witnesses]. When counsel asks you the questions, deny the whole thing, and say you made the statement because you were frightened by the police. They can't do anything to you." He grabbed my hand and said: "All right, I'll do what you say."

He did (more power to him !). To the consternation of prosecuting counsel he denied his own statement, and swore that Wilde had never been anything to him but a good friend. Counsel, of course, dropped him like a hot brick, he was told to "stand down," and walked out of the court having inflicted a very nasty jolt to the Prosecution, of which an intelligent counsel (if such a one had been appearing for Wilde) would have made tremendous use. I do not think it fair to give this young man's name, but a reference to the reports in the papers of the case would of course reveal it. I would not mention it if I did not think that what he did was greatly to his credit and perfectly justifiable. If all the other witnesses had replied in the same way, and by stating the fact that they only gave their evidence because it was a choice between the witness-box and the dock, the whole case would have been shoo'd out of court in a very short time, and one of the greatest and most far-reachingly disastrous scandals that ever afflicted this country would have been nipped in the bud.

CHAPTER XX

THIS prosecution of Oscar Wilde never had any moral force behind it, and as a result it produced nothing but a crop of evil and calamity. It was dictated by Vengeance and Hypocrisy, unaccompanied by any genuine moral purpose. The man who brought it about (although his direct part in the proceedings ceased after his acquittal at the Old Bailey) was an immoral man, a bad father and a worse husband, an avowed Atheist, a man who did not scruple to sacrifice his own son and break the heart of his long-suffering wife simply to gratify his feelings of revenge and his passion for notoriety. As exemplifying my father's moral attitude towards the whole business I may state that after Oscar Wilde's conviction he wrote to me offering, if I would give up Wilde for ever, to supply me with money and an allowance, and suggesting that I should go to the South Sea Islands where, he said, " you will find plenty of beautiful girls." His only idea of reformation was to substitute, as he supposed, one vice for another. If he had left me alone, and refrained from publishing the scandal to the whole world, my friendship with Wilde, which had already become quite harmless many months before the final catastrophe, would no doubt have gradually cooled off. It was not likely that I could have gone on indefinitely keeping up a sentimental friendship with a man whose ideas of what he describes in the "unpublished part" of *De Profundis* as his "great love" for me could yet allow him to live the kind of life of promiscuous nastiness with a dozen or more boy paramours which was revealed in his trial. The emotion of the great crisis fanned the waning fires of our devotion to each other. I was before the trial beginning to be a little tired of Oscar's "goings on" (even allowing for the fact that he of course concealed his "infidelities" as much as he could). We had had several acrimonious quarrels. In the ordinary course of events my infatuation for him would have worn out, and obviously his for me was a very much less enduring and tremendous affair than he himself imagined it to be. If it had not been so, he would scarcely have made such a complete *volte-face* in his attitude towards me after being in prison only nine months. I do not blame my father for trying to separate me from Wilde, but I do blame him bitterly for the way he tried to do it, and for acting as he did when he found that his efforts at separating us were unavailing. It is (and I defy anyone to say the contrary) perfectly obvious that he was not thinking of me and of my interests when he created the scandal which ruined my life and also (to a great extent) what was left of his own.

For his spectacular victory at the Old Bailey did my poor father no good. He was, metaphorically speaking, pursued by Furies ever afterwards up to the time of his last illness. A great number of people of his own class, who did not bother their heads overmuch about what happened to "Queensberry's boy" after his father had ruined him, yet definitely drew the line from that time forth at Queensberry himself. He was "cut" by many of his oldest friends, and politely cold-shouldered by others. My godfather, dear old Lord Robert Bruce (I am called, as my second name, Bruce, after him), who was in the Navy with my father, and up till then one of his greatest friends, told me himself, years after, that he never spoke to my father again after what he had done. He was for ever estranged from his son and heir, my brother Percy, and from Percy's wife and children, and though he received me back into favour for a short time, about a year before his death, our reconciliation did not last long. After formally "forgiving" me and embracing me with tears many times in the smoking-room of Bailey's Hotel, where he was then staying, promising me my allowance back again and actually writing to his cousin, Arthur Douglas, who managed his affairs, to that effect, and calling me "my poor darling boy," he whipped round on me again and wrote me an abusive letter in which he said that he did not intend to give me a penny until he knew exactly what my relations were with "that beast Wilde." This was quite gratuitous, as I had already explained in a letter to my cousin Algie Bourke (the Honourable Algernon Bourke, brother of the late Lord Mayo) exactly what those relations were, and he had shown my letter to my father, who had thereupon expressed a desire to see me and receive me back into favour. What happened was, precisely, that I wrote to Algie Bourke from Paris and told him that I should like to make friends with my father again, and I asked him to try to arrange it. I told Algie that I was ready to express contrition for what I had done, "but," I said, "I cannot undertake not to see Wilde from time to time. I can, however, give you and my father my word that my relations with him are entirely harmless and only dictated by my feeling that I cannot abandon him now that he is poor and broken after being his friend when he was rich and flourishing." I went on to say that I was sure my father would appreciate the situation that my intercourse with Wilde was chiefly confined to helping him financially whenever I could, and that I had already given my word of honour to my mother that I would never live in the same house with him or sleep under the same roof with him again. (I had given this promise to my mother when I left Wilde in my villa at Naples. In return for the promise my mother gave me £200 to give to Wilde.) I went on to say to Algie that I must ask my father to "consider the sort of dog's life I have had for the last few years and to meet me half way," and not make it impossible for me to bring about the reconciliation which I so sincerely desired.

Algie, kindest and most untiringly good-natured of men, immediately approached my father, showed him my letter, and wrote to me within twenty-four hours to say that it was all right, and that my father would be delighted to see me and had spoken in the most affectionate way about me. The interview I have described took place between us. This must have been in 1898, I think. The reconciliation lasted only about a week, and came to an end when my father wrote in the terms I have described. I made a "suitable" reply, in which I said that it was obvious that there was no possibility of any lasting peace between us, and once more hurling back the celebrated and legendary "allowance" with stinging words.

Very wrong and stupid of me, no doubt. If I had had enough tact I would have said nothing, and allowed my father to come round again in his own way. But in those days I had no sense, and I was, moreover, ill in bed with influenza at my mother's house, 18 Cadogan Place, when my father's letter arrived. I worked myself into a fever over it and replied in terms calculated to make the breach irreparable. My father was, I believe, very much upset by my letter. I saw him again only once in the street many months later. I was in a cab. I was struck with compunction at his appearance, for he looked ill and wild and haggard. I ascertained from my brother-in-law, St George Fox-Pitt, who was about the only member of the family who was at that time on speaking terms with him, that he was under the impression that I hated him, and that I was responsible for certain (purely imaginary) troubles from which he was suffering. He told my brother-in-law that he was being "persecuted by the Oscar-Wilders" and that they had driven him out of various hotels, and disturbed him at nights by shouting abusive epithets at him.

I felt dreadfully upset about all this, and, as it was quite obvious that my father was suffering from delusions, it struck me that the best thing I could do to remove them was to write to my brother-in-law a letter which I asked him to show my father. In this letter I said that my father was completely mistaken in imagining that I hated him or had any feelings about him except of kindness and affection. I explained that the last letter I had written to him was provoked by his own, which had reached me when I was in a high fever from influenza, and that I was scarcely responsible for what it contained, and in any case did not mean what I said and entirely withdrew it. I also sent him my love. St George gave my letter to my father. He read it, and it undoubtedly calmed his mind and put a stop to his delusions about persecutions. He made no comment on the letter, but my brother-in-law said : " I think he was pleased to see it." Not long afterwards he died, at the early age of fifty-three. My Uncle Archie (the Catholic priest) wrote me twelve years later, after I became a Catholic, a letter in which he told me that before my father died " a cloud seemed to lift off his spirit." He entirely renounced his Agnostic views, and professed his love for and faith in Jesus Christ, " to whom " he said, " I have confessed all my sins." My uncle gave him " conditional absolution," and he died happily and peacefully. My dear mother visited him just before his death, and he assured her she was the only woman he had ever loved. May his soul rest in peace. In spite of the hard things I have been compelled to say about him I have got back much of my old love for him as I had it when I was a child. Needless to say I have never ceased to pray for him, and I look forward confidently to seeing him " hereafter in a better world than this," when all misunderstandings and obstacles to love and knowledge will be removed for ever.

CHAPTER XXI

AFTER Oscar's conviction I remained in France for a time, and then went to Naples and Capri. I had a villa at Capri for about six months, and I stayed there right through the summer, spending most of the time in the water. During this period I wrote some of my best poetry. I then returned to Paris, and while I was there I was asked by the *Mercure de France*, the well-known literary monthly magazine, to write an article giving my version of the Oscar Wilde affair. I accepted the invitation and I wrote an article for the paper, in English, for at that time I did not know French well enough to write an article in the language, though I spoke French well and ended by speaking it almost like a Frenchman. The article was translated into French, and in it I included a quantity of extracts from the letters which Oscar had written to me while he was in Holloway Gaol, and while he was staying at the house of the Leversons, when he was on bail. I believe my article and the letters, if their publication had not been prevented by the possibly well-meant, but disastrous, interference of Robert Harborough Sherard, would have had the effect of completely rehabilitating Oscar at any rate in France.

Unfortunately, however, Sherard saw Oscar in prison and told him that I was going to " publish all his letters in a newspaper," and (knowing nothing whatever about my motives or the nature of the article, which I would have been glad to explain to him if he had taken the trouble to see me and inquire) entirely misrepresented the whole affair to Oscar. Ross, for his part, did the same. The result was that Oscar (according to Sherard's story) commissioned him to stop the publication of his letters.

Sherard was a personal friend of the translator of my article (whose name I have forgotten, but who was a well-known man of letters and a member of the staff of the *Mercure de France*), and he saw this gentleman and told him that Oscar begged that his letters should not be published. Consequently, the *Mercure de France* asked me to omit the letters from my article. I thereupon decided that it was useless to publish the article without the letters, and in view of the attitude towards me of Oscar, as retailed by Ross, who told me that he was commissioned by Oscar to demand the handing over of the letters to him (Ross). I have already described what I said to Ross when he approached me on the subject.

Thus for the second time Oscar Wilde, by his own misguided action, and acting on the bad advice of those who had the access to him which was denied (by his own fault) to me, dealt a fatal blow to his chances of rehabilitation. When he begged me, at Sir Edward Clarke's imperative behest, to leave the country before his trial, and put it out of the question that I should be called as a witness on his behalf, he threw away his chances of acquittal ; and now, when he prevented me (who at that time loved him passionately and had no thought but to try to help him and lift him up out of the gutter into which he had fallen) from defending him, as I could have done so effectively, he once again threw away his trump card. My article and his letters were designed to show that there was a fine and noble side to the whole of this business which Oscar's enemies, assisted by his feeble defenders and fat-headed friends, had dragged down into the kennel and the stews. I wanted to lift the affair out of the atmosphere of the police court and the Old Bailey into the higher air of romance and tragedy.

The letters which I intended to publish showed Oscar in a light which has never been revealed to anyone except myself and the few people to whom, at various times, I showed the letters. At the time he wrote them the anguish of his mind, coupled with what shone out at that time unmistakably as his real love for me, lifted him into realms of altruistic beauty and pathos which he never reached at any other time of his life or in any of his published works. I have never known anyone who could read these letters without genuine emotion. I have shown them to persons who hated and despised Oscar Wilde, and they have read them and shed tears over them. They showed him to be, at that time, one who had forgotten self in his love for someone else. They were a million miles removed from the artificial, slightly repellent epistles which were produced against him at the Old Bailey by my father as specimens of his attitude to me, with their Hylases and Hyacinthuses, "slim gilt souls," "flower-like lips," and all the other bag of tricks. These letters had the ring of genuine feeling, tragic emotion, sublimated passion. For once in his life, and for a period extending over many weeks, facing, as he was, a world which was one vast nightmare of unknown terror and hostile glares, he thought more about someone else than of himself. His letters were really noble and really fine. The alchemy of passionate sincerity transmuted his thoughts into pure gold. One of them contained an *apologia* for his whole attitude towards me, and what I meant to him, which would have gone far to disarm the criticism of his worst enemies. Once these letters had been published and read there would have been an end of that " terrible laughter of the world," which, as one of Wilde's characters says in *Lady Windermere's Fan*, is "a thing more tragic than all the tears the world has ever shed." I do not believe that my father himself could have read them without a feeling that here was something which he did not understand and which could not be spat upon without terrible risk to the spitter. I defy anyone who retains the least spark of honour to spit upon the real, essential love of one human being for another. And when

I say love, I mean love, and not physical passion or desire or anything else.

I say in *In Excelsis* :

> For Love essentially must needs be chaste.
> And being contracted to unchastity,
> Even in marriage, knows essential loss,
> And falls into a malady of waste,
> Squandering the expended spirit's minted fee
> For that which in itself is worthless dross.

As Oscar said to me in one of these letters : " Pleasure hides love from us, but Pain reveals it in its essence." He knew that then, but he forgot it all too soon.

I bitterly regret that these letters were not published at the time to which I refer. I bitterly regret that years afterwards I burnt them with my own hand on the advice of a " friend," at a time when I was fool enough to be ashamed of having received such letters from a man, and of having treasured them for so many years. If I had them now I would print them all in this book, provided, of course, that the executors of Oscar Wilde, or one or another of his " faithful friends," did not obtain an injunction to restrain me from doing so. As it is, they are lost for ever, and with them is lost for ever the evidence of what Oscar Wilde really was, once, at any rate, for a few weeks in his life. I have recorded in this book a few of the phrases from them that have stuck in my memory. I wish my memory were better. I wish I had stuck to my own original instincts, which are always right in this sort of matter. I wish it had occurred to me that the "friend" who advised me to burn the letters was also a friend of Robert Ross, and that the advice he gave me to destroy these letters was tendered only a few months before the trial of the Ransome action for libel !

A little while after this episode of the cancellation of my

article the *Mercure de France*, which is also, of course, a publishing house, offered to publish a collection of my poems. The volume appeared with a page-by-page French prose translation. The translation was ably done by the late Eugène Tardieu, a man of considerable talent and charming personality, who was on the staff of the *Écho de Paris*. The book was published at 3 francs 50 cents, and there were, if I remember right, fifty copies *de luxe* and twenty-five *de grand luxe*, priced at 10 francs and 25 francs respectively. I am informed that a single copy of the *édition de grand luxe* on Japanese vellum was sold about two years ago at the Maison Drouot for 10,000 francs (about £80 at the present rate of exchange). I do not myself possess a single copy of the book. Of those I had I gave away many, and the rest have disappeared.[1] The book has been out of print for at least twenty years. One thousand copies were printed. It was well received in Paris, and from the moment of its appearance my status as a poet was generously conceded by French men of letters and never afterwards disputed. The *Mercure de France* on at least two occasions asked me to consent to reprinting the volume, but this I declined to do, for the reason that it contained certain poems which, although there is really no harm in them (and, poetically speaking, some of them are exceedingly good), were brought up against me at the instance of Mr Ransome (or, I suppose I ought more properly to say, at the instance of Robert Ross, for I have long exonerated Mr Ransome from any blame in the matter of that libel action) in cross-examination at the High Court. I felt so aggrieved and disgusted at this that I have preferred to withdraw the poems altogether from circulation, and I accordingly refused permission to the *Mercure de France* to reprint the book containing them. No doubt they will be reprinted after my death, but meanwhile the book containing

---

[1] Since I wrote this my friend, Mr A. J. A. Symons, has kindly presented me with a copy.

them is practically unobtainable for love or money. I am glad to think that my first poems were published in France, a country which I have always loved, and I recall with satisfaction that Shelley's first volume of poetry was published at Pisa :

> From the beginning when was aught but stones
> For English prophets ?

I quote from one of the sonnets in my Collected Edition. Not that my poetry has been " stoned " in England. On the contrary, it was very well received when it first appeared in 1899, published anonymously, as *The City of the Soul*, by Grant Richards. But it was published in Paris, and appreciated by some of the finest writers in France (notably Mallarmé), three years before I could get a publisher to look at it in London.

CHAPTER XXII

DURING the last three months of his imprisonment, Oscar Wilde wrote the letter to me which constitutes the whole of the book called *De Profundis* and the "unpublished part," which is in the British Museum. I never saw it, or had the slightest knowledge of it, till more than twelve years later, and to this day I do not know whether Wilde really meant what he said, or whether he merely wrote it and then thought better of it. According to the account given by Robert Ross in one of his prefaces Wilde gave him the MS. on the day he left prison ; in another place Ross implies that it was sent to him by Wilde while he was still in prison, with instructions as to what he was to do with it. The two stories appear to be contradictory. Quite apart from what he did to me, which is related in Chapter VII. of this book, Ross is shown by Frank Harris in the "New Preface" to *The Life and Confessions of Oscar Wilde* to have been a truly monumental liar. His lies, like Falstaff's, were "gross and palpable." Harris points out that the account he gives in his *Life and Confessions of Oscar Wilde* of the death of Oscar as related to him by Ross is a pure invention of Ross's. Reggie Turner, who was in the room when Wilde died, has assured Harris that the account given by Ross (with its nauseating and disgusting details) is a lie from beginning to end. The same applies to Ross's account of the transference of Wilde's body to the Père Lachaise cemetery. I refer my readers to the "New Preface," where they can read Harris's own account of these amazing perversions of fact which were Ross's contribution to Harris's original book.

Knowing, therefore, that Ross's testimony on this, as on any subject, is utterly valueless, it is impossible for me to arrive at any certain conclusion about the matter. I am not on speaking terms with any of Ross's intimate friends. If I were, I would endeavour to find out the truth from them, supposing that they know it. Oscar Wilde's surviving son, Vyvyan, whom I have not seen since he was a little boy of seven or eight years, possibly knows the real truth, if he has not been deceived by Ross, which is quite on the cards. At the time when I wrote my book, *Oscar Wilde and Myself*, in collaboration with Crosland, just after the Ransome case, I accepted Ross's story that Wilde was privy to the plot of keeping his attack on me secret, and publishing it after my death. Now, however, I very much doubt the truth of this. I think it is quite possible that Wilde wrote the letter and thus purged his bosom of his rancour and unreasonable fury against my entirely innocent self, that he gave the letter to Ross when he came out of prison, telling him to send it on to me, or possibly telling him to keep it back for the time being (it seems difficult to believe that having taken the trouble to write the letter of over 60,000 words he deliberately refrained from giving me the opportunity to read it, which is apparently what Ross would have us believe) ; that then when he made friends with me again, as he did within three weeks of his release from prison, he put the thing out of his mind and thought no more about it. As it contained what he no doubt regarded as a lot of fine writing, his author's vanity would have prevented him from irrevocably destroying it ; and he may have had a vague intention of re-writing or revising it. It thus remained in Ross's hands, and when Oscar died Ross had it, and was free to do what he liked with it, and to tell any story he pleased (there being no one who was in a position to contradict him) as to Wilde's instructions and intentions about it. It is surely significant that nowhere and at no time has Ross ever stated publicly and definitely that Wilde told him to keep the MS. and conceal its existence from me. Ross left this to be inferred ; but there is no record, as far as I know, of his having ever put it into actual words.

Harris points out in the " New Preface " to *The Life and Confessions of Oscar Wilde* that Oscar after he came out of prison consistently behaved in a double-faced way about me. He wrote me a quantity of letters from Berneval, during the first three months after his release from prison, and before he met me again, in which he addressed me in the most affectionate terms. At the very time he was thus writing to me, calling me "My own darling Boy" and so forth, he was, as I only found out years afterwards, writing Ross abusive letters about me. Later, when he was taking large sums of money from me in Paris, he went about telling various people (everyone he met, apparently) that I had not given him a penny and that I refused to help him. As Harris says : "Such falseness and treachery are hard even to understand, but the facts remain."

In view of all these facts, and the utter unreliability as witnesses of both Ross and of Wilde himself, I do not see how it is possible that the real truth as to the *De Profundis* business can ever be known this side of the Day of Judgment. All I can say is that it is permissible to hope and believe that Wilde did not ultimately intend that his frantic abuse, and his ignoble laments about the money he had spent on enter-taining me to lunch and dinner in the days of his prosperity, should be published after my death. It is even possible to take it for granted that as soon as he made friends with me again he was heartily ashamed of what he had written.

My own evidence on this point is obscured by the fact that, as I did not know of the existence of the *De Profundis* MS. till years after Wilde's death, I may have missed references to it which perhaps he made under the impression that I knew of its existence. He may have believed that Ross had actually sent it on to me, and he may have thought that I had duly received it, or that my silence about it was deliberate and calculated. That he did have some such idea is suggested by the fact, which I have recorded in *Oscar Wilde and Myself,* that on one occasion when we were together he referred to something he had said or written about me in prison. Ross, while Wilde was in prison, had sent me a letter containing extracts from remarks which he alleged that Wilde had made about me, but whether these remarks had been written or merely repeated by word of mouth I did not gather, because, as soon as I realized the nature of Ross's letter (which was a very long one of many pages), I tore it to pieces in a rage and hurled the fragments into the River Marne, by whose banks I was living at the time. It is quite possible that this letter of Ross's contained extracts from Wilde's *De Profundis* letter to me. On the other hand, if Ross's story that Wilde gave him the letter for the first time on the day he left prison is true, his letter to me, which reached me at Nogent-sur-Marne some time before Oscar's release, could not possibly have contained any such extracts. All I can say with certainty is that on one occasion after I met Oscar again, after his release from prison, I reproached him about something or other in the course of a discussion we had, and he said words to the following effect : " Surely you are not bringing up against me what I wrote in prison when I was starving and half mad. You must know that I didn't really mean a word of what I said." It immediately, and naturally, occurred to me that he was referring to this letter of Ross's which was supposed to have contained extracts of things he had said or written against me in prison, and I replied to the effect that I had really not done more than glance at the letter, and that as soon as I saw what it was about I tore it in pieces and threw the pieces away and determined to put the letter altogether out of my mind.

As things are at present, and putting all the evidence together in my mind, I am very much inclined to think that he never intended the letter to be used against me and that Ross has deliberately misrepresented Oscar's attitude and intentions about the letter. If this is the case, it relieves Oscar Wilde of what is otherwise the blackest and most terrible charge that was ever brought against him. It was the belief (shared at that time by myself and I suppose by everyone who heard the evidence at the Ransome trial) that Wilde had really been guilty of this dastardly treachery and ingratitude which inspired Crosland to write his terrible and astonishingly brilliant indictment of Wilde, called *The First Stone*. If Oscar has been wronged, all I can say is that he owes it to his evil genius, Robert Ross.

By the time I started to write this book I had pretty well convinced myself that Wilde was not guilty in this respect; and it is this feeling (which does not however altogether amount to one of certainty) that has enabled me to cut out of my heart the sentiments of anger, resentment and indignation which inspired me at the time when, with Crosland's assistance, I wrote *Oscar Wilde and Myself*, in 1914. Having once arrived at this state of mind, it seems to me that I am bound to put it formally on record that I withdraw what I said about Oscar in that book. What I said does not, on the whole, represent the real truth, either about the facts of our friendship or my feelings for him. The whole book is distorted and wrenched out of focus by the bewildered resentment and indignation which overcame me when I first read the "unpublished portion" of *De Profundis* in the year 1913 or 1912. The Ransome case was tried in 1913, but the plea of justification, including a copy of the "unpublished portion" of *De Profundis*, was, I believe, delivered at the end of 1912.

What happened when I began to write that book was that Crosland, with whom I was then in close association (arising out of the fact that he had been my assistant editor on *The Academy* for more than two years), said to me : " You will never write this book as it ought to be written. Even now, after all that has happened, and after you have got the complete proof of what an unspeakable swine Wilde was, you are still too ' soft ' about him to put it right across him as you ought to do. Let me do that part of the book. In fact you had much better let me write the book altogether, you of course giving me the facts and revising it after I have put them into shape." In the end, after much discussion, I agreed to let Crosland collaborate. I paid him handsomely, giving him half of all I got for the book, although originally he asked only for £100. I gave him at least £250. On several occasions, when I had written what I thought was a fairly scathing piece of criticism, Crosland would say : " Yes, it's all very fine, and most admirably written, but you are still much too soft." He would then pace up and down the room and dictate (he nearly always dictated) a revised version of what I had written. In the end the book was really more his than mine. He certainly said things about Wilde which I would never have thought of saying myself. But once they were written I adopted them *con amore*. Crosland said : "What we must do is to knock this man clean off the pedestal on which his worshippers have erected him." A lot that the book contains is unfair and misleading. I hope I have learnt now once for all that it is always a mistake to be unfair even to persons who are grossly unfair to oneself. The fact that Ross and Harris and others have deliberately invented and circulated malicious lies about me, and that Wilde himself spent three months of his life in prison in a crafty and cunning attempt to blacken my character by means of gross and brutal misrepresentations, does not justify me in "hitting back" as I did by deliberately painting (and allowing Crosland to paint) a blacker and more biting portrait of the man than the truth warrants.

In *Oscar Wilde and Myself* I not only ran down Wilde unfairly —even to the extent of belittling some of his literary work which I place very much higher than I have there allowed—but I entirely misrepresented the strength of my own love and devotion for him, which persisted right up to the time when I read the "unpublished" *De Profundis* in 1913. In doing this I did less than justice to myself, because the only explanation of much of my conduct in regard to him is precisely that I really was (as I said once, in one of my cases, in the witness-box) "crazy about the man." The truth is that I really adored him. I think it is fairly certain that in spite of all his protestations about his "wonderful love" for me I really loved him far more than he loved me. His love for me, even allowing for the undoubted fact that pain and suffering did, for a time, transfigure it and touch it to finer issues, was yet chiefly founded on his mere admiration for what he chose to consider my personal beauty. I am sorry to have to say it, but I cannot but feel that the explanation of the shocking way he behaved to me, and about me, during the last two or three years of his life, after he came out of prison, was simply that I was no longer quite so attractive in appearance as when he first met me. There is a passage in *Dorian Gray* which gives quite plainly his own views on this point. Lord Henry says to Basil Halward (I quote from memory, for I have not read *Dorian Gray* for more than twelve years): "One day you will look at your friend and observe that his nose is a little out of drawing. You will resent it bitterly and feel that he has behaved very badly to you."

On the other hand, whatever devotion I had for Oscar was certainly (and surely I may say quite obviously) not founded on any physical admiration of mine for him. I loved him because he was brilliant and wonderful and fantastic and fascinating in his mind and in his conversation. His personal appearance, at any rate while I knew him, was always rather against him.

When I first met him I thought him comic-looking. Afterwards I got used to his strange aspect, and my admiration for his brain and the dazzling brilliance and spell-weaving enchantment of his conversation completely outweighed in my eyes the disadvantages of his appearance. When he got into his frightful trouble my love for him was deeply intensified by pity and compassion. There was nothing I would not have done for him. It is a mere commonplace of truth to say that I would gladly have died for him, or gone to prison in his stead.

That I am not now exaggerating the strength of the feeling I had for Oscar is easy enough to prove. I quote overleaf a sonnet that I wrote about him after he had been dead nearly three years. As evidence of the quality and enduring nature of my devotion to him it is overwhelming to anyone who can appreciate real and sincere poetry. Frank Harris is my great traducer, the man who has done more than anyone else to blacken me and calumniate me in the eyes of the whole world ; he claims to have sold 40,000 copies of his abominable book, *The Life and Confessions of Oscar Wilde,* in America, and, after admitting in writing that practically every word about me in that book is a deliberate lie or misrepresentation, after apologizing and expressing his deep regret and his desire to atone for the grievous wrong he had done me, he has broken his promise to incorporate the "New Preface" in future editions of his book and to put footnotes to the book explaining that the misstatements about me were, as he says, insinuated into the book by Robert Ross, and he has brought out a new edition of his book, published by Brentano in New York, in which every single one of his lying statements about myself is repeated. He does not so much as mention the "New Preface" containing his retractation, and if I had not brought it out myself, on my own responsibility and after being advised by my solicitors that I was entitled to publish it because it is a retractation of and apology for a series of gross libels, it would never have seen the light at all. Yet by a strange irony this same Frank Harris is the only now living really prominent man of letters who has written enthusiastically about my poetry. Harris, in the " New Preface " to *The Life and Confessions of Oscar Wilde*, after saying that as a writer of sonnets I can " stand with Shakespeare," quotes the sonnet in question as an example of a poem " which is as fine as anything that can be found in the whole treasure-house of English poetry."

Here it is, and let it end this chapter :

Alas ! that Time should war against Distress,
And numb the sweet ache of remembered loss,
And give for sorrow's gold the indifferent dross
Of calm regret or stark forgetfulness.
I should have worn eternal mourning dress
And nailed my soul to some perennial cross,
And made my thoughts like restless waves that toss
On the wild sea's intemperate wilderness.

But lo! came Life, and with its painted toys
Lured me to play again like any child.
O pardon me this weak inconstancy.
May my soul die if in all present joys,
Lapped in forgetfulness or sense-beguiled,
Yea, in my mirth if I prefer not thee.

CHAPTER XXIII

ON the day Oscar Wilde got out of prison he left the country. Before he left he went to the Brompton Oratory and asked to see one of the Fathers. He had then, as he thought, quite made up his mind to become a Catholic, and his idea was to get " received " at once if he could. In this hope he would, almost certainly, have been disappointed, for although he did really know rather more than the average Protestant does about Catholicism, yet many of his views were (as appears glaringly in the published part of *De Profundis*) not only entirely unorthodox, but grossly repugnant to Catholicism, or, indeed, one would suppose, to any form of Christianity. He asked for a certain Father, with whom he was personally acquainted. I do not know whom it was he asked for, but I imagine that it was probably the late Father Sebastian Bowden, a saintly old man who had formerly been in the Coldstream Guards. In any case, the Father he asked for happened to be away, and though he could of course have seen any of the others, and was invited to do so, he declined. Whichever of the Fathers of the Oratory had seen him would, I think, certainly have told him that he could not possibly be received without at least some delay for " instruction." This would probably have annoyed Oscar, for although in *De Profundis* he frequently refers to the supposed humility which he had acquired in prison, the book itself affords the strongest evidence that he had not even begun to understand the meaning of the word, in its true Catholic or Christian sense. The idea that he required " instruction " in a subject in which he set up as an expert would probably have offended him very much. Indeed, I more than suspect that it was the realization of the fact that he would certainly have to submit to instruction that caused him, when he got over to France, to drop the whole idea. He was seeing a good deal of Ross at that time, and Ross (himself a Catholic and a convert, though he afterwards, I am told, apostatized) would have been in a position to give him all the information he required as to the process of getting received into the Church.

That Oscar did really die a Catholic (being received into the Church by a Franciscan on his deathbed, and while he was unable to speak, but still able to make signs) I now believe, though for a long time I doubted the genuineness and validity of his reception. My reasons for doubting them were that Ross, with whom, at the time of Oscar's death, I was supposed to be, and imagined myself to be, on the best of terms, told me most distinctly and positively that Oscar was " quite unconscious " at the time of his reception, and that he (Ross) had only got the Franciscan friar to consent to receive him by swearing that Oscar had asked him before he became unconscious to go at once and fetch a priest, as he was determined to die a Catholic. Ross told me that, as a matter of fact, Oscar said no such thing, and that the only justification he had for the step he took was that Oscar, years before, had told him that he intended to die a Catholic, and that if he were in danger of death Ross, if he were present or available, was to send for a priest. Ross, according to his habit, told various stories about the event, varying them according to his own fancy and the effect he wanted to produce on his audience. At the time when he told me what I have just reproduced I was not a Catholic, and though not hostile, yet not particularly sympathetic to Catholicism. What Ross actually said to me in effect was : " I hope you don't mind ; you know how I feel about these things ; Oscar several times in his life did express a desire to be a Catholic, and said that it was ' the only Church to die in,' so when he was dying I took it on myself to fetch a priest and to tell him that Oscar had expressed an earnest desire to be received. I also thought it would make things easier in a Catholic country, and that it would facilitate arrangements for his funeral and burial."

I replied that I was very glad that he had acted as he did. Years afterwards the Right Reverend Sir David Hunter Blair, Abbot of Fort Augustus, as whose guest I twice spent a week in the Benedictine Abbey of Fort Augustus, wrote me a long letter on the subject, which, unfortunately, I have not been able to find. But I remember quite well what the letter contained, and that the Abbot told me that he had heard from the Franciscan friar who received Oscar, who assured him that Oscar was sufficiently conscious to hear and understand all that the friar said to him, and that, although he could not speak, he gave unmistakable signs of assent. " I satisfied myself," wrote the friar, " that he understood and assented." Thus at the very last moment of his conscious life,

> Betwixt the stirrup and the ground,
> Mercy he sought and mercy found.

I must say, in justice to myself, that when in 1914 I collaborated with Crosland in the book, *Oscar Wilde and Myself*, I was in my own mind quite convinced that Oscar had not died a Catholic. What Ross had told me seemed decisive, and I could imagine no motive for his misleading me. The difference it makes in the way I am able to think of Oscar is, of course, tremendous ; chiefly because the fact of his wishing to die a Catholic implies a certain state of mind which connotes a number of other things. For example, a man becoming a Catholic must *ipso facto*, if his conversion be genuine, " forgive all those who have injured him and ask pardon of all whom he has injured " ; he also implicitly renounces all heretical opinions and expresses contrition for all his sins, both of the flesh and of the spirit.

By the way, St Thomas Aquinas, who, Catholically speaking, is the ultimate word and touchstone of wisdom, lays it down that sins of the spirit are much worse than sins of the flesh ; and that is the chief reason why I think that the English attitude towards certain vices is indefensible (except, of course, in the case of persons who have never by thought, word or deed been implicated in them themselves), for hypocrisy is a spiritual sin. I must explain that I do not mean that a man who has committed sins of the flesh at one time of his life has not a perfect right to feel and express horror at such sins, once he has got to realize how horrible they are ; but I mean that such a man has no right whatever to persecute or hound down another for doing what he has done himself or condoned in others. It all comes down to the truly heavenly saying of Jesus : " Let him that is without sin among you first cast a stone." Nor do I think that a man can get out of this comfortably, as the average Englishman thinks he can, by saying that whatever he may have done in other (what he calls legitimate) ways, he has never, at any rate since he left school, gone in for Oscar Wilde's particular vice. I very much doubt if such a complacent view of the relative importance of his own and someone else's form of sin will " cut much ice " at the Day of Judgment. All sins of the flesh are mortal sins, and are on the one hand, from that point of view, equally deadly, and on the other hand equally easy to obtain absolution for, on the proper conditions. Hence the attitude of the criminal law in France is more logical and more Christian than it is in England, precisely, of course, because France is still a Catholic country. In France, Oscar Wilde could not have been sent to prison for what he had done, although French opinion was at that time quite as much against what is still sometimes called " Le vice Anglais " as English opinion.

Oscar Wilde left England for ever, as it turned out, and went
to the little village of Berneval, where a chalet was obtained for
him. When he left prison a sum of £800 was subscribed for him
by various friends, the largest contributor being Miss Schuster.
I was not asked to subscribe to this fund. The attitude of Ross,
who was chiefly responsible for getting up the subscription (to
which, however, I do not think he contributed, as he was at
that time and for a long time afterwards almost entirely without
money), was tacitly hostile to me, and his omission to ask me to
subscribe was, no doubt, intended as a deliberate slight. If I had
been asked to subscribe I might or might not have been able to
do so. I was living in Paris on a small allowance from my mother,
and I seldom had a penny to spare. On the other hand, if I had
made an urgent appeal to my brother Percy I might probably
have got fifty pounds or so out of him for the purpose indicated.
The "official" attitude of Oscar, instigated and kept alive by
Ross, was, however, that he wished to have nothing whatever to
do with me. I am amazed now when I think of the patience and
meekness with which I bore this offensive and utterly unmerited
treatment. If I had taken Wilde at his word, and neither
written to him nor attempted to see him again, the whole
course of my life would have been changed, to my advantage ;
nor would it ever have been in the power of either himself or
his "faithful friends" to reproach me. Instead of doing this,
however, I wrote to him at once, and said in effect : "I am
told that you now hate me and do not wish to see me or have
anything to do with me, but all the same I write to tell you
that I have not changed to you, in spite of all the efforts that
have been made to put me against you, that I have remembered
and kept my solemn promise to stick to you through thick and
thin, and that I long to see you again." It is, I think, almost
certain that this letter of mine and a lot more that I wrote
to Oscar about this time were among the number which Ross

K

appropriated and kept when Oscar was lying dead in the Hôtel d'Alsace. If so, it is almost equally certain that Ross's heirs or executors have still got them. Once more I ask that they should be given back to me.

Oscar replied at once, in a somewhat priggish, if not canting, tone. He said that he did not hate me and, on the contrary, still "loved me very much," but that at present he thought it better that we should not meet. Although it was "not a very nice letter," it certainly was a long way removed from the sort of thing I had been led to expect. Under the rather formal and lecturing surface of the letter it was easy for me to see that Oscar was very far from having arrived at the state of mind so much desiderated by the "faithful friends," who were so anxious, for reasons best known to themselves, to take charge of his actions and feelings. To put it plainly, I guessed at once that he was longing to see me, but that other people were putting obstacles in his way.

A number of the letters which Oscar wrote to me at this time have been published (not for sale) by a Mr William Andrews Clark, jun., in America. They have been magnificently produced in facsimile, and are supplemented by notes which are ably and fairly written. The writer of the notes points out at once that one of the letters completely disposes of the Ross-Harris version of the reunion of Oscar and myself. I will explain later in this book how I came to part with the letters, and how the promise made to me by the person who acquired them that they would not leave his possession during his or my lifetime was violated by his successors in business. At present all I need say is that the letters have been published. I think it rather extraordinary that Mr Andrews Clark did not have the courtesy to send me a copy of the book, which I saw and carefully went through when I was staying with Frank Harris in Nice in 1925. But possibly he did not realize that I would wish to have it.

The publication of the letters bears out what I have already said, that the more of Oscar's letters to me and my letters to him are made public the better it will be for my reputation and his own. The letters are entirely creditable both to their writer and their recipient.

CHAPTER XXIV

THE letters that Oscar wrote to me at this time began, as I have stated, in a lecturing and fault-finding tone which, for all my desire to be reconciled with him, I was not disposed to go on standing for long. I replied vigorously, and pointed out that his attitude towards me was unfair and ungrateful, that it was quite unworthy of him, and that it appeared to reflect the psychological results of his imprisonment in a way which he would probably soon grow out of when he got back the full use of his brains and intellect. The result was that Oscar soon dropped his fault-finding attitude. His letters became more and more affectionate, and he made no secret of the fact that he was longing to see me again and that it was only the necessity (chiefly for financial reasons) of " keeping in " with certain people, including, of course, Ross, who was apparently holding a great part of the money subscribed for Oscar and doling it out from time to time, that prevented him from rushing over to Paris to see me, or asking me to stay with him at Berneval. I may say, to prevent misunderstanding, that I do not blame Ross at all for his cautiousness about the money and for his, unfortunately fruitless, efforts to make it last a little longer than it did. In this respect he certainly acted entirely in Oscar's interests and with the best motives.

I must here emphasize what I have said before in this book, that the letters which Oscar wrote me at this time (even allowing for the fact that I later destroyed many of those which contained the most exaggerated expressions of affection and devotion) completely dispose of all the nonsense of his wild accusations against me in the "unpublished part" of *De Profundis*. Between the time when he penned this violent diatribe and the time when he wrote me these adoring letters nothing whatever had happened in relation to our friendship, except that he had got out of prison. If I was such a bad friend and so " unworthy of the great love I showed you," at the time he was spending his last months in prison, why did I now become his comfort and joy, his only hope for the future, and his " own darling boy " ? It is to be observed that when he wrote these letters he had not seen me for nearly two years, so that the disturbing and disastrous effects on him attributed to my presence and personality by Harris, Ross, Sherard, and others, had had no chance of being exercised.

The real truth is, unpalatable as it may be to Ross, and Sherard and Harris, and any other living person who could be named at that time, that Oscar cared more for my little finger than he did for all the rest of these persons put together, body and soul. It cannot be contended, either, that his devotion to me was a mere physical infatuation, because the facts, even according to my great enemy and detractor, Frank Harris, are admitted to be that I was, alone of those I have mentioned, not only the dearest friend of his bosom, but his intellectual peer. Harris cannot have it both ways. It is idle for him to endeavour to make out, as he does on one printed page, that I was a kind of (*Troilus and Cressida*) Patroclus to Wilde's Achilles, as interpreted and commented on by the foul-mouthed Thersites, when on another printed page he compares my sonnets to Shakespeare's and declares unhesitatingly that even in my extreme youth I was always a far better poet than Wilde himself.

As I believe in giving credit where it is due, even to those who have most grievously wronged me (and Harris has no excuse at all for his treatment of me, for I was for many years his intimate friend, and he once did me out of £2000 without losing my friendship or hearing any reproaches from me), I may say that I think it is really wonderful that he should have committed himself as strongly as he has done to appreciation of me as a poet and man of letters. At one time he knew many of my sonnets by heart, and used to recite them in his well-known sucking-dove roar in restaurants and other public resorts. (Seriously, his rendering of them was calculated to delight their author's heart, for he was and is now an accomplished reader or reciter of poetry.)   His charming and accomplished wife told me that, at one time, when he wanted to give the highest praise to any work of art, he used to say : " It's as fine as one of Alfred Douglas's sonnets."   It is then certainly to Harris's credit that his desire, for reasons best known to himself, to blacken my character, and hold me up to public contempt and reprobation, has not prevented him from expressing his honest opinion of my merits as a poet.   Unless indeed it be that this apparent honesty of opinion is only a clever device to lend more strength to his denunciations. As who should say : " You observe how fair I am, though I am obliged in the interests of truth to attack Lord Alfred Douglas's character I would not dream of denying him any credit that he deserved as a poet and man of brains and intellect."   I prefer to think that Harris really did feel that in his denunciation of me he must " draw the line somewhere," and that his literary conscience, being, like Oscar Wilde's, more sensitive than his moral conscience, did not permit him to speak falsely about my poetry even if he had no scruple in deliberately lying about my character and about facts well known to him in regard to my relations with Wilde.[1]

[1] To accuse a man of downright deliberate lying is a serious thing to do. I was willing enough to accept, without questioning it (whatever my private thoughts were), Harris's explanation that it was Ross who was responsible for misleading him and falsifying the facts. But as he has now repeated his libels in a new edition of his book, and reiterated them in an Introduction of a cheap edition of *De Profundis* published by the " Modern Library " in New York about a year ago, I can think of no other words to apply to what he has done but " deliberate lying."

Listen to what he says about me in the " New Preface " to *The Life and*

After Oscar and I had exchanged about half-a-dozen letters he wrote and definitely invited me to come to stay with him at Berneval. In a characteristically playful epistle he suggested that it would be advisable that I should assume some other name for the occasion. He said in his letter that he had been thinking of a suitable name for me, and was divided between "Le Chevalier de la Fleur-de-lys" and "Jonquil du Vallon." In another letter he informed me that he had "decided" that I was to be "Jonquil du Vallon," and referred to himself as "that strange purple shadow who is known as Sebastian Melmoth," which was in fact the name he adopted after he came out of prison, and by which I addressed him on the envelopes of my letters. All this, though it may now sound rather childish, was just like the old Oscar whom I had known and loved before the catastrophe. I was just getting ready to start when a telegram arrived stopping me and telling me to await a letter. The letter arrived, and contained a story that he had been warned that it would be dangerous for me to come, as my father was having him watched and would, certainly, intervene and create a fresh scandal. This, of course, was a pure *canard*, but no doubt he believed it. He lamented the impossibility of our meeting in moving terms, but declared that his devotion to me was only enhanced by our continued separation.

I wrote back, laughing at the idea of my father's supposed plot, and suggesting that we should meet somewhere else. He replied that he would not come to Paris as he " could not face Paris yet," but suggested Rouen. So we agreed to meet at Rouen, and did so, for one night and day at the Hôtel de la

Confessions of Oscar Wilde: " That I should have misjudged the foremost poet of this time is my keenest regret ; that I could have believed that such noble gifts could go with corrupt meanness of character, shows the malignant cleverness of his detractors.'' These are the words with which he finishes his Preface, and yet, within a year, he is republishing the book containing all his false statements and misrepresentations, and writing a fresh batch of them as an Introduction to a new book !

Poste, where I had stayed before and was known. This made the assumption of an assumed name on my part impracticable, which I really think was a cause of great disappointment to Oscar. The meeting was a great success. I have often thought since that if he or I had died directly after that, our friendship would have ended in a beautiful and romantic way. Poor Oscar cried when I met him at the station. We walked about all day arm in arm, or hand in hand, and were perfectly happy. Next day he went back to Berneval and I returned to Paris, but we had settled that when I went to Naples about six weeks later he was to join me there.

About a week later I went to Aix-les-Bains with my mother and sister. I stayed there about five weeks, and had a most delightful time. While I was there I wrote *The Ballad of St Vitus*, which I consider to be the best of my three ballads. My mother then went back to London and I went on to Naples, meeting Oscar on the train from Paris. We went to the Hôtel Royal, and I celebrated the occasion by running up a bill for £68 in the fortnight we were there. This bill remained unpaid right up to the time when I left Oscar at Naples, about two or three months later, when my dear mother sent me £200 to give to Oscar and also the money to pay the hotel bill and enable me to get back to Paris via Rome. I must explain that the proprietor, or manager, of the Hôtel Royal, being of course under the usual impression that obtains, or used to obtain, on the Continent, that an " English Lord " is invariably a millionaire, seemed quite undisturbed by my request that he should let the bill stand over. He expressed himself enchanted to oblige me, and beyond sending in the bill again after about two months he made no kind of demonstration. I would not have the cheek to do a thing like that nowadays, but in the year 1897 I still lived under the pleasing illusion that life more or less belonged to me, and that money was not a thing to take seriously.

While we were at Naples, Oscar finished *The Ballad of Reading Gaol*, and I wrote the four sonnets called *The City of the Soul*, my *Sonnet on the Sonnet*, and *A Triad of the Moon*. About a year before, I had spent some months in Rome with my mother, and I there had the pleasure of meeting, for the first time, my dear old friend, Harry de Windt, whose friendship to this day is one of my most valued possessions. Harry and I met in the bar of the Grand Hotel (he had known my father intimately for years, and also other members of my family, and he spoke to me directly he knew who I was), where he was engaged for several hours in an argument, which frequently threatened to culminate in bloodshed, with an exceedingly " tough " gentleman from the Colonies. What the argument was about I cannot now recollect, but the tough gentleman from the Colonies, who claimed to be (and really was, I afterwards found out) a bosom friend of my brother Percy's, several times " reached for a gun " which he carried in his back breeches-pocket. The discussion went on with varying degrees of ferocity (alternating with friendly interludes, when drinks were offered and accepted) till nearly half-past three o'clock in the morning, at which hour a truce, due to sheer exhaustion on the part of all concerned, was called, and the meeting broke up. Harry " saw me back " to the rooms where I was living with my mother. I then " saw him back " to the Grand Hotel. The process was repeated several times, and it was broad daylight when we parted.

A few months afterwards I met our colonial friend at Monte Carlo, where, hearing that I had just lost all the money in my pocket, he generously lent me twenty-five louis and insisted on entertaining me sumptuously at dinner at the Hôtel de Paris. He referred in feeling terms to Harry, who, according to his account of the affair, was a man to whom he had immediately felt irresistibly drawn by magnetic attraction at first sight, and who had reciprocated the feeling in the strongest way. I saw him a week later, when, I am glad to be able to state, I paid him back the twenty-five louis, for the next thing I heard about him was that he had committed suicide. I cannot remember the poor fellow's name.

Harry de Windt turned up at Naples while Oscar and I were there. He knew Oscar well, and admired his work and his conversation. We dined together in a café, and I afterwards happened to go away and leave them together. Harry de Windt told me years later that when he read the accounts of the Ransome trial in the papers he was amazed and disgusted to read the letter which Wilde wrote to Ross in which he describes how I left him at Naples. "As soon as there was no money he left me," says Wilde in this abominable letter, and the rest of the letter (which is reproduced in Harris's *Life and Confessions of Oscar Wilde*) is in the same strain. No mention is made in it of the £200 I gave him. Harry told me that while I was away Wilde's conversation with him was one long eulogy of me, and of how I had stuck to him through thick and thin and was his best and most faithful friend. Harry told me that if he had known about the Ransome action he would have been pleased to come and give evidence on this point. I described in detail in Chapter XIV. how I was forced to leave Oscar in Naples because my mother, when she found out that he was with me, immediately wrote to me and said that unless I left him she would discontinue my allowance. What possessed Oscar to write this disgusting letter to Ross, which I read for the first time fourteen years later, I cannot even conjecture. As Harris says in the " Preface " : " Such hypocrisy and falsehood are hard even to understand, but the facts remain."

Oscar and I were fairly happy at Naples, though we had several quarrels. He had nothing beyond an allowance of £3 a week from his wife and I had very little money, only about £8 a week. The constant worry about ways and means was trying, and Oscar did not adapt himself as easily as I have always been able to do to making the best of a small income. All the same we were still great friends, and when my mother's ultimatum came as a bombshell to break up our association we were both very distressed. Obviously, however, there was nothing for it but for me to leave him. We were neither of us in a position to raise a penny, and it was merely a question of getting enough money to carry Oscar on till he could get more from some other source. I left him in my villa with three months' rent paid in advance. With ordinary care the £200 I got for him would have kept him in Naples (where everything was amazingly cheap) in comfort for at least five or six months. I had lived myself on less money for as long a period in France without complaining. But as a matter of fact Oscar remained only a few weeks in Naples. He then went to Paris.

CHAPTER XXV

WHILE Wilde was with me at Naples he was in good health and good spirits. He was chiefly engaged in finishing his *Ballad of Reading Gaol*, of which he had concluded the rough draft at Berneval. He worked at it very hard, thus bearing out the contention I have always made, that all good poetry is the result of struggle and effort, and that good poets do not " pour out words " like inspired gramophones.

I have been reminded of his struggles to get the ballad " just right " by reading the collection of his letters to Robert Ross written from my villa at Posilipo (Naples), recently brought out by Mr More Adey. *En passant* I note that he refers in eulogistic terms to three sonnets, called *A Triad of the Moon*, which I wrote at that time and which appeared in *The City of the Soul*, and have been reprinted in subsequent volumes. He says in the first letter in the collection : " Bosie has written three lovely sonnets, which I have called the *Triad of the Moon*. They are quite wonderful. He has sent them to Henley. I have also got him to send his sonnet on Mozart to *The Musician*." I had forgotten till I read this letter that it was Oscar who gave me the name *Triad of the Moon* for my three sonnets. I had also forgotten all about the sonnet on Mozart. I now remember quite well writing it, but I cannot recall more than two lines of it. All I know is that *The Musician* evidently did not publish it. In view of Wilde's contemptuous remarks about my " undergraduate verse," made when he was in a rage and quoted by Harris, I am glad to have this independent evidence that he did not always despise my poetry.

It is instructive to note, from what he says in these letters, that my influence over him in the poetical line prevailed over that of Ross in at least two instances. Ross objected to his fine phrase for a judge, " the man in red who reads the law," in *The Ballad of Reading Gaol,* saying it made him think of " the man in blue," for a policeman. It was I who insisted on Wilde keeping in the expression and overruling Ross's foolish objection.

Again, Ross said the poem ought to end at the words " outcasts always mourn." Wilde says in one letter to Ross : " You are quite right in saying that the poem should end at ' outcasts always mourn,' but the propaganda, which I desire to make, begins there." The fact is that Ross was a poor critic, and if he had had his way he would have spoiled *The Ballad of Reading Gaol,* which is the one entirely fine and sincere poem Wilde wrote, forgetting his " art for art's sake " heresies which Ross encouraged. It was I again who influenced him here. If the poem had ended at the point suggested by Ross it would have been a heavy loss to literature. It is exceedingly lucky that I happened to be with Wilde at the time he finished writing this fine poem (far the best thing he ever did in poetry), for otherwise he would certainly have succumbed to some of Ross's inept attacks on his best phrases. " The black dock's dreadful pen " he defends against Ross, and he kept it in spite of Ross's efforts to make him change it. It is a fine phrase. His struggles and his (astonishingly humble) pleas to be allowed to write his own poem in his own way remind one of Byron's similar pleas on behalf of *Don Juan* when it was continually being assailed by the mediocrities who assembled to criticize it, canto by canto, as Byron sent it in, in Murray's " Back Parlour."

I do not for a moment claim that I helped Wilde to write this great poem. I can recall only one passage which owed something to a sonnet (unpublished) of mine which I had written while Oscar was in prison and which I showed him at that time. It had two lines :

> Into the dreadful town through iron doors,
> By empty stairs and barren corridors.

Those who know *The Ballad of Reading Gaol* well will recognize that there is an echo of these two lines in the ballad : " That night the empty corridors," etc. etc.

Wilde apologized for " borrowing," and I assured him he was quite welcome, and I meant it. That is the only passage which owed anything at all to me, except that I, as a fellow-poet, for whom he really had a respect as a poet, stiffened him against the " clever " criticisms of Ross. All I did was to maintain then, as I would now against all comers, that Wilde was a much better judge of what is and what is not proper to a poem than Ross, who could not have written a dozen lines of poetry to save his life, and whose critical faculty can be gauged by the fact that he considered Shakespeare " very much over-rated," and inferior not only to Marlowe but also to Webster !

I am afraid that my reminiscences of life at the Posilipo villa are very vague. I remember that we had a cook called Carmine, a maid, Maria, and two boys called Peppino and Michele, who waited on us. Servants cost little more than their keep in those days at Naples, and the cost of feeding Wilde and myself and the servants was about twelve francs a day! I also remember that the villa, which was charmingly situated, with a terrace and marble steps leading down to the sea, was full of rats—so much so that I, who have always been terrified of rats and (if the truth must be told) not by any means exactly mad about mice, was reduced to the ludicrous pass of having to hire a room in a house opposite the villa to sleep in. After a time, however, we got rid of the rats, partly by means of a professional and orthodox rat-catcher, but also (and chiefly, according to Oscar's opinion) owing to the ministrations, hired for a small fee, of a potent witch who was recommended as infallible by Michele, and who came and " burned odours " and muttered incantations, which she assured us no rats could resist. She also told both our fortunes, and Oscar professed to regard her as a wonderful and powerful sorceress. In appearance she was quite the witch of literature and drama. She had a distinct beard and "with age and envy was grown into a hoop." Anyhow the rats dis-appeared, and I was able to return to the villa, where I remained till I was obliged to leave because my allowance was threatened with extinction if I remained longer with Wilde.

It was after I left him in possession of my villa, and with £200 of my money in his pocket, that he penned his celebrated letter to Ross, to which I have already referred, in which he says that " as soon as there was no money left Bosie left me," and describes the incident as " the most bitter experience of a bitter life " ! Considering that I was forced to leave him much against my will, and that he for his part was also threatened with the loss of his pittance of £3 a week from his wife if he continued to live with me, and that consequently we both agreed that it was necessary to separate, this letter is one of the most astonish-ing products that the history of literature has ever recorded. The letter is not included in Mr Adey's collection, called *After Berneval*, but it is now being offered for sale (with my consent) by Messrs Dulau, of 32 Old Bond Street. As an example of the amount of reliance which can be placed on Wilde's statements (spoken or written) it is perhaps the most powerful piece of evidence in my favour that the whole of this melancholy history of our friendship can provide. I commend it to those who go on refusing to believe that anyone could possibly have behaved so badly as I accuse Wilde and Ross of having done. I include Ross because he used the letter against me at the Ransome case although he knew perfectly well, and had known all along, what were the true facts, and that I was not only innocent of the slightest offence against Wilde, but treated him with the greatest generosity, and was also heart-broken at being obliged to leave him.[1]

[1] It occurs to me that I have omitted to make any mention of my translation of Oscar Wilde's French play, *Salomé*, and though it belongs to a period long before that which I have reached in these memoirs, I may now suitably bring it in, in a chapter devoted chiefly to literary matters.

I translated *Salomé* at Oscar's request while I was still at Oxford, and I wrote an article eulogizing the French play in my undergraduate paper, *The Spirit Lamp*, in which paper I have just remembered that I also printed the sonnet addressed to me by Oscar, to which I referred in the first paragraph of Chapter XII. of this book.

When I had finished the translation, to which I devoted a great deal of time and careful work, Oscar did not like it. In fact he actually yielded to the solicitations of Aubrey Beardsley, who declared that he could do a splendid translation and that he thoroughly understood the spirit of the play, and who begged Oscar to let him do it. I was, not unnaturally, somewhat offended at this, and was rather gratified, I must confess, when a month later, after Oscar had received and read Beardsley's translation, he declared that it was "utterly hopeless," and that he would, on second thoughts, rather have mine, the manuscript of which I had meanwhile taken back. I told Oscar that if my translation was any use to him he could use it, and that anything in it he did not like he could alter. But I added that if he altered it, it would no longer be my translation, and that in that case it would not be advisable for my name to appear as the translator. Oscar used my translation, making a few alterations. Really I believe he originally wrote the play in English and translated it into French with the assistance of Pierre Louÿs and André Gide. So that to get anyone at all to "translate" it was a rather ridiculous pose. At the time Oscar wrote this play he did not know French well enough to write a play in the language, and André Gide told me later that Oscar's first draft was a mass of blunders and misspelling. Pierre Louÿs and he knocked it into shape, and when it came to a translation into English, Oscar just put it back more or less into his own original language, altering my translation where it differed from his own words. Consequently I do not regard the present translation, which is usually attributed to me, and which is dedicated to me as the translator, as mine at all. I do not claim it as my translation. I think my own translation, as a matter of fact, was much better!

CHAPTER XXVI

DURING the next two years I saw Oscar constantly in Paris, where I was living in a small flat in the Avenue Kléber. I was still very hard up, but, out of what little I had, I did what I could for him. As a matter of fact, during that time he really had far more money than I had, for, though he had no regular income except his £3 a week, he was helped by a great number of people, including Frank Harris. I must do Harris the justice of saying that he is, and always has been, generous with money. I do not for a moment doubt what he tells me about the money he gave Oscar. Harris at that time owned and edited *The Saturday Review*, which he ultimately sold at a large profit, and he was very well off. He declares that he alone gave Oscar more than enough for him to live comfortably during the whole time between his release from prison and his death. I could mention a dozen other persons who gave him money, including Ernest Leverson, Dal Young and Claude Lowther. He also got a good lot from Smithers, the publisher, over *The Ballad of Reading Gaol*, and he sold the scenario of the play, *Mr and Mrs Daventry*, which Harris afterwards wrote with Oscar's consent, to at least half-a-dozen different people. The way he behaved about this scenario is enough in itself to indicate that he had by this time pretty well lost all sense of honesty and honour, for he really defrauded all the various persons who gave him sums of money under the impression that they were buying exclusive rights in a valuable property.

I prefer not to say much more about these last years of his life. I have already related what happened when my father died and I came into a modest amount of money—less than

£15,000, of which I received only £8000 at first. Oscar
lived only a year after my father's death, and during that year
I gave him at least £1000, while he for his part (as I only
found out years later) went about telling everyone he met that
I refused to give him a penny or to help him in any way. I
believe he did not do this out of malice against me, for the extraordinary thing is that, in spite of what he was doing behind
my back, he remained outwardly on the most affectionate terms
with me, and we spent many a delightful evening together
after I had entertained him to dinner at Paillard's or the Café
de la Paix or Maire's or the Grand Café. I think his sole reason
for acting as he did was his desire to get money out of other
people. He found that his "pitching the tale" that, although
I was now rich, I had deserted him and left him without
money was very effective in loosening the purse-strings of those
to whom he poured out his tale of woe. Their pity for him,
coupled with their indignation against me, made them generous.
I judge that this was his motive, partly because I can think of
no other, and partly because he applied the same principle to me.
Whenever I met him he was always full of "the meanness
and want of imagination"—a favourite phrase of his at this
time — of Frank Harris, Robert Ross, and anyone else who
helped him in any way. He did not tell me that Harris had
not given him a penny for the simple reason that I happened
to know otherwise, having been present at lunch at Durand's
on at least two occasions when I had with my own eyes seen
Harris hand him 1000 francs (in those days a thousand francs
really was a thousand francs, or £40). But later when, as I now
know, Harris was giving him a lot of money, he complained
bitterly to me of his "meanness," though really he had not
the slightest claim on him.

Unlike Harris and unlike Ross (both of whom at that time I
liked and looked upon as friends) I discounted these statements

of Oscar's. Knowing by this time from experience that he was, since he had come out of prison, quite unscrupulous about money, and that he was liable to abuse his best friends for no particular reason, I did not repeat what he said. It "went in at one ear and out at the other." Harris and Ross, on the other hand, treasured up everything Wilde said against me, and did everything they could to spread what they must have known to be his false and wickedly ungrateful accusations against me. When I say that both Ross and Harris spread these accusations, I must qualify this by explaining that I do not think that Harris did so till many years later ; because, although he entirely suppresses the fact in his *Life and Confessions of Oscar Wilde*, he and I were, at the time I am now referring to, on terms of great friendship. He called me "Bosie" and I called him "Frank." I liked and admired him, and the way he went on sticking up for Oscar and making a point of entertaining him at Durand's, which at that time was a favourite resort of the British Embassy people, greatly appealed to me.

Harris, in his *Life and Confessions of Oscar Wilde*, gives a grossly garbled account of an interview I had with him (he says in Paris, but really the meeting took place at the Hôtel Condé, at Chantilly, where I was then living). He represents me then as speaking meanly and bitterly about Oscar, and as giving indications that I grudged him even the "small sums of money" I was then giving him.

What really happened was that Harris came to Chantilly, and we had dinner, and passed the evening together sitting up talking till two in the morning. He informed me that Oscar had complained to him about my "meanness." In reply I told him that I had given Oscar a lot of money (several hundred pounds) and that I fully intended to go on giving him more, as long as he needed it, and as long as I had it to give. But I told him, what was the fact, that a few days before Oscar had tackled me on the money question and had bluntly told me that it was my bounden duty to give him a large sum, several thousand pounds, or at any rate "a couple of thousand." I told Harris exactly how I was situated financially since the death of my father, and I put it to him whether he thought it was reasonable to expect that I should hand Oscar £2000 out of my small patrimony, of which I had at that time received only about half. I told Harris that I had no intention of giving Wilde £2000 in one lump, though I did not doubt that he would get far more than that out of me in the long run. Harris said that he entirely agreed with me, that it was preposterous of Oscar to ask for such a sum, which he would probably spend in riotous living in a few months, and he went on to suggest that instead of giving Oscar £2000, if I would give it to him (Harris) he would put me into a scheme which he was then floating which would bring me in £2000 a year for life. "This," he said, "will put you in a position to treat Oscar in the most handsome way and still have plenty for yourself."

I have not the slightest doubt, in view of what subsequently happened and of what I now know of Harris's character and methods, that he came to Chantilly on purpose to rope me into this scheme of his, or rather, I may say simply, to "touch me for £2000." I imagine that until Oscar had complained about my "meanness" Harris had not realized that I had come into money, and that there was any question of my being able to dispose of such a useful sum as £2000. Directly he found out that I had money and was, so far from being mean about it, on the contrary, recklessly generous and open-handed with it, he conceived the idea of exploiting me.

He did it very cleverly—he was a past master at the game and I was a mere child in his hands. He said to me : "Do not decide anything about it now, but come and stay with me as my guest in my hotel at Monte Carlo. I am running an 'hotel for millionaires,' and I have put in Césari [the celebrated *maître d'hôtel*] to manage it for me. This hotel will shortly be paying fifty per cent. on the capital, and, if you like, I will let you into the company ; but I have another much bigger thing on, a real gold mine. I prefer to say nothing about it now, but come to Monte Carlo any time you like within the next four weeks and I will show you everything. Then, if you are convinced that it is a good thing, you can be right in on the rock bottom and get a hundred per cent. for your money. Meanwhile do not mention a word of this to Oscar or to anyone else."

A week or two later I went to Monte Carlo and stayed with Frank Harris at his hotel, which was called Césari's Hotel. It was a small hotel, and consisted entirely of beautifully furnished and ultra-expensive suites (bedroom, bathroom and sitting-room). Harris's idea was that he would attract American, South African and other brands of millionaires who really enjoy paying enormous sums for special comfort and luxury. He had a splendid cook, and the hotel was undoubtedly something quite out of the ordinary. Indeed I think that Harris's idea was an excellent one, but no doubt he had not enough capital to run it long enough to " turn the corner."

Harris entertained me sumptuously, and drove me out the day after I arrived to the Restaurant de la Réserve, at Eze, for lunch. We had an excellent lunch on a terrace looking over the sea, a Hungarian band was playing, and the restaurant was full of clients and appeared to be doing a roaring trade. When the liqueur and cigar stage had been reached, Harris told me that the restaurant belonged to him. " You see for yourself the sort of business we are doing," he said ; " this is my gold mine." I said : " Well, it seems a good sort of speculation, but I don't quite see where the hundred per cent. profit you spoke of is going to come in." Harris leaned across to me and clutched my arm. " My dear man," he said, " this is nothing. The real gold mine is not yet revealed to you ; but listen to this. I have a concession from the French Government allowing roulette and trente-et-quarante to be played here ! " I was much impressed. No doubt, if Harris really had had such a concession, the place would have been a veritable gold mine, and I was too young and foolish and inexperienced to reflect that in that case he would hardly have been so anxious to take so much trouble to secure my modest £2000. To cut a long story short, I parted with the £2000, giving him a cheque that day for £500 and a further cheque for £1500 a week or two later in Paris. In return I received two thousand shares in what was called "The Césari Reserve Syndicate."

I never got so much as sixpence back. I afterwards discovered that at the time I lunched there with Harris the restaurant was mortgaged up to the hilt ; and it was closed down less than a year later. I also discovered that Harris's story about the gambling concession was a pure invention. No such concession had been promised, nor has any concession for playing roulette and trente-et-quarante ever been granted by the French Government during the last fifty years, these two games being illegal by French law, which, however, does allow baccarat and petits chevaux or boule. When I found out that I had been "done," as I did little by little during the next twelve months, and that Harris's references to the promised "gold mine" gradually grew less frequent and finally petered out altogether, I took stock of the situation. It occurred to me that I had been a "mug" and a fool. I thought it exceedingly unlikely that I would ever be able to get anything out of Harris, and I came to the conclusion that the best thing I could do was to cut the loss and say no more about it. I was in those days incredibly foolish about money. I could never get myself to believe that I could not get plenty some time or another whenever I really started to "go after it," which is just exactly what I have never done.

So I said, literally, nothing. When Harris finally admitted that the whole scheme had gone to pieces and that he had been, as he expressed it, "done out of the promised concession," but that he intended to "make it up to me" in another way before long, I simply shrugged my shoulders and said : "All right, old chap."

I can truthfully say that I never bore Harris the slightest grudge about what he had done. I never reproached him with it, and I told very few people about it. I had almost forgotten all about it when, in the year 1920, while I was editing *Plain English*, I for the first time read the lies that Harris had published about me in his book, *The Life and Confessions of Oscar Wilde*, and particularly his account of the interview I had with him at Chantilly. I then told the story of the real facts about that interview and its sequel in the columns of *Plain English* very much as I have told them here.

CHAPTER XXVII

DIRECTLY after my father's death the South African War broke out. By the time war was declared I had already bought two or three horses, and they were being trained by George Woodhouse, at Chantilly. As soon as I heard the news I returned to London and offered myself as a trooper in "Paget's Horse." Colonel Paget said to me: "You had much better join 'The Duke of Cambridge's Corps,' which is being recruited entirely from gentlemen who are prepared to pay for all their own equipment." I accordingly went straight to the depot of the corps, joined it, after passing the riding, shooting and medical tests, and gave the secretary a cheque for £250 to pay for my horse and equipment. Two days afterwards my cheque for £250 was returned to me, with a letter informing me that my services were not required. In face of this deliberate and cowardly insult there was nothing to do but what I did—namely, to write to Lord Arthur Hill, who was responsible for raising the corps, and to tell him in plain English what I thought of him and also of the Duke of Cambridge! Having thus relieved my feelings I returned to Chantilly and bought another horse.

I bought a horse called "Hardi" out of a selling race for £250. He belonged to Edmond Blanc, the owner of the Casino at Monte Carlo, and had been leading his horses in their work at Chantilly. He was six years old and had never won a race, and he was a gelding, a beautiful chestnut horse. I put him in a race at Lille, and he ran there and won during the time I was with Frank Harris at Monte Carlo.

I had an extraordinary run of luck on that occasion at Monte Carlo. In the intervals of "talking business" and lunching and dining with Harris I went into the Casino with twenty-five louis (that was then, of course, £20). I determined that I would not lose more than this, and that the moment I lost it I would come out of the rooms and not go back. This was the third time I had been at Monte Carlo. I went once with Oscar, just before he prosecuted my father at the Old Bailey. We stayed at the Hôtel de Paris, and I won about seventy or eighty pounds. Then I went nearly two years later with my mother to the Hôtel Windsor. This was the occasion when, as I have described, I was at first refused admission to the rooms on the ground that I was too young, although really I was twenty-seven. This was also the occasion on which I met again and dined with the colonial who had had the historic argument with Harry de Windt at the Grand Hotel in Rome.

On the third occasion, when I was with Harris, who, although at one time he had (so he says) been a big gambler, now never went into the rooms, I determined that, as I had just bought horses and was also going in for Harris's " gold mine," it really would be foolish to start " chucking away money at the Casino." However, I could not resist the idea of " giving twenty-five louis a chance," so after registering all sorts of mental vows that I would not lose more than this sum, I went in and put a louis on the number thirteen, which promptly came up. I doubled my stake and it came up again. In those days play at the Casino was in real gold and notes. When you won with an *en plein* louis you were paid with a five-hundred-franc note and ten louis in gold. I went on backing *en pleins* at haphazard, five or six at a time. Every time I won one I put the note in my pocket and went on with the gold. After about two hours I lost my last gold piece and went out with nine or ten five-hundred-franc notes in my pocket (about £200).

I gave this money to Césari and told him to put it in a big envelope, together with any other notes I might win. I told him he was on no account to give me the envelope till I was actually getting into the train to go away. After dinner that evening I again went in with twenty-five louis. I went on backing five or six *en pleins* each coup, and doubling my stake when I won. But I never had more than two louis on a number. I repeated my plan of pocketing the notes and going on with the gold as long as I had any left. The result was just about the same as that of my morning *séance*. To cut a long story short, I went on doing this every day while I remained at Monte Carlo. I was there only four days, and I went into the rooms three times a day. I never lost my twenty-five louis till the last day, when I went in—at what hour I forget ; but I know that my train was due to start about an hour later and that I had instructed Césari (who looked after me during all the time of my stay with special attention) that he was to be at the station with my luggage and that I would be there to catch the train. For the first time I lost the twenty-five louis. I rushed out to the bank and changed a cheque for £50. I went back and lost it all. The gambling fever was on me and I went out to cash another cheque, but on the way to Smith's Bank I looked at my watch and saw that I had just five minutes to catch my train. I hesitated for a moment, and then dashed to the station. When I got there I found the train in and Césari, with my luggage, looking wildly round for me. I just had time to get in, my bags were hurled after me and the train began to move. Césari handed me the sealed envelope containing my winnings and I sank back on the seat. I had lost count of what I had won, and I eagerly opened the envelope. It contained forty-two thousand francs—£1680. So I actually got away with over sixteen hundred pounds, allowing for the seventy I had dropped that day. If I had been what is called a " really good gambler," and had played up my luck as such a gambler would have done, I could easily have won twenty or thirty thousand pounds with the luck I had. But being "a really good gambler" cuts both ways, and I never was one.

When I got to Nice I was within an ace of getting out and going back to Monte Carlo for another flutter in the Casino. But I resisted the temptation and went on.

I stopped the night at Marseilles (in those days there was no "blue train"), and found a telegram from Woodhouse, my trainer, to say that my horse had won at Lille. This was the first race I won. It was worth only three thousand francs (£120), as far as I remember, but I was perfectly delighted. I had entrusted Woodhouse with fifty louis to back the horse for me. In the provinces in those days, in France, if you had fifty louis on your horse he was pretty sure to start favourite, and I think I got only about 6 to 4 for my money.

Two or three months later my horse Hardi ran in the selling race (a mile and a quarter), which was the opening race on the card, on the day of the French Derby at Chantilly. There was a good enough market there, as at all the meetings round Paris. There were plenty of bookmakers in those days (now done away with), as well as the Pari Mutuel. I fancied my horse, and told all my friends to back him. Just because I was a novice, and also looked like a schoolboy, though in reality I was in my thirtieth year, nobody seemed to believe that I could win a race, and I doubt if any of my friends benefited by this, which was really something of a *coup*. Two other horses in the race were backed for money, and my horse started at 6 to 1. I had 300 louis on him, and he made all the running and won in a canter by two lengths.

My horse was a gelding, and there were in those days in France very few races for which geldings were qualified. On the Friday after the race I have referred to there was a five-furlong race at Maisons-Lafitte for *chevaux entiers, hongres et juments*. I had insisted on entering Hardi for this race, against the advice of my trainer, who said the horse had no chance over any distance less than a mile (1600 metres). However, my chief object was to see my colours, and I also had an odd feeling that the horse would win. Woodhouse was, I think, really rather annoyed that I would insist on starting the horse. There were about eighteen runners, and my horse was quoted at 50 to 1. I had 50 louis " each way " on him. I was watching the race with my glasses, and half way from home saw my horse in the ruck and apparently having no chance, but in the last two hundred yards he came with a rush, went right through the beaten horses, got up on the post and made a dead heat. I forget the name of the other dead-heater, but we divided the stakes, and my bet brought me in over 1600 louis.

Dear old Hardi, whom I used to ride myself before break-fast at exercise, wound up the season in France by winning a £500 handicap at Maisons-Lafitte by a short head, beating some of the best handicap horses in France and starting at 50 to 1 in the book. He brought in 689 francs for 10 in the Pari Mutuel—roughly, 68 to 1, and 330 odd for a place, 32 to 1. As luck would have it, he won this race on the only occasion in France since his victory at Lille when I was not present to see him run. If I had been on the course I would certainly have had at least 25 louis each way on him, as in those days I always had a bet on any horse I ran, even when, as in the present case, I did not think he had a chance. He was running apparently " right out of his class," but the fact is that at this moment he was a really good horse, and I would not have taken £1000 for him. If he had not broken down a little later he would have been worth a fortune over jumps, as he was a perfect natural jumper.

It happened that on the day the race was run it was pouring rain. I did not get up to go out riding at exercise, and I was still in bed in my villa at Chantilly when Woodhouse came in about ten o'clock in the morning and said : " Are you going racing to-day, my lord ? " I said : " No, I shall give it a miss ; this rain will make the ground very heavy, and that will settle any possible chance our horse could have in this sort of company. Besides, I have arranged to take a friend out to lunch in Paris and I would not be able to get away in time. I shall not back the horse," I added. Then, just as Woodhouse was going out, I called him back and gave him 200 francs, and said : " Put me 100 francs (£4) each way on him in the Pari Mutuel."

I went up to Paris, where I had an appointment to meet a young French girl, whom I had met at Trouville (Deauville, apart from the racecourse, scarcely existed in those days, and Trouville was the place), and with whom I was at that time slightly *épris*. I took my young lady to lunch, and for a drive in the Bois afterwards. I parted from her on the Boulevard, and towards six o'clock drifted to a chair on the pavement outside an American bar near the Gare du Nord, to await a train back to Chantilly. A boy selling the *Paris Sport* (evening sporting paper) passed. He grinned ingratiatingly at me and said : " *Achetez-moi un journal, mon beau petit prince.*" I gave him a couple of francs in return for his compliment, took a paper, saw that my horse had won by a short head, and was divided between pleasure at the gallant performance of the old horse and disgust that I had not backed him. It is true that with the value of the stakes and my tiny bet I had won about £900, but the thought that if I had been on the course I would have won at least four times as much was maddening ; especially as things had not been going very brilliantly from the racing point of view at that time. This was Hardi's last race. He had previously distinguished himself by running second (beaten a short head entirely owing to the jockey hitting him with his whip when he had been warned that if he touched the horse with a whip he would stop) in the Oos Handicap at Baden-Baden, a race worth nearly £1000. When this happened I was not present, having gone instead to Deauville, where I had 500 louis on Fourire for the Deauville Cup at 5 to 1—the horse, who won in a canter by two lengths, being disqualified and the race awarded to Codoman. This action of the stewards, which I have never been able to understand, and which made a difference to me of 3000 louis on the wrong side, caused a riot, the mob from the *pelouse* booing and howling for three-quarters of an hour, and being prevented only by a large force of police from " rushing " the stands and the judges' box.

My racing career received a set-back from which it never quite recovered with this misfortune, which followed on a run of bad luck of all kinds. I had one or two other winners, notably a good horse (a jumper) called Guara, who won a race at Auteuil and another at Enghien. I kept the horses on for some time after Hardi's win at Maisons-Lafitte, but did no more good with them. Poor Hardi in the end bolted at exercise, chucked off the boy who was riding him and ran away for about five miles down the La Morlaye road at Chantilly. This was the result of a hard frost, which stopped all work for more than a week, and the horses were all doing walking exercise and " jumping out of their skins." The road was like iron, and when Hardi was caught he was broken down badly all round. He had already been fired before I bought him, and he never got sound enough to race again, and in the end, with great grief, I had him shot when I sold the other horses, because I knew that as a gelding he would inevitably end up in a cab if I sold him. It was a pity, as if I had known anyone who would have given him a good home I would have gladly handed him over for nothing. He might still have been hacked about, or even hunted, though of course he was rather a handful to ride for anyone who was not used to riding thoroughbred racehorses.

I have had English friends come out at exercise at Chantilly who were by way of being first-class men to hounds, and when they rode in a gallop the horses nearly always got away with them. There is all the difference in the world between riding a well-schooled hunter and a thoroughbred horse in full training, even for a good horseman. My idea is that no one who has not had some experience of riding thoroughbred horses in gallops really knows how to ride. If you can ride a hard-pulling horse in a string and keep him in his place you can ride anything. However, as Bacon remarks, " these be toys."

CHAPTER XXVIII

DEAR old Dick Luckman (later the original "Scout" of *The Daily Express*) was at that time racing correspondent to the Paris *New York Herald*, owned by the American millionaire, Gordon Bennett. He and I were great pals, and used to meet regularly at all the meetings round Paris. When my horse Hardi won at Maisons-Lafitte, paying 68 to 1 in the Pari Mutuel, Dick Luckman had a good enough win—as he was never tired of recalling in after years—to get his whole family, consisting of his wife and three children, " out of pawn," as he expressed it.

He had been with them at Dieppe, and as he was " going very badly " just then (by no means an uncommon experience with him, or with any racing man for that matter) he was quite unable to settle up the hotel bill, which had been running on for many weeks. He had particularly noticed, as I ought to have done myself, that just a week before Hardi won the race I have alluded to, " Le Prix de L'Escaut," he had run in a similar handicap on the same course, meeting a similar class of horses, and had put up a fine performance, looking very like winning the race two hundred yards from home, but being caught at that point, and finishing about fifth in a big field. On this form, coming on the top of his fine performance at Baden, and noticing that the horse was looking extraordinarily well, and being, as he told me afterwards, " pretty well desperate," he put all the money he had left in his pocket on Hardi to win and a place. The money he had in his pocket—which was also at that time all the money he had in the world (though of course he had his salary from *The New York Herald* to come in later)—amounted to only a few louis. But such as it was it brought him in enough to pay up the Dieppe bill and release his family, whom he had left behind " in pawn," and also to give him a handsome sum to go on with.

Dick Luckman was my constant companion at Deauville, or rather I should say at Trouville, where I was staying at the " Roches Noires." He dined with me one night at the Casino with two Americans from New York, with whom we had made friends, a Mr Jennings and his very pretty wife. After dinner I went into the more select of the two " clubs," where the big gamblers were, though I doubt if the play, except at one table, was as high as it is now, from what I hear. I took a hundred-louis bank at baccarat, the fair Mrs Jennings cut for me, and I ran my bank into rather more than £1000. We went out and " celebrated " in a convivial supper. The sequel is sad to relate, for I regret to say that I went after supper into the other club (where I fully believe they " got up a game " for me), took a bank, and lost the whole of my £1000, as well as a bit more besides. The next day I bitterly reproached Dick for not having seized the money that I had won and refused to give it me back till the following day. But, as he pointed out, this was " easier said than done," for I was obstinately determined to go on gambling, though he did his best to try to persuade me to stop.

I have related here the few occasions that stand out in my memory when I won substantial sums of money. But in truth I was at this time betting in the most idiotic way, and losing large sums of money on balance. From a financial point of view my French racing career was disastrous, though it is some satisfaction to be able to say that I am still " well up " on the Casino at Monte Carlo ; for after I got away with that £1600, as described in my last chapter, I did not go back there for more than ten years, when I remained there a week and lost £200. Since then, my gambling days being finished, I have neither

M

lost nor won there more than a few thousand francs, which at the present rate of exchange is not worth mentioning.

While I am about it I may relate another sad story which belongs to this period. On the same day on which, by the disqualification of Fourire, as already described, I was landed with a loss of 500 louis in place of a win of 2500 louis, dear old Parfrement, the trainer (father of the well-known jockey who rode Lutteur II. to victory in the Grand National some years later), came up to me in the paddock and told me that he had a horse running in the maiden three-year-old hurdle race on the last day of the Deauville Meeting. This was a hurdle race for three-year-old horses that had never run. He told me his horse was sure to win this race, for which there was a huge field, that he had at least a stone in hand, and that I could get "any price I liked" about it. He asked me to buy the horse for 10,000 francs (£400) and run it in my name, back it and win a small fortune.

At the time when he spoke to me I was worried to death. I had just received a telegram from Woodhouse, at Baden-Baden, that Hardi had been beaten by a short head in the Oos Handicap, and two horses of my own that I had brought with me to run at Deauville had both gone wrong owing to the neglect of a man who had been engaged by Woodhouse to look after them in his absence. This man, an ex-steeplechase jockey who at one time had been a crack rider, had gone off on a drunken "bust" and had left my horses to look after themselves, with the result that they were in a hopeless state, and had not been taken out to exercise for two days. I found this out only by chance, from one of the stable lads, and I had of course immediately "sacked" the ex-steeplechase jockey, whose name I will not mention. The Fourire incident coming on the top of all this had reduced me to a state of deep depression and irritability. I was fool enough to think that Parfrement was trying to "plant" me with a horse he wanted to get rid of. I told him that I could not dream of buying the horse, that I had had a frightfully bad week and was losing a lot of money, and that in fact I would have to rush back to London to arrange an overdraft with my bank to meet my bets. I said : " I couldn't give you £40 for a horse, let alone £400." Parfrement replied by saying that it did not matter a bit about the money. "Take the horse, pay me when you like and put me fifty louis on it. Put a few hundred on for yourself and we shall all be in clover."

I can hardly bear to write this story now. It really seems to me that I must have been mad not to do what he suggested. I knew him for a splendid fellow ; I knew he liked me and was as straight as a die, and anyone who knows anything about racing can easily believe that a man in his position (a small trainer who had been at that time " out of form " for some time) might be just in the condition of having a really good thing and not a penny to back it with. I had unlimited credit in the ring, and I had plenty of money still available at home, and yet I absolutely refused to do what he asked me to do. I could have easily backed the horse to win £10,000, but I did not even have a penny on. The fact is I disbelieved his story and thought he was trying to sell me a horse he did not want. The horse, starting at 50 to 1, won the race by about twenty lengths, after being in front, right out by himself, the whole way in a field of about twenty-five runners. Almost the worst part of the whole thing is that dear old Parfrement was bitterly offended (as he had every right to be) and would hardly speak to me again.

Evidently Providence was determined to get me out of the racing business, for over and over again I missed big things by perverse luck or, as in this case, by stupidity and bad judgment. I missed getting a horse called Gratin in a " claiming race " by 500 francs.   A claiming race is, or was, peculiar to France. The principle is the same as that of a selling race, only instead of the horse being sold by auction you write on a piece of paper how much you will give for the horse and put it " blind " into a box which is opened after the race.   The highest offer on paper takes the horse.

Woodhouse told me that Gratin was, to his certain knowledge, a really good horse, and that I ought to buy him.   He was in a claiming race, entered to be sold for about 6000 francs, as up till then he had done nothing.   I asked Woodhouse how much would get him and he said that 8000 francs would do it easily, as he did not think that there was anyone after the horse.   I determined to make sure, so I wrote " 9000 francs for Gratin " on a piece of paper, signed it and put it in the box.   Gratin won the race, for which I had backed him to win enough to cover the cost of my " claim."   The box was opened, and it was found that the horse had been secured by a well-known Parisian *demi-mondaine*, Madame Ricotti, for 9500 francs.   This horse subsequently won the Big Steeplechase (*Le Grand Steeple*) at Auteuil, worth nearly £5000.   He won half-a-dozen other big races, and was in fact a real " smasher," and worth many thousand pounds.   If I had put in another twenty guineas I would have got him.   That of course was sheer bad luck, as I would just as soon have made my bid 10,000 or 12,000 francs if Woodhouse had named that price.

This concludes the account of my short racing career in France.   Although I lost a lot of money and acted very foolishly, as with my little bit of money I had no right to be dabbling in racehorses, I have never greatly regretted it.   The eighteen months or two years during which I had the horses were the happiest days of my life.   After all the misery and beastliness of the Oscar Wilde affair it was a grand thing to get back to the clean, wholesome atmosphere of my entirely sporting little racing stable.   Getting up for two hours before breakfast to ride glorious gallops in the splendid morning air made me so fit and well that I renewed my youth like the phœnix.   The sort of life I had been living in London, Naples and Paris was very unhealthy.   Up till the time when I bought the horses I had not been on a horse's back, fired off a gun, or played a strenuous game of any kind, for at least six years.   Oscar Wilde, who, during those years, even when I was not actually in his company, completely overshadowed my life, hated sport and games of all kinds.   He had " no patience " with my love of horses and racing. Harris relates, in his *Life and Confessions of Oscar Wilde*, how he sneered at " Bosie's ridiculous horses about which he understands nothing at all."   (I don't profess to give the exact words, but that was the effect of it.)   He resented my spending money on racing instead of giving it to him.

I, for my part, have always had the two distinct sides to my nature.   I love literature and poetry and art and music with a passionate love.   But I am equally fond of sport.   If I had my life to live again I might even go in more for sport and less for literature.   Even now I am not quite sure that I would not rather have ridden the winner of the Grand National than have done anything else.   Anyhow, I believe that my eighteen months, on and off, at Chantilly added twenty years of health and vigour to my life ; while my trainer, Woodhouse, whom I always re-garded and treated as a personal friend, was one of the best and most loyal natures I have ever come across.   At about the same time I began to get fond of shooting again, and at the time when Oscar Wilde died I was in the Highlands of Scotland, where I had taken a small winter shooting.   His death was a terrible blow to me.   I arrived too late to see him alive, a fact for which Ross is solely to blame.   For he wrote to me, at Oscar's request, and told me that he was ill, but that it was " nothing serious," and two days later telegraphed that he was dead.

If I had had any inkling of the seriousness of his state of health I would have rushed over to Paris at once, and if I had seen him before he died, and while he was still conscious, the whole course of future events would surely have been altered. For one thing, Ross would not have been able to appropriate my letters as he did, and for another thing it is possible that Oscar would have said something about his letter to me, the *De Profundis* MS, supposing that he really knew, as Ross would have us believe, that Ross had the original MS. in his possession. At any rate, Ross would not have dared to touch any of the letters and MSS. without my consent. As it was, he told me when I arrived that he had been through Oscar's papers and found "nothing of the slightest importance," but he was careful to ask me what I wished done about them. It was not disputed at that time, by anyone, that I was the person to decide such questions, any more than it was questioned that I should be the chief mourner at the funeral and pay all the expenses. I told Ross to do what he thought best about the papers, and I never bothered my head any more about them. The base use to which he put my letters of which he thus obtained possession has already been related.

When I reached Paris poor Oscar had been dead two days, and was already in his nailed-up coffin. Robert Ross and Reggie Turner, who were both with him when he died, gave me an account of the last days of his illness. Ross said not a word to bear out the horrible story of his end which is related in Harris's disgusting book, on the authority of Ross. Reggie Turner has categorically denied the story, and declares that Oscar died quite quietly and peacefully. I have no doubt that Ross's story, with its revolting details, is a pure lie, though what can have induced him to invent such a story about the man he professes to have loved so much must always remain a mystery.

Oscar was buried according to the rites of the Catholic Church, in the cemetery at Bagneux, after a requiem mass in the beautiful old church of Saint Germain-les-Près. I took the part of chief mourner at the funeral, and was in consequence taken by some of those who were present for his son, or some other near relative. Someone (a lady) asked Ross (as he afterwards told me) who the " youth " who acted as chief mourner was, and Ross told her that it was Lord Alfred Douglas ; whereupon she said : " But the one I mean was a mere boy, it couldn't be Lord Alfred Douglas, who must be about thirty." There were several persons at the funeral who were unknown to Ross and Turner and myself —including this lady, and two others. One of them I afterwards discovered was a friend (or *protégée*) of my grandmother, the Honourable Mrs Alfred Montgomery, who, being a Catholic, and knowing of my connection with Wilde (as of course all the world did), came to pray for him. She wrote to me and told me this afterwards, but I cannot recall her name.

I have no personal knowledge about the facts of the removal of Oscar's body from the cemetery at Bagneux to Père Lachaise, which took place many years later under the direction of Ross.

CHAPTER XXIX

I WENT back to London after Oscar's death, and lived in rooms in Duke Street, Portland Place, and with my brother Percy in a place called Smedmore, in Dorsetshire, which he had taken. My brother Percy (now become Queensberry) inherited no place (except the small house, Glen Stewart, in Dumfriesshire, which was let to my uncle and aunt, Sir Beaumont and Lady Florence Dixie, and about 2000 acres ; all the rest of the property and the family place, Kinmount, had been sold by my father). Percy inherited, however, about £300,000. Unfortunately, he had already borrowed large sums on his expectations, at exorbitant rates of interest, and nearly half of his inheritance was immediately mopped up by moneylenders. Owing to the quarrel with my father, which took place over the Wilde business and was never made up, there had been no resettlement of the property.

As it is the fashion for the Ross-Harris school of Wilde worshippers to assert that I " ruined Oscar Wilde " I may observe that it would, on the same principle, be easy for me to argue that Oscar Wilde not only ruined me, but also ruined my whole family. The Ross-Harris argument, reduced to its ultimate form, is : that if Wilde had never met me my father would never have interfered with him, and that in that case he would never have been exposed and ruined. This was, in effect, the essential part of the argument by which the defence in the Ransome trial, when I sued for libel, " justified " their libel and won the case. Following the same line of " reasoning " I might say that if I had never met Wilde I would never have quarrelled with my father and been " saved " (in plain English, ruined) by him, that my brother Percy by espousing my cause would never have become involved in a lifelong feud with my father, and that but for this feud there would have been a proper resettlement of the property on to Percy's son, the present Marquis, which would have made it impossible for the property which had been in the Douglas family for so many hundred years to have been alienated from that family for ever.

However, this sort of speculation as to what might have been, if something else had not happened, is fruitless and foolish. Even after Percy had satisfied his rapacious creditors there would still have been enough money left for him to have at least six or seven thousand pounds a year, and he might have settled the reversion of this income irrevocably on his elder son, and made provision for the younger children. But unfortunately for him he was " in the City," and certain City sharks, or as Shylock would say " land rats," got hold of him, and relieved him of all his money in a very short time. Poor Percy was ruined really, in a way, by his early success in finance. He left the Navy when he was only about nineteen, and after spending a few years on a ranch in the Western States, and in a tea plantation in Ceylon, he went to Australia, accompanied by his great friend, the Honourable David Carnegie (youngest son of Lord Southesk), and made tracks for Perth and the goldfields. David and he, after many adventures, got to the goldfields at the very beginning of the " rush." They staked out claims, and Percy returned to London to try to sell them. After he had made all sorts of fruitless attempts in the City to dispose of his and David's properties, the West Australian gold-mining boom suddenly came. The result of the boom was that Percy made quite a lot of money, about £20,000 or more. At that time he was Lord Percy Douglas, a younger son with no particular prospects. When my eldest brother, Francis (Viscount Drumlanrig), was killed by the accidental explosion of his gun, Percy became the eldest son and heir to a large fortune.

Having found it so easy at such an early age to discover gold, and to make money, Percy conceived what proved to be the fatal idea that he was destined to be a millionaire. When he became eldest son he already had plenty of money at his disposal, for, needless to say, he treated the £20,000 or so that he had made, not as capital, but as money to spend. He started speculating on a large scale, and raised money on his expectations in order, as he thought, to make a rapid fortune. Unfortunately he drank a good deal, a habit he acquired in his ranching and gold-digging days, and when he was under the influence of this tendency of his he was an easy mark for the unscrupulous.

Although he really had a great flair for " good things," was a good prospector, and over and over again discovered or originated properties from which other people have made fortunes, he never could protect his own interests. He rediscovered and had in his own possession for several years the " Bruce Mines " copper mine, which is now one of the largest sources of the wealth of Sir Alfred Mond. In the end he got " frozen out " and others reaped where he had sown. I could mention half-a-dozen similar cases. The late Alan Stoneham, who died an exceedingly rich man, benefited enormously by my brother's " good things," beginning with the properties in Western Australia to which I have referred.

Poor old Percy was recklessly generous, confiding and extravagant. In certain moods he would almost literally " throw money out of the window." On one occasion he went down the Embankment on a bitterly cold night and distributed nearly £1000 in bank-notes to the men and women " down-and-outs " who were spending the night on the seats there. He had an enormous number of friends of all classes all over the world, and at his funeral, which took place in the Catholic Cathedral at Westminster, in 1920, hundreds of people who were unknown to his family turned up to pay a last tribute to him. At the same time it cannot be denied that his accession to the position of eldest son by the untimely death of my dear brother Francis was the cause of the *débâcle* of the family fortunes, which his son, my nephew, the present Marquis, has already done much to repair.

I had a good time with Percy at Smedmore, where the shooting was good, and still more so at Colonsay, a beautiful island in the Hebrides, which he took for a year. Colonsay consisted of about twelve to fourteen thousand acres. There was a charming house and plenty of coverts for pheasants (a very unusual thing in these islands, which are generally bare of trees). The " bag " was a really good all-round one, for in addition to a (not very good) grouse moor there were several hundred brace of partridges to be shot, at least five hundred woodcock, and any quantity of duck and snipe. I myself, with one other gun, an Argyllshire laird called Graham, in the month of February 1902, shot one hundred and forty-seven woodcock there in five days' shooting, when there was a hard frost on the mainland, which did not reach the islands and sent in swarms of woodcock. If we had had two more guns we could have shot double the number during the days that the frost lasted.

Just before this time (in October 1901) I went over to the United States. I still had my horses at Chantilly, but my financial position was distinctly " rocky." When I came into my money at my father's death I regret to say that it never occurred to me for a moment that I could live on the interest of my capital, which would have been about six or seven hundred pounds a year (more than I have got now !). I spent the money freely, having fully decided (though I blush to have to say so) that before it was all gone I would " marry an American heiress."

In pursuance of this noble ambition I scraped together about
£800 and went off to New York, armed with a few letters of
introduction, including a letter (not of introduction, because I
already knew him) from my uncle, Percy Wyndham, to his
nephew and namesake, my cousin, Percy Wyndham (son of Sir
Hugh Wyndham), who was Second Secretary at the British
Embassy in Washington.

I must say honestly that there would have been no difficulty
at all about the heiress. I might have had the choice between
at least three, one of whom had quite £20,000 a year ; but,
unfortunately for the success of my scheme, I had fallen in love
before I left for America with the lady who is now my wife, Olive
Custance. When I left England in search of an heiress, although
I was already very devoted to Olive, I did not think that I had
the slightest chance of marrying her. We met in a romantic
way, for it started by Olive, who was a distinguished poet (her
book, *Opals*, had then been published by John Lane about a
year before), writing to me expressing admiration for my poetry.
I replied in suitable terms, and it was not long before we met.
We fell in love at sight ("Who ever loved that loved not at
first sight ? "), and, thanks to the good-natured assistance of
Olive's cousin, the lovely Lily, Marchioness of Anglesey, now
Mrs John Gilliat, we met every day for about ten days in Paris,
where Olive was staying then with Lady Anglesey and other
friends at a hotel in the Champ Élysées.

Olive and I had already on several occasions met sur-
reptitiously in London. She came to see me the first time
(chaperoned by her maid) in my rooms at Duke Street after
we had made an appointment at the South Kensington Museum,
which owing to my going to the wrong door (or the wrong room
—I forget which) had failed to bring about a meeting. We were
both very shy, but the romance ripened rapidly. Olive introduced me to her mother, Mrs Custance, and on that occasion,

at an hotel in Dover Street, we made the exciting discovery that we had met before at the wedding of my cousin, Rachel Montgomery, to the Reverend Reginald Knatchbull-Hugessen at Trinity Church, Sloane Square, and afterwards at the house of my Uncle Alexander and Aunt Rose (Sir Alexander and Lady Montgomery), at 56 Cadogan Place. On that occasion I was still in Eton jackets and little Olive was a ten-year-old bridesmaid. Neither of us remembered the meeting, but obviously we had met on that occasion.

Shortly afterwards Olive wrote from Dinard to say that she and Lily Anglesey, with whom she was staying, were going on to Paris, and that if "the Prince" (that was me) would come over he could meet his "Page" (herself) as often as he wished to do so. Needless to say, I at once went to Paris to the Hôtel Rastadt, Rue Daunou, where we afterwards spent our honeymoon.

For the next ten days I saw Olive every day. At meals, at Lily's hotel, a separate table "for the children" was provided, and we also went out by ourselves to lunch and dinner at restaurants and spent a day at Chantilly, looking at my horses and wandering in the forest, holding each other's hands. "And all our talk was delicate and shy," to quote one of Olive's poems written a month or two later.

Then I went off to America very much depressed. No question of marriage with Olive had arisen. I had no money, and it appeared utterly unthinkable that we could ever marry. But when I got to New York Olive wrote to me often, and I replied, and the "heiresses" began to appear less and less attractive the more I saw and heard of them. I must explain that I never got to the stage of "making up" to any one particular "heiress"; all that happened was that I had reliable information (in two cases it was actually in their own writing) that I would not be rejected if I chose to proceed. All this sounds rather sordid, but this is a true story and I am not concealing anything.

After a month or six weeks in New York, and a week or two in Boston, in both of which places I had an agreeable time and met pleasant people, I went on to Washington. I landed up at an hotel there, and my cousin, Percy Wyndham, who had heard from our joint Uncle Percy that I was coming, came to see me. He treated me with the greatest kindness and hospitality. The Ambassador, Lord Pauncefote, left a card at my hotel. I returned his call, and next day Percy Wyndham came to see me and invited me to leave the hotel and come to his rooms as his guest. I accepted and went, and for about three weeks I enjoyed a most cheerful and lively time and met, and was entertained by, a number of charming people. Percy made me an honorary member of the Metropolitan Club (I think that was the name), which was, I believe, by way of being *the* smart club of Washington. Then, after about a fortnight, some charming person or other at the club raised a question about my being an honorary member, in view of my " connection with a disgraceful scandal." I strolled into the club one day and ordered a drink, when a man, unknown to me and whose name I do not know, who was sitting with a group of members, made an offensive remark about Oscar Wilde in a loud voice, evidently intending that I should hear. Like the young lady of Sweden " when they cried Weeden station," I made no observation, but finished my drink and went back to my cousin's rooms. There I found that my cousin Percy had received a letter from the committee of the club, asking for an " explanation " of the fact that he had introduced me as a member.

Percy Wyndham replied that no explanation was required, that I was his cousin and guest, a man of high social position, that I was on intimate terms with the British Ambassador and Lady Pauncefote, that I was a member of one of the most exclusive clubs in London, and that he had no doubt that in view of the attitude adopted by the committee of the Metropolitan Club I would be extremely unlikely to have any desire to go into their club again. As this was quite unanswerable the committee wisely refrained from making any answer, and there the matter ended, except that the newspapers " got hold of the story " ; in other words, it was deliberately given to them by one or more members of the club. *The New York Herald* came out with headlines, and the other papers followed suit.

I was at that time frightfully sensitive to anything of the kind, and I told my cousin that I should leave Washington at once. He begged me not to go, the naval attaché asked me to lunch, and all the rest of the Embassy staff " rallied round." Lord Pauncefote sent for me and told me that the Metropolitan Club was a " pot-house " of the deepest dye, that the members never lost a chance of being rude to anyone who was on friendly terms with the British Embassy or himself, and that it was beneath my dignity to take the slightest notice of them. He then told me that Lady Pauncefote was expecting me to dinner next day to meet someone or other (I forget who it was, but I rather fancy it was Mr Choate), and that she wanted me to take her to a concert that afternoon. I went to the concert with Lady Pauncefote and attended her dinner-party, but after that I felt I could not stand it any longer. The whole thing got on my nerves. I was bitterly hurt and disappointed. I felt instinctively that my cousin, although he begged me to stay on, really would be delighted to get rid of me (subsequent events proved that I was right in my conjecture), and I insisted on going back to New York. I must say that my cousin behaved quite correctly, as well as kindly and generously. I really think he liked me, and enjoyed having me to stay with him. He was a delightful person, and had a great sense of humour and a very kind heart, and we had much in common. Up till the time when the incident of the club occurred we had got on splendidly. But there never has been a diplomat yet who, with one eye on the Foreign Office in London, has not got cold shivers at the idea of any kind of newspaper scandal. He could not, being an Englishman, have been expected to do more than he did, and dear old Lord Pauncefote and Lady Pauncefote were kindness itself. It was just one of the numerous occasions on which I have had to pay for having been associated with Oscar Wilde.

Three days after I got back to New York an invitation to dine with Senator Cabot Lodge (who, I understand, was considered rather an important person) was forwarded on to me. No doubt if I had stayed at Washington a little longer many people at Washington, besides the Embassy, would have made a point of being kind to me, but my lacerated feelings did not allow me to take any chances of further snubs. I remained in New York, where I was made an honorary member of the University Club, for another fortnight. I wrote a long letter, which appeared in *The New York Herald*, giving my version of the Metropolitan Club incident, and I then left for England. I also, as I have just remembered, wrote a not very good sonnet, which was published in *The New York Herald*, in which I let out at America generally. Since then I have been more abused and blackguarded and libelled and insulted and lied about in America (for no reason at all and without the slightest provocation, but I imagine chiefly by the admirers of Wilde and what he stands for) than I have been in all the other parts of the globe put together—which is saying a good deal! It does not worry me at all, and individual Americans whom I have met from time to time have invariably got on famously with me, as I have with them. The people who abuse me in America have never met me, and necessarily they know nothing whatever about me, except what Mr Frank Harris has told them. Consequently, it is not surprising that they do not like me. It would be absurd for me to resent the fact that the caricature of my real self, which is all they know of me, does not appeal to them.

CHAPTER XXX

DIRECTLY I got back to London I wrote to Olive and begged her to meet me. Immediately after my return I had been flabbergasted by getting a letter from her in which she informed me that she was "engaged to be married to George Montagu." George Montagu, now Earl of Sandwich, had been a small boy in my house at Winchester during my last two years there. He was consequently about three or four years younger than myself. He was, at Winchester, a fair-haired, blue-eyed, pretty boy, with engaging manners, and I was very fond of him, though he later told me that I used to "brock" (Winchester for bully) him at school. I think my "bullying" only amounted to "teasing," which at school is often a sign of affection. At any rate, I took a good deal of notice of him, and when he was a little older I became a great friend of his. When I came down from Magdalen to Winchester for the day, as I did whenever I could get a chance or an excuse to do so, I always made a bee-line for George, or "Jidge" as I used to call him. My mother was a great friend of his mother, Lady Agneta Montagu, and I had stayed with his family at Wherwell Priory, the beautiful old house on the River Test where they lived at that time.

After the Wilde affair I went abroad, and remained out of England for two or three years. When I came back many of my "friends" cold-shouldered me and others "cut" me outright. Knowing what I did about their own private lives, and also knowing that their attitude towards me was (in ninety-nine cases out of a hundred) dictated not by moral considerations but simply by snobbishness, hypocrisy and cowardice, I mentally consigned them all to the Devil (who, by the way, appears to have taken me at my word in a good many cases), and I cultivated a habit, which I have kept to this day, of never speaking to acquaintances who did not speak to me first, and of seeing people without appearing to look at them.

All the same, there were still quite a lot of good fellows who were apparently just as pleased to see me and to frequent my society as they had been when I was in the heyday of my social prosperity. Curiously enough (or perhaps, when you come to think of it, not curiously at all) it was just those whose private lives were the least reputable who were most inclined to be " nasty " to me. Anyhow, George Montagu was one of those who was just as friendly and pleasant to me as he always had been ; and just before I went to America, for a period of two or three months in London we had been almost inseparable. George in those days was kept very " short " by his parents, and his uncle, old Lord Sandwich ("Hinch"), was by no means what might be described as a " cheerful parter," at any rate as far as his nephew and heir was concerned. Although in reality I was already getting to the end of my financial tether, I was still in those days never without plenty of money in my pocket. This no doubt did nothing to lessen my attractions in the eyes of George and other gilded youths who still had no objection to being seen about at restaurants, clubs, music halls and other " places where they sing," in company with Lord Alfred Douglas.

Just at the time when I was most friendly with George, and when he was in the habit of lunching and dining with me as my guest nearly every day, and using my rooms as if they were his own, his family arranged that he was to stand for Parliament. His father and mother, hearing that he was constantly in my company, told him that he must drop me as a preliminary to starting his election campaign. This he did, as Malvolio would say, " without any mitigation or remorse." I was very much annoyed and very much hurt, and after a while, when I grasped what the situation was, I wrote and told him what I thought of him. I also later wrote a sonnet about him, called *The Traitor*, which can be read in my *Collected Poems*.

As always happens in such cases, the person who has done the injury poses as the injured, and ends by considering that he has been very badly treated. George had nothing to say for himself in reply to my letters, and instead of seeing me, and explaining things to me, he simply ignored the two letters I wrote to him. It was at this stage that I wrote my fairly devastating sonnet, and sent it to him. I think now of course that my sonnet was absurd (though considered merely as poetry it is one of the best I ever wrote). George's conduct to me was just typically English and nothing more. I believe that he honestly did not understand why I was " making such a fuss." It appeared to him to be merely natural and inevitable that, if and when the moment came when it was convenient to drop his friend, he should do so. To me as a Scotsman, and with my poetical temperament, his conduct appeared in the light of the blackest treachery ; to him it was merely common sense and worldly policy. So, as I have said, he ended by thinking that he had been very badly treated, and went about saying so.

Then I went to America, and just about that time George met Olive. Olive's interest in him began simply through his former friendship and association with me. She entertained his acquaintance because she liked to hear him talk about me and tell stories about me. George told her that I had behaved very badly to him and showed her my letters. He got no sympathy from Olive, who, on the contrary, told him frankly that she considered that his conduct to me had been mean and unworthy. George took this to heart, and entered into long explanations and excuses. He also, being a clever mimic, used to delight Olive by giving imitations of " Bosie doing " this, that or the other. The result of all this was that they became very intimate. Olive made no secret of the fact that she adored me, but she agreed with what George said, and constantly repeated to her —namely, that a marriage between us was not practicable and that I did not want to marry her and had never seriously thought of such a thing. Under these circumstances, when he told her he was in love with her, and repeatedly asked her to marry him, she ended by accepting him. Her mother, who was quite aware of her infatuation for me, did everything she could to encourage her with George. My wife admits that she did wrong to become engaged to George. When she accepted him she fully meant to marry him. But she says, quite rightly, that to have gone on with the marriage when she found out, as she did afterwards, that I really wanted to marry her, and in view of the fact that she loved me and did not love George, but only " liked him very much," would not have been right to him or to me or to herself.

I do not wish to say a word against George Montagu. He was at one time my friend and, quite obviously, I was much fonder of him than he was of me, for I would not have dreamed of giving up his friendship to oblige my " people " or to conciliate my constituents. When he treated me as he did, I naturally felt bitter against him. When I returned from America and found that he was engaged to marry " my girl " the blood of a hundred Douglas ancestors surged up, and I said in my heart : " No, you don't ! " Leaving out the question of money, I knew that there was nothing against me as a husband for Olive which would not apply with at least equal force to him. George's treatment of me did not encourage me to think that his love for anyone would be likely to be of a lasting or irrevocable kind, and I determined to act swiftly and vigorously. I asked Olive to dine with me. She came, and when she told me, as she did, that she had agreed to marry George only because she thought

that I did not want to marry her, and that I had irrevocably
made up my mind to go in for the " American heiress," I told
her in reply that, of course, she must know that I adored her,
that I had never cared two pins about any other girl, that I had
given up all idea of the American heiress and had come back
to England simply because I could not live without her, and
that I had always wanted to marry her, but had not thought it
fair to ask her because I had no money at all, and would in
future be almost entirely dependent on my mother. This interview took place in Kettner's restaurant. In the end, after much
discussion, and in view of the fact that Olive did not for a moment
deny that she cared more for my little finger than for George's
body and soul put together, I asked her to run away with
me. I told her that it was the only possible way we could be
married, as if her people got wind of it such pressure would
be brought to bear that we would inevitably be separated for
ever.

Olive made an appointment to meet me a few days later.
Curiously enough, we met on this momentous occasion, as we
had done before, in the upper room of Robert Ross's little
picture shop, " Carfax," in Ryder Street, with his consent.
Olive was then due to go down on the following day to spend
the week-end at Hinchingbrooke, Lord Sandwich's place in
Huntingdonshire, to meet George's family. She told me that
Mrs Custance had, that morning, received a letter from the King
congratulating her on her daughter's engagement to George. I
told her that I would get a special licence while she was away
at Hinchingbrooke, and that if she was " game " to do it I would
be awaiting her at St George's, Hanover Square, at nine o'clock
on the following Tuesday morning, which was 4th March 1902.

I did not see her again till the time specified. Up to the
last I did not feel perfectly certain that she would turn up. She
was staying in Dover Street with her mother, and had to pack

her things the night before, with the assistance of her maid, whom she took into her confidence. She told her mother that she was going to spend the day with her former governess, who lived somewhere in the suburbs, and she got out of the hotel without exciting any suspicion or comment, her maid going on to the station with the small portmanteau which was all she could manage to smuggle out with her.

I, in the meanwhile, arrived at the church ten minutes before nine, accompanied by my sister, Lady Edith Fox-Pitt, in her carriage-and-pair. I had persuaded her overnight to come with me to keep us in countenance. This she very kindly and loyally did, though, as was to be expected, she was blamed and abused for it afterwards. I had also told my mother at the last moment what I was going to do. My darling mother gave me £200, her fondest blessing, a diamond ring for Olive, and the promise of an allowance. My friend, Cecil Hayes, the well-known barrister, who was then private secretary to Lord Denbigh, and who afterwards appeared as my counsel at the Ransome trial, and later when I was convicted and sent to prison for libelling Winston Churchill, came to the church to support me, and afterwards saw us off for Paris at Victoria Station. My darling little Olive arrived "dead on time," and we were married. Before leaving Victoria, Olive sent a telegram to her mother informing her of what she had done and giving our address in Paris. I subsequently discovered that Robert Ross during the marriage ceremony was in the church in the background. I had taken him into my confidence because, as I have already said, Olive and I used to meet occasionally at his little picture shop in Ryder Street. For some extraordinary reason Ross always seemed to resent my marriage. All the same, I continued to be on good terms with him for several years after it took place, and he professed to be devoted to Olive, and made every effort to ingratiate himself with her. My wife, who sometimes has wonderful intuitions about people, never liked him or trusted him.

Needless to say, our runaway marriage created a fearful rumpus. King Edward was (so I was told) " very angry," though what on earth it had to do with him I have never been able to make out ; the Montagus and the Yorkes with one accord " gave tongue," and worked themselves up into a fearful state of indignation and fury (this does not apply to poor George, who was merely sorrowful and dignified). Mrs Custance was naturally in a great state of consternation, and Colonel Custance, who had only just returned from the South African War, where he had commanded the Norfolk Regiment (he was formerly in the Grenadier Guards), went through all the usual motions which are proper to the outraged father of an absconding daughter on such an occasion. I do not in the least blame him. Of course it was a frightful blow to him that his elder daughter and heir (for his property was entailed on her) should have thrown aside a very eligible young man like George, heir to an earldom and about £30,000 a year, to run away with a penniless younger son who was, moreover, under a cloud, and who had been mixed up in the worst scandal that had occurred in London for about a hundred years (if there is anything else that I have forgotten in this list of my ineligible qualities the reader can please supply them *ad lib.*).

The first thing Colonel Custance did was (funnily enough) to rush round to Scotland Yard and make inquiries about me ! He was no doubt disappointed to be told there that nothing whatever was known against me, and that as far as their information went I was a model of every virtue. Years afterwards, when he applied to the Chancery Court in an endeavour to take my only child away from me, the only charges that he could manage to rake up against me were that I was " very bad-tempered " and that I " attached far too much importance to religion " ! Within a few weeks of our marriage, however, he declared that he had " forgiven " us, and asked us to come down on a fortnight's visit to his house in Norfolk, Weston Old Hall. Up to this point I must say that he behaved exceedingly well, and the same applies to Mrs Custance.

Meanwhile Olive and I were having the time of our lives in Paris at the Hôtel Rastadt (now extinct). Out of the dust of the past, and surviving all the welter of the mud and stones that for more than thirty years have been thrown at me, and incidentally (though by no means always accidentally) hit my wife and made her life next door to impossible for her, our marriage still survives. Though we were subsequently separated eleven years later, and though almost superhuman (and I might add entirely diabolical) efforts were made to smash up our marriage and force us into divorce or separation, we are still married, and still love each other. It is the astonishing fact that certain persons, including one who has the best of all reasons to know the contrary, have tried to make out that our marriage was always a failure, and that after our brief honeymoon had been followed by the birth of our son, Raymond, it was one " in name only." Nothing more fantastically or more grotesquely untrue could be devised by the brain of a lunatic. I am not concerned to produce proofs, though they exist in superabundance in the shape of letters exchanged between us covering the whole period of our marriage up to within a few months of our separation ; and again with intervals of estrangement right up to the present day. Nor would one in the ordinary way think it necessary to say anything about what is after all a private affair between one's wife and oneself. But in view of posterity, which is as certain to be concerned in all this business as it is certain that there is a sun in the heavens, I put it here and now and once for all on record that the wicked efforts that were made to break up my marriage and to alienate my wife's affections never

really succeeded. In the year 1907 I published in *The Academy*
the series of sonnets which appear in my *Collected Poems* under
the title *To Olive*.

Those sonnets remain, and all the water in the sea will never
wash them out. Here is one of them :

TO OLIVE

When we were Pleasure's minions, you and I,
When we mocked grief and held disaster cheap,
And shepherded all joys like willing sheep
Who love their shepherd ; when a passing sigh
Was all the cloud that flecked our summer sky,—
I floated on an unimagined deep,
I loved you as a tired child loves sleep,
I lived and loved and laughed, and knew not why.

Now I have known the uttermost rose of love,
(The world is very strong but love is stronger).
I love you so, I have no time to hate
Even those wolves without. The great winds move
All their dark batteries to our fragile gate.
The years are very long but love is longer.

CHAPTER XXXI

SINCE I finished my last chapter I have consulted my wife, and she agrees that I should print extracts from some of her letters written at this time. In an ordinary way such letters would be considered quite private and sacred, but there is nothing ordinary about our history, and to ignore that fact is only to court trouble and pave the way to future misunderstanding. Both my wife and I are poets. I have always been very jealous and particular about the use of the words " poet " and " poetry." However much I may like a man or a woman, and however much I may desire to please him or her, I will not say that he or she has written good poetry (a very rare thing, especially in this age) unless I really think it. When I say that my wife is a poet I mean it, and I consider that she has written better poetry than any other woman of my time, not excepting Mrs Meynell, for whose work I have the greatest admiration.

To say, as I dare say will be said, that I call her a good poet just because she is my wife would be putting the cart before the horse. It was just the fact that she had written such really beautiful stuff that, combined with her exceptional beauty and grace, drew me to her and differentiated her from all the other girls I had ever met. As I am at least as good a judge of what is and is not fine poetry as any man now living, I have a perfect right and qualification to estimate the value of her work. This being the case, and granting therefore that my wife and I are both considerable poets, and seeing that I have been, very much against my will and inclination, forced for years into a fierce glare of publicity, it is merely foolish to ignore the certainty that after we are dead everything we have done, said or written will be the object of public interest.

The few remaining letters written by Oscar Wilde to me which I did not destroy, including some of those he wrote to me at Berneval directly after he came out of prison, were sold by me, directly after the Ransome case, to the late Mr Bernard Quaritch, who was at that time lying ill in bed. I sold them because I was, for the time being, ruined and penniless, and because it was absolutely necessary for me to raise money, chiefly in order to be able to fight the Chancery case against Colonel Custance for the custody of my son, then a boy of eleven years. Mr Quaritch was too ill to see me when I offered him the letters (about thirty-five of them). He offered me, and I accepted, as far as I remember, £350. At the time I sold the letters (and also, for two or three hundred pounds, all the autographed copies of his own books which Oscar Wilde had given me) I hated the very name of Wilde. My idea was to disassociate myself as far as I could for ever afterwards from him and from any memory of him. I remember thinking at the time when I sold the books and letters that this was the only good turn Wilde had ever done me. I understood when I sold the letters, through a member of his firm, to Mr Quaritch, that Mr Quaritch pledged himself not to sell the letters during his own and my lifetime. This stipulation which I claim to have been made (and, indeed, voluntarily made by Mr Quaritch himself) is denied by those who at present control the firm. So, as it is merely a case of my word against theirs, I will say no more about it. But it is a fact that Messrs Quaritch sold the letters very shortly afterwards, after the death of Mr Bernard Quaritch, and that they subsequently changed hands several times. In the end they were bought in New York by Mr William Andrews Clark, to whose privately printed edition of the letters I have already referred, for the large sum of £2000.

My own letters to Wilde (most of which are, I suppose, in the possession of the heirs or executors of the late Robert Ross, who stole them) will be just as valuable when I am dead. The same applies to my letters to my wife, and hers to me, many of which will also, sooner or later, almost inevitably be given to the world. So that if I publish extracts from a few of them now I am only anticipating what is bound to happen.

Here is one of Olive's letters, written before I went to America :

Dear Sweet Prince,—I am thinking of you every moment and praying that your " luck may turn " and that things may be better soon. . . .

The little Princess is most unhappy about the dear, beautiful Prince. . . . She cried when his letter came and wished—oh, how she wished to be " rich and powerful," that she might help him in some way. . . .

I was too sad to dream yesterday . . . so I took up my *Imaginary Portraits* and read about Denys l'Auxerrois because he reminds me of you . . . " a flaxen and flowery creature " . . . and then I read Shakespeare's sonnets and wondered why people should have worried so much who they were written to . . . because, you see, I know it was *you*. . . . Shakespeare *must* have met you in another world !

> " When in the chronicles of wasted time
> I see descriptions of the fairest wights.
>
> .   .   .   .   .
>
> I see their antique pen would have expressed
> Even such beauty as you master now.
> So all their praises are but prophecies
> Of this our time, all you prefiguring."

Dear Prince . . . let me see you on the 30th, if only for a moment.   Opal.

Olive was called " Opal " by her friends (though I always preferred to call her Olive), partly because her first volume of poems was called *Opals*, and partly because she suggested that beautiful stone. She always wore opals at that time. The rows of dots . . . in her letters are characteristic, as she seldom used commas and full stops. None of her letters at this time is dated, which makes it difficult to fix the order in which they arrived, but the next was almost certainly written just after we first met.

WESTON HALL, NORWICH.

BEAUTIFUL PRINCE,—I must send a few words to you by the early post . . . just to thank you for your sweetness to me. . . . It was so lovely to look into your clear brave eyes and talk to you . . . and hear your voice and your laugh. . . . It was so lovely that I can hardly believe it was not all a dream. . . . When shall I get another letter from you . . . and tell me are you pleased with your little Princess ?

No ! I am not your Princess. . . . *She* will be very beautiful . . . but meanwhile love me a little please, kind and beautiful Prince.   OPAL.

The letter that follows was evidently written just as I was starting for New York :

WESTON HALL, NORWICH.

MY OWN BOY,—What a joy to get that last little letter from you . . . but now at last I feel you have really gone and I am miserable without you. Last night I dreamed of you and woke to find my pillow wet with tears . . . and I stretched out my empty arms to you and called you, my Prince, very softly . . . but you were too far away to hear. . . . Oh how I miss you . . . your sweet golden head . . . your small red mouth . . . always it seems a little shy of my kisses . . . and above all your great blue eyes . . . the most beautiful eyes a boy ever

had, like two blue flowers under water (as I told you once) and
those " carved lids fringed with lashes thick and long " (I think
I wrote that poem to you !) how my lips love them . . . if
only I might kiss them to-night. . . . But if I were to write for
ever I should not be able to tell you how much I love you. . . .
[Here a page and a half are omitted.]   I will send you the photographs as soon as they are ready and I will also send you to New
York a little cigarette case for your birthday on the 22nd (isn't
it ?).   I seem to be scribbling dreadfully . . . but I forget even
to write well when I write to you. . . . I forget everything
except that I love you. . . . See ! What a child I am ! But
you will understand because you are a child too, my Darling
. . . my own Bosie whom God made for me I think. . . .
Goodnight my Poet (and you must write a poem to *me* I think ?)
I dream beautiful dreams to-night and I will pray that they all
come true.   Your loving   OLIVE.

The Basilisk sends his love to you and the " young boy
Basilisk," if he is not lost ! The little heart is safe. . . .

" The young boy Basilisk " was a ring with an emerald
snake's head and ruby eyes which Olive gave me, but who the
other basilisk was I cannot now remember.
  Here is another letter, evidently written after I got back
from New York :

                                      19 DOVER STREET, W.

DARLING PRINCE,—When are you coming to London ?   I
am so *longing* to see you. . . . I have taken two stalls for *The
Importance of Being Earnest* for next Saturday afternoon . . .
could you come . . . it would be a way of meeting. . . . I
shall say I am going with George . . . so that will be all right.
. . . My Beautiful, London is very dark without you . . .
come out of the " Clouds " my sunbeam.

                                      YOUR PAGE.

This last letter was evidently written to me when I was staying at Clouds, the place in Wiltshire of my great-uncle, Percy Wyndham.

I give two more letters. The first written before I went to New York and the second after I came back :

WESTON HALL, NORWICH.

MY OWN PRINCE,—The little heart is sweet . . . [this was a locket I sent her with a lock of my hair] and I shall always . . . always wear it . . . even when you have forgotten me and married the beautiful rich princess who will give you all those lovely things you ought to have. . . . I miss you more than I can say . . . for I love you beyond everything in the world . . . and I think we shall never be happy together again. . . . Write to me soon . . . soon and tell me you love your little Page and that one day you will come back to "him" . . . my Prince, my Prince. . . .

I found Mummy rather unhappy as "Tannie" [her governess] had told her we met that time in London . . . wasn't it horrible of her ! However Mummy has forgiven us and all will be well if she doesn't find out about Paris. . . . She would never forgive any of us *then* I am afraid !

Good-bye my Darling . . . may all your dreams come true. I cannot write more. . . . Goodbye. . . .

OLIVE.

The next one appears not to be signed, and breaks off abruptly, but probably a sheet is missing :

MY OWN BOY PRINCE,—Send me the photograph *at once please* . . . it will be something to look at till I see you my Darling my Beautiful. . . . I have another photograph for you . . . better than the last, and I am having it tinted for you. Don't stay too long away from London as I shall certainly be up on the 30th . . . and write to me to 19 Dover Street Piccadilly W. . . . as your friend's writing is so utterly unlike yours they would never guess anything . . . tell him not to forget to put Miss *Olive* Custance . . . as then they cannot give them to Mummy by mistake !

A dreadful thing happened to your last wire ! It was opened by Daddy ! However " Bosie " conveyed nothing to him . . . so I said it was from Nathalie . . . and soon after sent myself a wire from her to say she was going to Italy as Mummy doesn't like her ! I think you will laugh at all this. . . . But oh why, why does fate make it so difficult for us to meet. . . .

I have no doubt that some of my critics will say that I ought not to have chosen letters which make flattering reference to my personal appearance. My answer is twofold. In the first place, I cannot choose other letters which are free from such a reference, for the simple reason that they do not exist. Every letter Olive wrote me at this time (and, for that matter, for a good many years afterwards) contained such references. My second answer is that this admiration of the girl for the boy is in itself beautiful and brave and right and classic, even if it does not commend itself to modern stupidity. Shakespeare's heroines, who are the model of everything that is perfect in womanhood, did not hesitate to express similar sentiments. " Swear by thy gracious self who art the god of my idolatry," says Juliet to Romeo, and, also referring to him, " O serpent heart hid with a flowering face," and she retracts the " serpent heart " part of it immediately afterwards and accuses herself bitterly for it. I could give a hundred more instances. Indeed, so far from being the least ashamed of the fact that a lovely girl thought me a " beautiful boy prince," and said and wrote it on every possible occasion, I glory in it. These letters are, moreover, a crushing answer to Frank Harris, who, not content with attacking my character with foul lies and misrepresentations, goes out of his way in his ugly book to make half-hearted but spiteful attempts to run down my personal appearance as it was when I first met Oscar Wilde. This is all part of the modern Bolshevik hatred of Beauty in any form which is typical of much of the tendency of modern art and literature. I will never be a party to it, nor to the idiotic convention which makes so many—who really think it—afraid to say that a boy may be, and frequently is, just as beautiful as a girl. As a model of what may and may not properly be said or written on any subject, Shakespeare will always be good enough for me.

o

CHAPTER XXXII

THERE is another aspect of this episode of my life which I have no intention of shirking. My idea is that for a man to write what purports to be the history of his own life and to leave out the most interesting and psychologically revealing part of it, is dishonest and stupid. It would be easy for me to write a book representing myself to be other than I really am. To a certain extent I have already done so, with the assistance of Crosland, in *Oscar Wilde and Myself*. At the time I wrote or endorsed that book I had really persuaded myself that it presented a true picture of me. In truth it merely presented a picture of what at that time I wished to be supposed to be. At my age, and believing as I do that the battle of my life is over, I decline to put on any of the convenient cloaks and masks which convention has at our disposal whenever we need them.

It is fairly evident from the letters I have quoted, and from the story of my marriage as I have here related it, that I was in the whole affair of my marriage more the pursued than the pursuer. I firmly believe that in the end, after we had been married for some time, I loved my wife more than she did me. I have often told her so. But at the time of our " courtship " period she courted me more than I did her. The reasons for this were twofold. The first reason was that, as a result of the social decline I had suffered as a consequence of the Wilde affair, I had definitely adopted the attitude which I have already described—the attitude, that is, of avoiding even any appearance of making advances to other people, either in the way of friendship or love, or mere acquaintance. I was so sensitive to slights that my whole life was ordered on the basis of a line of conduct which would make it difficult, if not impossible, for slights to be offered to me.

Towards marriage my attitude was quite definite. I said to myself : " I will never make love to a girl of my own class and ask her to marry me. If any girl wants to marry me she will have to do it all herself. I refuse to go after any girl with a view to marriage." I was, moreover, at this period of my life not preoccupied with girls, and I took very little notice of them when they came my way. Before the Wilde scandal broke out, when I used to go a great deal to dances and stay in country houses, I had a few girl friends, but although I was fond of them, and even had sentimental feelings about at least two of them, I never got within a hundred miles of thinking about marrying them.

After the Wilde affair I subconsciously came to the conclusion that marriage with any English (or I should say of course, properly, British) girl was out of the question. The " American heiress " was obviously another pair of horses. My idea was that I would marry for her money an American girl (she had to be American) who had a superabundance of it, and that she would marry me because I had a title and an historic name, and because I knew, and could easily show her, or anyone concerned, that, with plenty of money, there would not be the slightest difficulty in getting back again into the social circle from which I was then partially (though never altogether) excluded. I have less compunction in mentioning these sordid ideas because after all they never got beyond the region of ideas. I think it is exceedingly unlikely that I would ever have married any girl, however many millions she had, unless I had loved her. One proposes to do things, and Nature laughs at one and says : " All right, go ahead, my dear child, but you will soon find out where I come in."

For me to be married at all, therefore, to an English girl

was something of a miracle. In order that it should happen it was necessary that there should be a girl who loved me very much, who had the very great courage to despise and ignore what was then the conventional attitude of society towards me, and who was prepared to take every risk. In addition to that she would have to make the first advance, and a good many other advances after that. On the top of all this there was also to be considered that I was exceedingly fastidious, that I would not have so much as looked at a girl who was not, on the one hand, well born, beautiful and outstandingly attractive and, on the other hand, intellectual and appreciative of poetry and literature. As I have never been good at mathematics I refrain from any attempt at calculating the odds against any such girl being found to fulfil all the conditions. Yet there she was !

The second reason for the lines into which our courtship period fell is to be found, I believe, in the obscure psychology of sex. I believe that almost everyone is more or less bi-sexual. All my life, up till two or three years ago, I have angrily and violently resented the suggestion that I ever had anything feminine about me. If anyone wanted to " get a rise " out of me, at any time from my schooldays onwards, the way to do it was to make some such suggestion. When I was a schoolboy I was so determined to be " manly " that I deliberately went about insufficiently clothed in winter. I used to shiver without under-clothing unless someone took the trouble to insist that I wore it, which of course did not happen at school. Although by nature rather nervous and apprehensive, I cultivated insensibility to pain, and whenever any danger appeared I trained myself to rush out to meet it more than half way. Harris in his book, so often referred to, speaks of my " insane courage and aristocratic contempt for convention."

Well, within the last two or three years, having got into a backwater of life, and being determined if possible to look steadily at everything, I have come to the conclusion that I really have all the time had a great deal of the feminine in my nature. What is more, I believe that I have been most successful in life when, acting naturally and without thinking what I was doing, I have allowed this part of my nature to assert itself. "Letting myself go," so to speak. Everyone should try to control his nature, but to try to distort it or force it is a great mistake, and leads to all sorts of miseries and misunderstandings, both for oneself and for others. One should never allow one's nature to run away with one, but, on the other hand, one should be careful not to resist or repress it too much.

It also occurs to me with great force that what Harris calls "insane courage and aristocratic contempt for convention " are really feminine qualities and not masculine. The average woman is far braver than the average man. The common kind of courage —that of the soldier who disregards the danger of death—belongs to the majority of men in the last resort. I mean that if it has to be exercised they exercise it without making a fuss about it. But when you come to moral courage it hardly exists at all among men. There is only one man in ten thousand who will brave the full violence of public opinion. Women, on the other hand, will often do it, if they are in love or to defend their children. I used to think that the Englishman was the most cowardly creature (morally speaking) on earth. But I believe now I was doing him an injustice. Moral cowardice is not peculiar to the English, any more than to the French or the Italian or any other nationality, but it is characteristic, with exceptions of course, of men as opposed to women. The bravest men are those who have a good deal of woman about them. On the other hand the same men have, of course, the defects of their qualities.

To understand the psychology of sex one must be outside the circle and beyond the tyranny of the sexual motions. I do not mean by that that one must be sexless or unaffected by the " sex urge." A man or a woman who is in that condition can really understand nothing at all about it. Chastity to such a man or woman is not a virtue, but an indifferent condition. I have been chaste, solely through religion, for fourteen years roughly, and I am therefore able to look dispassionately at my own sex psychology. Looking back at it from these serene heights, I am able to see, what I would have probably indignantly denied at the time when I was in the vortex, that up till the time when I became a Catholic the guiding principle of my life was the desire to be loved and admired. Of course I understand now, when it is too late, that these feelings and instincts which were perfectly natural to me, and which I could no more help than I could help the colour of my hair, might have existed combined with absolute purity and chastity. When I say that they might have existed I am putting it much too low. The fact is that they did exist and did operate in innumerable cases quite outside any avowed question of sex. Whether I liked it or not, I did for years attract persons of both sexes with a very powerful attraction. When I was at Oxford I even suffered greatly from the jealousy of my friends. Each was anxious that I should believe that he was *the* friend to the exclusion of others. It was a common experience for me (so common indeed that I used to enjoy ecstasies of secret laughter every time it occurred) for a friend to warn me against other friends. Then, when (as of course was bound to happen) the friend realized that he was not accepted at his own valuation, and to the exclusion of others, he had a grievance against me, and very often ended by nearly disliking me.

What kept me away from girls at the period of my life (1900-1902) which I have now reached in these memoirs (except in the lower form of very infrequent casual *liaisons*) was just that I did not for a moment intend to put up with less love and admiration from a girl than I had been in the habit of getting (without any conscious effort on my part) from innumerable male friends. I certainly was not going to marry any girl who did not get at least as sentimental about me as my friends at Oxford, and later, had been in the habit of getting. This is only another way of saying that I was very spoilt, and that I was determined, in so far as I thought about it at all, to have nothing but the very *crème de la crème* in the way of marriageable love.

Naturally enough having these feelings (even though I was not quite aware of them and had not analysed them) I got what I wanted. In exactly the same way I had got Oscar Wilde, the most brilliant man of his age. I never set out to attract him, which is what Harris tries to make out. If Harris knew anything about the psychology of either Wilde or myself he would know that it was precisely because I made no effort at all to attract Wilde that he became infatuated with me. It took him a year's hard work, and every bit of brain he had, to get me half as interested in him as he was in me from the moment he first saw me.

In the case of Olive it was of course different. I fell desperately in love with her, not really quite at first sight, but after I had known her for a very short while. In the end, after we were married, I was more in love with her than she was with me. Then of course the moment that happened I was, comparatively speaking, lost, as far as my supreme position in her eyes was concerned. It was a dreadful business, but I do not see that I could help it or was to blame. Moreover, even if I had known then what I know now, I could only have prolonged the agony of our love. But how could I know or guess that the very thing she loved in me was that which I was always trying to suppress and keep under : I mean the feminine part of me ? As soon as I was married I deliberately tried to be more and more manly. The more manly I became the less attractive I was to Olive. I can see now, looking back at it all, that she was always desperately trying to recapture the "me" that she had guessed and seen and loved, and only occasionally finding it concealed under various cloaks. If we had never married we would have gone on for ever adoring each other. But marriage (which I for my part, entirely agreeing with St Paul, believe to be a quite " second-best " institution as compared with chastity) gradually destroyed our love. When I say destroyed our love, I only mean that it destroyed our passionate love; another kind of love still remains. My only consolation, now that I at last understand, is that if she had married anyone else her disillusion would have been ten times more rapid, and quite as complete. Moreover, what pair of lovers in the world is going to believe that their only chance of preserving their love for each other at its highest point is not to marry, and that from the moment they marry their love will begin to decline? Yet I feel quite certain that this is the case with those who are spiritually minded :

> Love is a flame whose fuel is the flesh,
> Which, burning in that unconsuming fire,
> Distils the milky dew of chaste desire
> Whose secret sap wells ever sweet and fresh.

If it be said that I am trying to run down marriage, I reply that I am not trying to do anything ; I am merely stating what I believe to be the facts. I wish as much as anyone else that married love could be eternal, and that it did not feed upon itself and consume itself. That it is not eternal and that it does consume itself is part of the curse of Adam and Eve from which there is no escape, except by the pains and suffering of renunciation and sacrifice, out of which sometimes another kind of love emerges. I feel on this subject as I do about Hell. The modern idea is that Hell is " unthinkable," and that it is much too horrible to be true. But is anything too horrible to be true ? And what is the use of refusing to believe in something because one does not like it ?

And so it is with this perhaps the most terrible curse of all, the impermanence of married love, the impossibility of going on loving your wife or your husband to the end, *in the same degree* ; there is something that will beat it, something that will make it " all come right in the end." Moreover, after great suffering and anguish, even when they are blind and misdirected, sometimes a miracle occurs, and in the wilderness waters break out and the desert rejoices and blossoms like the rose.

CHAPTER XXXIII

AFTER our marriage the next few years were uneventful. Our son was born in a house in Chelsea. We went abroad to Corsica and the Riviera; then back to London, and then to Wiltshire, to a beautiful farmhouse called Lake Farm. We owed Lake Farm to my cousin, then Mrs Edward Tennant, later Lady Glenconner, and now Lady Grey of Fallodon.[1] At that time she and I were friends, and had been so from childhood. It was she that pointed out to me the beauties of Lake Farm, which was half-a-mile from her house, Wilsford, and arranged with our landlord, dear old Mr Lovibond, who occupied the beautiful old Elizabethan Lake House, that I would be a suitable tenant for his farmhouse.

Lake Farm was on the lovely road that runs between Amesbury and Salisbury. It was only about a hundred yards from the River Avon, one of the best trout streams in England. During the time I was there, about two years, I had the run not only of Mr Lovibond's water but of that, extending over several miles, of our neighbours at Amesbury Abbey, Sir Edmund Antrobus (" Strobus ") and Lady Antrobus ("Wavie "). Farther down the river I also had leave to fish in the water of Mr Devenish, and sometimes in that of Mr Louis Greville, uncle of the late Lord Warwick. So I had miles of the finest trout fishing in England for nothing, and I became a fairly skilful dry-fly fisherman.

I must put it on record that I was taught to fish by my father-in-law, Colonel Custance, at Weston, where he had a splendid

[1] Since this was written the deeply regretted death of Lady Grey of Fallodon has occurred.

trout stream. He was a magnificent fisherman. Up to the time of my marriage I had never fished at all ; but I ended by loving it quite as much as shooting. I believe I caught one day, with dry fly, the second-largest basket of trout ever secured on the Amesbury Abbey water. As far as I remember, and it could of course be verified in the trout-book kept at the Abbey, I got eighteen fish, all over a pound and a half, eleven of them over two pounds, and one of three pounds. In addition to that I put back quite a dozen just under a pound and a half, the rule of the water being that you kept only fish over a pound and a half. The record basket was made the same year a few days before by Mr Payne Galway.

While we were at Lake, the Tennants (afterwards Glenconners) were, with Mr Lovibond, our nearest neighbours, and showed us much kindness. But our great friends were the entirely delightful " Strobus," who had formerly commanded the Grenadier Guards, and the equally delightful, if eccentric, "Wavie." Their constant kindness and hospitality contributed largely to make our stay at Lake about the happiest period of our married life. It is tragic to think that both Strobus and Wavie are dead, and that their only child, " Toots " (Grenadier Guards), was killed in the war. The present owner of the Abbey (which, by the way, was built by my collateral ancestor, the Duke of Queensberry, who resided there with Kitty, Duchess of Queensberry, celebrated for her patronage of the poet Gay, who wrote *The Beggar's Opera* at Amesbury Abbey, and for her " aristocratic insolence " to George the Third) is Sir Cosmo, brother of the late Sir Edmund ; but I believe he does not live there and the magnificent Palladian house stands empty.

It was while I was at Lake, in 1907, that my cousin, Pamela Tennant (Lady Grey of Fallodon), induced her husband, Eddie Tennant (afterwards Lord Glenconner), to buy *The Academy* and to make me its editor.

It is very difficult to write on this subject. My cousin Pamela, to whom I had always been devoted, is too well known both for her beauty and her talents (she is a considerable poet) to make it necessary for me to say anything about her from those points of view. Any feeble tribute that I could make to her would be completely drowned and overwhelmed in the constant flood of appreciation and adulation that has followed her from her earliest youth down to the present day. All I need say is that she was very kind to me and that her action in getting me the editorship of *The Academy* was a piece of pure good nature and friendliness, which I have never ceased to appreciate and be grateful for. But the unfortunate truth must be told that while the general consensus of opinion—I think I may say without much fear of contradiction — puts my editorship of *The Academy* on record as synonymous with the " palmy days " of that journal (which rapidly declined and died after I was pushed out of the editorship), Pamela and I were never able to see eye to eye about it. From the moment I started editing it there was constant friction and trouble. Whatever I did I never seemed able to please the proprietor of the paper and his wife. I was constantly being found fault with, and whatever success the paper achieved while it still belonged to the Tennants was in the teeth of much opposition and detraction from this quarter.

Part of the trouble was no doubt due to the fact that I was a strong Conservative, of the " Diehard " variety, and that Eddie Tennant (Mr Asquith's brother-in-law) was a Liberal, and M.P. for Salisbury. At the same time I must say that my running of the paper in the Conservative interest, and in the strongest opposition to Messrs Asquith, Lloyd George and Winston Churchill, whom I regarded then, and regard still more now, as jointly responsible for the ruin of the country and the " smash up " of almost everything that used to make life in England worth living, was not carried on in opposition to the wishes of the man who was finding the money to run the paper and to pay my salary (£300 a year, which barely paid my out-of-pocket expenses, and which was less than half what might have been considered a fair salary for what I was doing).

Some member of my own family said to me one day that it appeared to be " rather rough on Eddie Tennant " that I should be using his paper and his money to attack his party and his brother-in-law. This caused me to have qualms about the matter, and I wrote to him and told him what had been said and asked him if he objected to the political line of the paper. " If so," I said, " I will drop it. I cannot, of course, change my views or those of the paper, but if you wish it I will drop politics altogether and stick to literature alone." Eddie wrote back at once, and said in effect : " Not at all. I don't mind it a bit ; in fact, I think it very lively, and a great deal of what you say I entirely agree with." Much relieved at the receipt of this letter I went ahead, and about two weeks later I wrote a very strongly worded attack on Mr Asquith for his suppression, at the last minute, of the procession which had been arranged to celebrate the Catholic Eucharistic Congress. (Incidentally I must mention that during the whole time I controlled *The Academy* I ran it as a High Church Anglican paper. I did not become a Catholic till the year after I lost the editorship.)

To my great surprise and indignation I received what I can only describe as an extremely offensive letter from Eddie Tennant (he afterwards admitted that it was offensive and withdrew and apologized for it). He told me that he considered that my article on Mr Asquith was " in the worst possible taste," and he went on to say (for about the third and, as it turned out, the last time) that he had definitely decided to sell the paper and cut all connection with it.

I felt very indignant at this treatment, and the idea of losing the paper, of which I had then held the editorship for only about eight or nine months, was utter misery to me. It seemed to me a cruel thing, and yet entirely characteristic of the casual want of consideration of the very rich man in regard to the feelings and rights of the "mere man of letters," who also happened to be his wife's cousin and, according to her own oft-repeated account, one of the foremost poets of his age. At that time Crosland had come on to the paper as my assistant editor, and he laughed at my fears of losing the paper. He put into my head an idea which would certainly never have occurred to me in my wildest dreams—the idea, namely, that I was not just the poor dependent on the half-contemptuous whim of the million-aire *nouveau riche* who paid my miserable little salary, but the editor of a powerful paper installed in a position from which, if I showed fight, it would be no easy job to oust me. Primed by Crosland I took up the attitude (which I am bound to say I consider was entirely justified) that Eddie Tennant had no earthly right to make me editor of a paper on the tacit under-standing of continuity and then, just as I was beginning to get hold of my job and to understand what I could do, and just as I was involved in half-a-dozen controversies which covered matters of principle and the welfare of letters, as opposed to log-rolling and corrupt cliques, to whip round on me and tell me that he was going to sell the paper to my enemies and push me out into the cold.

Even as a matter of bare legal right I was, as an editor, en-titled to six months' notice, but not a word about any such thing had been said, nor any suggestion that it was recognized that I had any rights at all in the matter. I do not suppose that Eddie Tennant had any idea that he was behaving in an arbitrary and ungenerous manner. He was, in matters of business, largely under the influence of his *homme d'affaires*, who had always greatly disapproved of *The Academy* and the, to him, utterly unprofitable expense it involved. All he wanted was to get out as quickly as possible from a responsibility which he ought never to have assumed, and which he was constitutionally incapable of shouldering with any degree of credit and dignity.

Crosland told me that if I attempted to conduct the negotiations I " wouldn't have a dog's chance with these people," and that the only thing for me to do was to give him authority to go to Tennant and make the best terms he could for me. I told Crosland to go ahead. Crosland's methods were never very pleasant or amiable. He adopted a bullying and aggressive tone which, I believe, was quite unnecessary. I believe now that if I had seen Eddie myself, and told him exactly what my side of the case was, he would have seen it, and that he would have done what he actually did, without any necessity for all the " rough stuff " that Crosland imported into it. On the other hand, if it had not been for Crosland in the first crisis I would have been simply squashed out of existence and my paper taken away from me, for it would never have occurred to my simple mind that I had any possible chance of " vindicating my helpless right " against Tennant and his *homme d'affaires*.

To cut a long story short, Eddie ended by handing over the paper (for which he had paid £2000) to me, together with a sum of £500, for which I gave him a bill, which I am bound to say I never had the slightest intention of taking up. If he had done all this of his own accord it would have been generous, and an act of grace. As it was, he was more or less forced into it. The gift of the paper was not really so generous as it appears, for it was at that time running at a loss of at least two or three thousand pounds a year, and as a condition of keeping it going I had to find this money myself as soon as the £500 (which lasted about three months) was exhausted. I feel pretty certain that Eddie himself and Mr Asquith—who was in the offing, so to speak—did not give me six months of life for my paper.

Eddie wanted a peerage, and, putting two and two together, it is not difficult to guess that Mr Asquith was not going to give him one as long as he was supplying his wife's cousin with the money to run a paper which was a constant source of annoyance and a very real menace (as any well-written and sincere paper must be to those whom it opposes) to himself and all his most cherished schemes. As it happened, I ran the paper for more than two years after this date, and Eddie Tennant did not get his peerage till after I had sold it (through the intermediary of Pamela's brother, my cousin, George Wyndham) to Lord Fitzwilliam and Lord Howard de Walden. Altogether I edited *The Academy* for rather more than three years. In that time I doubled its price and more than trebled its circulation. At the end I sold it for £2000. But I lost heavily over the whole transaction. To keep it going I raised money on a reversionary interest I had in my mother's property, and altogether, by the time I got rid of it, I was quite £2000 out of pocket.

It has always seemed to me a scandalous and a discreditable thing that there was not one solitary rich man in the country who would back me. If I had had anything like a decent backing I would easily have " turned the corner " and made the paper pay a good profit. But, as things were, I kept it going only by great sacrifices and a succession of " miracles."

The only person who helped me was Lord Howard de Walden, who put up £2000 in return for quite worthless debentures. When I sold the paper he surrendered these debentures, as I did mine, representing the money I had sunk. But whereas what I lost represented nearly all that was left of my small fortune, I do not suppose that his loss of £2000 worried Lord Howard de Walden. Had he continued me as editor when he and Lord Fitzwilliam bought the paper I would, with the financial support which he then gave it, have easily made the paper into a paying proposition (it was already when I had it a powerful and influential paper and a great *succès d'estime*), but he handed the editorship to a Mr Cowper, who was utterly without experience in journalism or letters (I believe he was by profession a land agent), and who killed the paper. The moment I left the editorship the circulation dropped to about half the figure up to which I had gradually worked it, and in a few years it was so depreciated and discredited that it was offered to me by the then proprietors for £25 ! I declined the offer, and it then expired, after an existence of nearly fifty years.

CHAPTER XXXIV

I HAD met Crosland for the first time two or three years before, when he was introduced to me at a music hall one evening by Mr Hannaford Bennett. Crosland told me, on that occasion, that he had been " reader " to Grant Richards when the question of publishing my volume of poetry, *The City of the Soul,* had come up in 1899. Crosland told me that it was he who induced Grant Richards to publish it, and that in his opinion it was far beyond any contemporary poetry. Whether or not this statement of his as to his share in bringing about the publication of my volume was accurate I have no means of knowing. I think that, as a matter of fact, it was my cousin, Wilfrid Blunt, who arranged with Mr Grant Richards to publish my book, and I doubt if Crosland had anything to do with it, though I do not question for a moment that he read it in MS. and greatly admired it.

Some years later he begged me to allow him to write an introductory note to the edition of my sonnets which was published by " The Academy Publishing Company " while I was editing the paper. In that " Note " he claimed that the best of my sonnets were equal to the best that had ever been written, and that " several of them will endure as long as poetry is read and as long as the English language is understood." It was natural that I should be pleased to meet a man who had such a high opinion of my work, and from that day I saw a lot of Crosland, and later I was for several years on terms of the greatest friendship with him. He was a most extraordinary man. Someone once wittily described his appearance by saying that he looked like " an inspired bus conductor." Undoubtedly he had genius. He has written some very fine poetry (some of the best of it

226

appeared in *The Academy* under my editorship), and also a good deal that is nothing like so fine, and occasionally gets perilously near to doggerel, especially in the poems he churned out week by week during the war. But all poets must be judged by their best work, and at his best Crosland was superb.

All his best sonnets were written when he was with me on *The Academy*. He had what I can only describe as a slightly defective ear for rhythm, as far as his own work was concerned. It appeared to be impossible for him to produce a sonnet which did not contain at least one line with too many feet in it. As long as he was with me I used to employ every art I possessed in the way of tact and cajolery and argument to make him correct these blemishes. He would argue fiercely that they were not blemishes and that he wrote the lines in question in that way " on purpose to produce a rugged effect." If everything else failed, I used to adopt an air of aggrieved resignation (Crosland called it " sulking "). In the end I invariably got my way, and he would change the sonnet according to my wishes. The result is that all the sonnets he wrote for *The Academy* are correct in form, and every single one he wrote for other papers is incorrect in form.

Up till the time when I met Crosland I knew of him only as the author of *The Unspeakable Scot*, a book I have never read to this day. I asked Crosland about it, and wanted him to lend me a copy to read, but he declared that he did not possess a copy, and that if he had possessed one he would not lend it to me. He begged me not to read it, and I promised I would not do so, and I have kept my promise. He told me it was " mostly rubbish," and that he wrote it partly as a pot-boiler to get money and partly to " get even " with two or three Scottish journalists in Fleet Street whom he particularly disliked. " As a matter of fact," he said, " nearly all the few people who have been decent to me have been Scotsmen, to say nothing about you, the best and dearest friend I have ever had." After he quarrelled with me, Crosland returned to his foolish, pointless and half-witted abuse of Scotland and Scotsmen, but as long as he was associated with me (on and off for seven or eight years) he carefully avoided anything of the kind.

Crosland was a delightful companion when he was in good form, which in those days was pretty nearly always the case. He was, I think, at that time really fond of me, at least I try to think so, though when he could get no more money from me he basely deserted me. He was a perfect cormorant for money. His salary on *The Academy* was supposed to be £7 a week. (It must be remembered that £7 before the war was worth nearly twice what it is now.) It was, of course, grossly inadequate for what he was (the only journalist in London who was also a genius and a fine poet), but it was more than he had ever got before. In any case, as I invariably gave him at least £10 a week (often much more), besides having him to lunch with me every day as a matter of course, and frequently to dinner as well, during the whole time he was my assistant editor, he certainly had nothing to complain of. I do not wish to emulate Wilde's laments in *De Profundis* over the money he alleges he spent on entertaining me to dinner and lunch, and I do not grudge Crosland a penny of what I paid and gave and spent on him (*e.g.* I gave him £250 as a free gift when I sold *The Academy*), but I do feel his subsequent ingratitude very much. However, this is a matter on which I do not wish to enlarge. I prefer to remember that Crosland taught me all I know about journalism and editing a paper, and that in the long run he was nearly always right in his views about people and things. He did a lot for *The Academy* in one way, and he lifted me clean out of cheap cynicism, log-rolling and determination-to-be-smart which are the bane of budding literary amateurs (I was an amateur in those days, except of course as regards poetry). His own articles in *The Academy* (as later in *Plain English*) were models of the literary journalist's art. As a writer of articles there has never been anyone to touch Crosland in my lifetime. He had a fine style, which was based on a most intimate knowledge of Shakespeare and all the best poets. He had infinite wit and a really Shakespearian sense of humour. Merely as a contributor, he would have made the fortune of any paper in the long run, as certain wooden-headed newspaper proprietors at last began to find out just when his best period was nearly over.

But as a manager or financial adviser on a paper he was positively fatal. His views on finance may be best exemplified by an actual instance : about two or three years before I had *The Academy*, Crosland brought out a paper called *The English Review* (no connection with the present journal of that name), for which I wrote a series of light or nonsense verses. He was associated in this venture with the late Julius Beerbohm. On one occasion I was sitting in the office of the paper (it was one small room in a street in Soho) with Crosland and Beerbohm when another member of the " staff " suddenly entered the room, with a pale face and tragic mien, uttering the words : " Look here, do you know what has happened ? The d——d bank has honoured that cheque for £50 ! " " Good God, the dirty dogs ! " ejaculated Crosland, rising from his seat. " Well, that just about finishes us." He and Beerbohm then hastily left the room, after excusing themselves to me (they had asked me to lunch).

After they had gone I extracted from the member of the staff who had brought the sad tidings the explanation of this curious scene. The balance at the bank was, it appears, something like £17, 10s., just enough to pay for lunch for the next day or two for Crosland, Beerbohm and myself, and anyone else connected with the paper who cared to turn up, for they kept " open house " although, as I subsequently discovered, they never paid their contributors.   Meanwhile they owed £50 to someone, and were being pressed.   Crosland's solution was simplicity itself : "We will give him a crossed cheque for the money ; he will pay it into his account, which will keep him quiet for two or three days ; our bank will of course dishonour the cheque, and meanwhile we must see what turns up ; and we shall still have £17, 10s. to go on with."

The horror and indignation of Crosland on discovering that the bank had paid the cheque, which had been " specially cleared," and that instead of having £17, 10s. to their credit he and Beerbohm were owing the bank about £32, was one of the funniest things I have ever witnessed.

Crosland's ideas of finance during the two years when we were associated on *The Academy* were based on his assumption that as a " lord," and related to a large number of rich and powerful families, it was obvious that I was entitled to, and would ultimately and inevitably get, " stacks of boodle," as he expressed it.   His visions of the future prospects of *The Academy* were golden and rosy.   He said to me once when I was depressed : " In about another couple of years this paper will be making at least £10,000 a year.   You will hear people in the streets whispering : 'Who is that fair youth ? '   And the reply will be : 'That is the wealthy Lord Alfred Douglas, who owns *The Academy*.'   Then they will ask : ' And who is that dazzling object by his side ? ' ' That's Crosland,' will be the reply."

The essence of humour is, I believe, incongruous contrast. The idea of Crosland as a " dazzling object " was irresistibly funny, for he was the most strange and uncouth-looking person I have ever seen.   He was always untidy, and somehow conveying the impression that he had been to bed in his clothes ; his hair hung dankly over his forehead, and when annoyed he had a positively ferocious aspect.   On the other hand he was sometimes unexpectedly soft-hearted, and had many generous impulses and feelings. His appearance when he was "smartened up" and forced into evening dress, I myself having tied his tie and brushed his hair—a process which occasionally took place, with many groans and protestations on his part, when I was going to drag him out to dinner to meet respectable people or to go to the theatre—was really not bad at all ; and he had fine eyes. Those who want to find out what was in his soul at his best, and beneath all the outward stains of financial unscrupulousness and what almost amounted to savagery, will find it by reading his best poetry—for example, the beautiful *Swan Song,* his best sonnets, and a glorious poem called *The Finer Spirit,* which is full of magical lines.

CHAPTER XXXV

ALTHOUGH Crosland did a lot for *The Academy*, and although its undoubted success at this time was due really more, I believe, to him than to me, he let me and the paper in for all sorts of trouble which would never have come our way but for him. He involved me personally, as well as the paper, in all sorts of rows and feuds, which really were his own and not mine at all. He was not over-scrupulous about using the paper to fight some of his private battles, under the guise of attending to the " public interest," and I as editor got all the " credit " for what he did and wrote. The articles were nearly always unsigned, and, of course, I willingly accepted responsibility for everything that appeared in the paper. The result was that I drew upon myself a pretty large volume of anger and hatred. Some of the people who were angry and hated me were persons for whose good will and countenance I had no hankering at all, and I regarded their attitude towards me as a compliment and an asset.

On the other hand, it is idle to deny that *The Academy* made me a great many unnecessary enemies. Some of the people we " went for " were those whom I would go for again to-morrow " every time," if I had a paper, but others were comparatively harmless people who might well have been left alone. Almost the worst turn that Crosland did me, and one which let me in for an enormous amount of unpleasantness, grief and regret, was that he forced me into a terrible fight with poor Freddie Manners-Sutton (the Honourable H. F. W. Manners-Sutton, afterwards Viscount Canterbury), which ended at the Old Bailey in a triumph for Crosland and myself, which was, all the same, too dearly bought at the price of the sacrifice of my friendship with Freddie, who had been a great friend of my wife's before I married her, and who had, by the time I had got *The Academy*, become one of my own greatest friends.

Poor Freddie is now dead, and I rejoice to say that, after an estrangement which lasted about seven years, we made friends again. I was with him, staying in his London house as his guest, only about a week before he died, and we had then been reconciled and on terms of the greatest friendship for at least two years. Our reconciliation was brought about by my wife, who never ceased to regret the quarrel into which I was reluctantly forced.

In justice to myself I must put it on record that, before Freddie Canterbury and I were actually reconciled, and while the negotiations towards reconciliation were in progress, I wrote to him and told him frankly that as a preliminary to such reconciliation, which I greatly desired, it was absolutely necessary that he should recognize and admit that the responsibility for what had happened was not mine, and that by obstinately persisting in his attempt to get Crosland, who was then not only my friend but my paid *employé*, locked up for " criminal libel " he had put me into a position from which it was impossible for me to retreat without loss of honour. Crosland, in a fit of rage and temper, brought on by Freddie's feline sarcasms and banter, which always maddened him (he was also very jealous of him with me), wrote him a violently offensive letter, containing all sorts of abuse and accusations. Freddie was then ill-advised enough to go to a magistrate with his solicitor and apply for a summons against Crosland for libel. Crosland was served with the summons in the office of *The Academy* in my presence. He was prosecuted at Bow Street, and committed for trial at the Old Bailey, where he pleaded " justification," and was acquitted after I had, on his behalf, successfully, and indeed devastatingly, repelled a violent attack made on me in cross-examination by Mr, afterwards Sir Edward, Marshall Hall, who had the bad taste (which probably lost him and his client the action) to bring up the Oscar Wilde matter in an attempt to discredit my evidence.

This was the first of the long series of actions and trials in which I became involved, and it was the first time I had ever been in the witness-box. I had been warned that Marshall Hall was going to attack me on the Oscar Wilde matter, and that he had publicly boasted that he was going to " smash " me, although the Oscar Wilde matter had nothing whatever to do with the present action, and its introduction by Marshall Hall was merely an attempt to revive old-fashioned methods of bullying and brutality which are now popularly (but quite erroneously) supposed to be foreign to the " best traditions of the Bar."

I should be the last person to complain of what he did, for his doing so enabled me to win the enthusiastic sympathy of the jury and to make the useful discovery that I was an exceptionally good witness.   F. C. Philips, the well-known writer of the novel, *As in a Looking-Glass,* with whom I had some acquaintance and who was a great friend of my friend, the late Rowland Strong (formerly Paris correspondent of *The Morning Post*), was a barrister, and he was among the tightly packed group of members of the Bar who assembled to see me " smashed up " by the great Mr Marshall Hall.   F. C. Philips's account of my cross-examination, which lasted only about forty minutes, as retailed to me afterwards by Strong, was :   " My dear boy, Douglas simply ate him, he *ate* him ;   there's no other word for it.   I never saw anything like it in a law court before."

The case was tried by the Common Serjeant, Sir John Bosanquet (known in the Temple, by a coincidence, as " Old Bosie "), and half way through my cross-examination Marshall Hall was appealing to him for protection against me, for I was not content with answering his questions, I carried the war into his camp, and " made speeches to the jury " as he bitterly complained. Marshall Hall, like all the other " deadly cross-examiners " and " irresistible advocates " that I have ever crossed swords with (with the solitary exception of Carson), had really very little in him. The moment I tackled him he collapsed like a pricked balloon. My brain was twice as quick as his, and I simply played with him. He never had the slightest chance with me, and he appeared to have shrunk to half his imposing height when he had finished. He got no help at all from the Common Serjeant, who, rigidly fair, declined to interfere with me. If only all the judges were like that !

I think it is almost certain that if he had not attacked me in the unfair way he did, and roused all my latent powers of defence and personality, Marshall Hall would have won the case. For Crosland's plea of justification was very thin, and even the great skill of our counsel, Mr Valetta, one of the most brilliant men at the Bar and worth two of Marshall Hall any day, would have hardly pulled him through but for the chance which I got and took so successfully. As it was, the jury were so indignant at the way I had been treated, and so pleased with the " first fine careless rapture " of my maiden appearance in the witness-box, which, honestly (unlike Browning's thrush), I never have been quite able to recapture, that they gave Crosland a verdict after a very short retirement. Crosland himself was very good in the witness-box, and if I outshone him on that occasion it was simply because I had the better chance. In short, if I myself had " put up " or " squared " counsel on the other side to play into my hands he could not have done it more completely and effectually than Marshall Hall did. Whether he afterwards became a really great advocate or not I cannot say. I doubt it very much. The fact that he was so proclaimed *ad nauseam* by the Press every time he defended a murderer, and whether

he " got him off " or not, does not prove anything one way or
another. The Press invariably singles out the worst and most
incompetent judges for the most constant and fulsome praise,
and never mentions the few really fine ones. Its praise of Sir
Edward Marshall Hall as a great advocate, as a consequence,
rather inclines me to doubt that he was ever anything out of the
ordinary run of " Nature's sale-work." I strongly suspect that
the persons whom he successfully defended on charges of murder
were acquitted simply and solely because they were innocent.
About those that were hanged we may give him the benefit of
the doubt.

CHAPTER XXXVI

As soon as I had sold *The Academy*, which I did, with George Wyndham's assistance, only when I had got into the position of being utterly unable to find any more money to go on with it, I became (although I did not then know it) a mark, and ultimately an easy prey, for my enemies. George Wyndham not only sold the paper for me, but while the negotiations for the sale were going on he gave me £200 to "carry on" with. The negotiations however took several weeks, and if I had not had the luck to go to Ascot and back eleven winners in the four days' meeting (one of them being Winkipop, at 14 to 1) I could not have held out. As it was, when I collected the £2000 for the sale of the paper, there was an overdraft at Cox's Bank (Guards Office), my bankers and *The Academy*'s (separate accounts though I controlled both), of £800. By the time I had given Crosland £250, and paid up the printers and all other outstanding creditors, there was not much left of the £2000.

As long as I had my paper my enemies gave me a wide berth, especially after we had won the Manners-Sutton case at the Old Bailey. During the whole time I had *The Academy* (more than three years) I never had an action for libel brought against me. The reason for this was that, although we continually criticized and attacked with the utmost frankness and outspokenness, and always made a point of "going for" big people and disregarding the small fry, we were always sure of our ground. Instead of bringing actions for libel against us, the persons attacked frequently salved their wounded feelings by libelling me.

The libels always took the same form : insinuations or insults on the subject of Oscar Wilde. When this happened I issued writs at once, and in every case the libellers " climbed down," apologized abjectly and " paid up." The sums I got for compensation from persons who libelled me, and squealed for mercy when I writted them, were for a long time, in a small way, quite a source of income to me. Among the sums paid as compensation, and in consideration of the discontinuance of legal proceedings, were fifty guineas from *The Isis*, the Oxford undergraduate magazine, and fifty guineas from *The Cambridge Magazine* (paid by the dons who ran the paper). In both cases the undergraduate editors were dismissed and their dismissal was taken into consideration " in mitigation of damages." I could of course have extracted much larger sums than those I actually accepted, but my idea was to be generously contemptuous of this sort of petty spitefulness. I took fifty guineas and the dismissal of the editors just to " teach them a gentle lesson."

I have been trying to add up all the actions for libel which I have had to take in my life, and really I find that I have lost count. On the spur of the moment I can think of at least eight. I lost only one of them, my action against Ransome already referred to. By far the greater number of them were settled out of court by payments and apologies to me. As I write now I have a crop of actions, or at any rate (so far) threatened actions, in respect of booksellers who will persist in selling in a hole-and-corner way Harris's book, *The Life and Confessions of Oscar Wilde*, knowing full well that it contains gross libels on me.[1]

It is exactly what one would expect, and quite characteristic of the sort of way " history " is written or gets accepted, that I am regarded and described by many people as " a man who is always libelling people." I have been twice convicted for libel at the Old Bailey, once for libelling my father-in-law,

[1] Since this was written I have obtained damages in respect of three libel actions, only one of which got into court. In each case the defendants were booksellers who sold copies of Harris's book.

Colonel Custance, by accusing him of defrauding his daughter, and once for libelling Winston Churchill, by accusing him of writing a deliberately false account of the battle of Jutland with the object of enabling a group of Jews to make a financial *coup* on the American stock markets.

With regard to the first libel, I will only say that I subsequently repeated it quite as strongly, and at much greater length, and supported it by chapter and verse, in a twenty-page " Postscript " attached to a poem called *Eve and the Serpent*, of which I printed and circulated about a thousand copies. (The poem without the " Postscript " appears in my *Collected Satires*, published by the Fortune Press.) No proceedings were taken against me, though my late father-in-law consulted the late Sir George Lewis about the advisability of such proceedings. Sir George Lewis advised him that he had better not take any proceedings against me, and this advice was certainly not given out of any consideration for me, for Sir George and Colonel Custance were both up to the day of their deaths my most implacable enemies.

I will further point out that when I won my action for libel and was awarded £1000 damages against *The Evening News*, for stating that I was " violently eccentric and had shown marked signs of degeneracy," the solicitors for *The Evening News* were once more Lewis & Lewis, who had all the documents and all the information about my libel on Colonel Custance in their possession. My attack on Colonel Custance was brought up by them as part—indeed the principal part—of *The Evening News's* justification for their libel on me. The whole thing was thrashed out exhaustively in court. I was cross-examined on it for at least two out of the six hours during which I remained in the witness-box, my cross-examiner being the (of course) " deadly " Sir Douglas Hogg, the Attorney-General, now Lord Hailsham. The result was that I certainly convinced the judge (Mr Justice

Horridge) and the jury that I was entirely justified in what I had done in the case of Colonel Custance. The judge in his summing up, of which I have shorthand notes, even directed the jury very strongly on the point. He said : " You have heard the plaintiff's account of the whole matter. If what he says is true (and no attempt has been made by the defendants to dispute it) you are certainly not likely to come to the conclusion that he was ' violently eccentric ' because of the attitude he took up about the way he was treated in regard to his son and his wife."

It is, in short, perfectly obvious that if I had not been entirely justified in my attack on Colonel Custance (even admitting, as I do, that the form my attack took was unfortunate and in-judicious, and made things very awkward for my wife by putting her into the dilemma of having to choose between supporting her husband or her father) I would in the first place have been prosecuted by Colonel Custance a second time, when I repeated the libel in much greater detail, and certainly sent to prison (on the first occasion I was merely " bound over "), and in the second place I would have had no earthly chance of winning my action against *The Evening News*.

That I lost the case when Custance prosecuted me at the Old Bailey in 1913 is solely due to the fact that, distressed and disheartened as I was by the defection of my wife, and the loss of the Ransome action a few days before, I threw up the sponge, did not put in a " plea of justification," or go into the witness-box, and thus practically allowed the case to go against me by default.

With regard to the occasion in 1923 when I was convicted and sentenced to six months' imprisonment for libelling Mr Winston Churchill, I have not the slightest intention of saying anything which might be regarded as a repetition of the libel. But what I can and will say is (and I will make Mr Justice

Avory and all others concerned a present of the usual retort which is always employed on such occasions, I mean the retort about "disappointed litigants") that my trial was a farce. I do not for a moment say that if my trial had been differently conducted I would have established the truth of my libel, but I do say that if I had been allowed to explain to the jury how I came to print it (three years before my trial, in my paper, *Plain English*) I would have convinced them, and any reasonable being, that I acted in perfect good faith, without the slightest malice and in what I considered to be the public interest. As I had pleaded "justification" that would not have won me the case, but it would at least have made it practically impossible for the judge to send me to prison. The vindication of Mr Churchill from the charges I had brought against him would have been at least as complete if nearly all my counsel's questions to me had not been overruled by the judge, or again if Sir Douglas Hogg had given me a chance to explain myself in cross-examination.

As it was, Sir Douglas Hogg asked me two questions and then sat down. This was very smart of him, and it was also the greatest compliment to my powers as a witness that has ever been paid to me. It was an admission that he did not dare to give me the chance of giving the jury my version of the facts. It was very unfortunate for me that Sir Douglas Hogg, the Attorney-General, happened to be the very counsel who had cross-examined me two years before for six hours on behalf of *The Evening News*, when I won my action against that journal. Sir Douglas knew what a formidable witness I was. He had seen me win a case for myself out of the witness-box against tremendous odds, and he had seen that I had done it simply by "getting the jury," as I always have done when I have had fair play in a court of law. Consequently the next time he was opposed to me he took the very unusual course of not cross-examining me. It was a great moral triumph for me, especially as my counsel, Mr Cecil Hayes,

with my consent, went out of his way to " put in " my character.
This was a direct challenge to Hogg to say a word, if he dared,
against my character, moral or otherwise.   It was so pointed
that the judge, Mr Justice Avory, with an appearance of fairness
to me which did not, I must say, impress me very much, inter-
rupted Mr Hayes and said meaningly : " Are you putting in the
defendant's character, Mr Hayes ? "   Mr Hayes replied without
hesitation : " Certainly I am, my Lord ; let my learned friend
ask him any questions he likes relating to his moral character."
In face of that, Sir Douglas Hogg's failure to cross-examine me
was, as I say, a great moral triumph for me, but unfortunately
(like most moral triumphs) it was in the nature of a Pyrrhic
victory.   For the result was that I got no chance at all of using
my brains and my gifts of speech and personality in my own
defence.   It really does not matter a pin now.   My imprisonment
nearly killed me, as I shall explain later on in this book, but from
a social point of view it has proved to be the turning-point of
my life.   I have made more friends and converted more enemies
by going to prison as I did and in the cause which I represented
(the cause of fearless criticism of public men, however powerful)
than I had ever hoped to make again in this world.   From that
point of view, Mr Churchill, who doubtless goes in for being a
magnanimous man, when he is not actually engaged in getting
his critics sent to gaol, will be pleased to hear that indirectly he
has done me one of the best turns that it would be possible for
one man to do for another.

While I am about it, I think I ought to put it on record that
Sir Douglas Hogg's cross-examination of me in *The Evening News*
case, when I won, was conducted with the utmost politeness
and good breeding, although, acting on the instructions contained
in the brief prepared for him by Lewis & Lewis, he put all my
stolen letters to Wilde to me, and dragged up again the whole
question of my relations with Wilde and my quarrel with my

father. I can thus say that both methods, the brutal and the suave, were employed against me, the first by, among others, the then Mr Marshall Hall and the second by Sir Douglas Hogg, and that both equally failed. I think perhaps, all the same, that it is fairer to say that the failure in Sir Douglas Hogg's case was certainly less conspicuous than in the case of Marshall Hall, because I really "knocked out" Marshall Hall in about forty minutes, while Sir Douglas Hogg lasted a full number of rounds, through a whole day and a half. There was no knock-out; I won on points.

With regard to the Ransome case, which I lost, I have of course to admit that to that extent Sir James Campbell, who cross-examined me, got the better of me, but I do not consider that his victory was due to any "deadliness" on his part. He had overwhelming ammunition in the shape of my stolen letters sprung on me for the first time, and I, for reasons which I have already suggested and which I would like to amplify, but cannot without making serious allegations against someone else, was fighting with one hand, metaphorically speaking, tied behind my back. Just as I ultimately completely turned the tables on Colonel Custance by my publication of my "Postscript" to *Eve and the Serpent*, and also by my answers in cross-examination and victory in *The Evening News* case; so I completely turned the tables, I will not say on Mr Ransome, because I have already explained that I do not regard him as more than a figurehead or stalking-horse for Ross in the action which he defended against me, but on Robert Ross, when I justified all my terrible charges against him at the Old Bailey in 1914.

To sum it all up and to get back to what I was saying, before I got off into details of my various cases, it is not true that I am a man who is "always libelling people." What is true is that I am a man who is always being libelled. I have dealt with the only two cases in which I was accused of libelling a man, that of

Colonel Custance and that of Mr Winston Churchill, and I have shown that one of those cases must go by the board considered as anything against me in that respect. That leaves one case in which I have been proved legally to have libelled a man, and that one case certainly does not give anyone the right to say that I am a confirmed libeller or that I delight in libel for libel's sake. Even my worst enemy must admit that I had nothing to gain by libelling Winston Churchill. It has never been suggested that I had the slightest ill-feeling against him, nor as a matter of fact did I ever have any such feeling against him, nor have I any such feeling even now. All I did was to write about him what I believed to be true, at great risk to myself, because I thought it was my duty to my country to do so. For doing that I was sent to prison, where I was nearly starved to death, and from which I emerged broken in health. It has taken me three years to get over the effects of my imprisonment, and even so I can say that I have never been, and am very unlikely ever again to be, as well and strong as I was before it took place.

On the other hand, and to the credit side of the account, it is to be remembered that I wrote what I consider to be my finest poem, *In Excelsis*, in the prison hospital. "So find we profit by losing of our prayers," and also by losing of our law-suits—sometimes.

CHAPTER XXXVII

A YEAR after I sold *The Academy* I became a Catholic. During the time I was editing *The Academy* I was a High Church Anglican, and I ran the paper from that point of view, as far as religion was concerned.

From the time I went up to Oxford right up to the time when I became editor of *The Academy*, a period of about seventeen to eighteen years, I had really no religion. I was what most Englishmen actually are, whether they admit it or not, a pagan. (I am not exaggerating. I saw the other day a table of statistics which gave the number of people in England—outside the Church of Rome—who went to church on Easter Sunday last year as seven per cent. of the whole population.)

Soon after I started editing *The Academy* I began to get contributions from Mr Arthur Machen. It was these contributions of his which first sent me back to Christianity. I gave Mr Machen a perfectly wonderful show in *The Academy*. I printed columns from him week after week. I even reproduced in the paper, in weekly instalments, a whole book of his, called *The Views and Opinions of the Revd. Dr Stiggins*, a fiercely ironical attack on Protestantism, and paid him for it (or rather Sir Edward Tennant paid him) at the full rates on the highest scale for contributors. Mr Arthur Machen's way of showing his gratitude for what I did so successfully to bring his name before the public was to write the " obituary notice " of me in *The Evening News* when that journal published a false report of my death in 1921.

What changed me from High Anglicanism to Catholicism was simply that reading history, and finding out all the lies that had been taught to me as truth at school and at Oxford, convinced me that the High Anglican position, however attractive it may be, does not hold water. The theory that the Church of England is a " branch of the Catholic Church," and that the continuity was never broken at the Reformation, seems to me to be demonstrably false. I held it for a long time, and abandoned it, reluctantly, only because the evidence was too strong for me. What finally converted me to Catholicism, though I did not actually become a Catholic till more than a year after I read it, was Pope Pius X.'s *Encyclical Against Modernism.*

This stately and magnificent piece of argument was, I suppose, sent round to the papers for notice. At any rate, a copy of it was sent to *The Academy.* The original is, of course, written in Latin, but the copy I got was an English translation. I thought of sending it out for review, but picking it up and reading a few lines I became interested, and took it home to read myself. It had the effect of convincing me that the Catholic Church, in communion with the See of Peter in Rome, is the only true Church. I definitely made up my mind to become a Catholic, but I put it off chiefly because, as appears from what I have just written, my conversion had come entirely through the intellect. I felt no emotion about it. On the contrary, I felt in some ways that to become a Catholic would be a tiresome necessity. I would have avoided it if I could. " At any rate," I thought, " there is no particular hurry."

The emotional side of Catholicism did not reach me till some time after I had been in the Church. When I first joined it I was cold about it. The ritual, although I always liked it and thought it beautiful, did not influence me in the very slightest degree, nor has it ever done so to this day. When I had been a Catholic for about eighteen months I underwent the most violent persecution, which lasted, on and off, for at least ten years. The result of this persecution was to force me deeper and deeper into my religion. For years it was my only support and consolation

in a succession of almost unbearable miseries. Instead of being
cold I became very devout and mystical. I lived on reading *The
Lives of the Saints,* and such mystics as St Teresa and St John
of the Cross. I got to the stage of glorying in the persecution
I was undergoing, and regarding it as a special sign of grace,
which, of course, it undoubtedly was. I even had supernatural
experiences, but I cannot speak of them in this book, except
in one instance which I will refer to later on though I am not
definitely sure that it was really supernatural.

It is with deep regret that I say that I am now less devoutly
religious than I was during those years. I have never, as far as
I know, fallen out of a state of grace, and I am just as determined
to live and die a Catholic as I ever was. But the wonderful
feelings I used to have have gone. So have the supernatural
experiences; and though a priest in confession told me that this
was simply because I no longer needed them, and that it was
greater merit for me to go on simply being a good Catholic
without them, I believe in my heart that this is not really what
has happened. The fact is that, at the time I am speaking of,
I intended to become a saint, which was a perfectly laudable
ambition at any rate, however hopeless it may have been. Now
I do not want to be a saint, I am afraid. When one considers
this, it is enough to make one shed tears of blood, but that is the
plain truth. Perhaps I shall change again. Meanwhile I have
become, I fear, much more worldly than I was during those
terrible years when I was, apparently, "hated of all men," and
persecuted and even cast into prison more than once.

The persecution began with the attack on me in Ransome's
book inspired by Robert Ross. I have already dealt with this
case, and I do not want to become tedious to my readers by
going into details of all my various actions at law. My quarrel
with Ross began about two years before Mr Ransome's book,
Oscar Wilde, a Critical Study, appeared. All that happened was

that I made up my mind, after various incidents and in view of information I had, that I did not want to go on knowing Ross, and that I did not choose that he should come to my house and associate with my wife. My reasons for this were that I had grown far less tolerant than I had been before my marriage, and even for some years later, of the sort of things which Ross boasted publicly of doing. I did not want to have any open quarrel with Ross, but I wanted to drop him.

However, he refused to accept this. I had given orders to my servants at my house, 26 Church Row, Hampstead (a beautiful Queen Anne house which belonged to Eton, my landlords being the Provost and Fellows), that if Ross called we were always to be "not at home." Ross came once or twice, and was not received. He thereupon wrote to my wife and demanded the reason why he was refused access to our house. My wife gave me his letter, in which I detected an undercurrent of insolence and menace. I was very angry that he had written to her. If he wanted to write at all I thought he should have written to me. I wrote back and told him, in a letter which I have no doubt is still preserved (or was, at any rate, as long as he was alive), that, as he insisted upon forcing me to tell him why I did not wish to keep up my acquaintance with him, I would tell him that it was " because I no longer care to associate with persons like yourself who are engaged in the active performance and propaganda of every kind of wickedness, from Socialism to Sodomy."

Ross made no reply, but I heard from various sources that his rage was extreme, and that he stated openly that he was going to "get even " with me. I treated these threats with utter contempt, rashly as it appears, for it is always a mistake to undervalue one's enemy—as Ross himself was to find out before the end came. I had not the slightest idea that Ross had a quantity of my old letters to Oscar Wilde, nor if I had known it would it have made the slightest difference in my conduct, and, badly as I thought of Ross, it never occurred to me for a moment at that time that he was capable of such villainy as he actually put into practice. I also, obviously, knew nothing whatever about the "unpublished part" of *De Profundis*. When I read Ransome's book I immediately determined to take proceedings. My wife, as she reminded me only a short time ago, was strongly against my taking proceedings. She and I will never agree about what happened and the attitude she took then or when she left me (not on account of anything connected with Ross or Oscar Wilde, but as the result of my attack on her father, which yet, I must say, was made at least as much on her account as on my own). All I wish to say here is that although her leaving me just before the Ransome action was a frightful blow to me, and really took all the heart out of me, and caused me to throw up the sponge when her father prosecuted me for libel at the Old Bailey, I entirely exonerate her and acquit her of any intention or desire other than to do what she thought was right in a very difficult situation. Although at the time I felt exceedingly bitter about it, what has happened since has proved that she never really turned against me in her heart.

Those who still think that I made a mistake in taking proceedings against Mr Ransome, and that all would have been well if I had simply ignored the libel in his book, which most people would not have noticed as it did not mention me by name, ignore the whole nature of the attack on me and what was behind it. If I had ignored the libel it would simply have been repeated more boldly and more openly as time went on. Everything that happened in my life after the Ransome case followed logically and inevitably from that case, including the ultimate smash-up of Ross. The Ransome case (though of course I did not know it at the time) was simply the first battle in a campaign in which, in the long run, I ended by driving all my

enemies out of the field. It was losing the Ransome case that
made me take the fearful risk of publicly and persistently libelling
Ross till I forced him into the open to prosecute me. Looked
at in the proper light the ultimate result of the Ransome case,
with all its apparently deadly knock-out blow to me, was that I
afterwards smashed Ross, defeated *The Evening News*, and put
Colonel Custance and Sir George Lewis out of action. (Sir
George Lewis's firm, Lewis & Lewis, were the solicitors against
me in all four cases mentioned.) Omelettes cannot be made
without breaking eggs. I had to go through the humiliation, and
the chastening and hardening effect of losing the Ransome case,
before I was turned into the tempered steel which was more
than a match for all this formidable group of enemies, even
hampered as I was by extreme poverty, in a fight against
unlimited money. In short, if I had not sued Ransome for libel
I might as well have committed suicide, as far as any prospects
in this world are concerned.

CHAPTER XXXVIII

JUST before the Ransome case came on the feud between my father-in-law, Colonel Custance, and myself came to a head. After my marriage I became quite friendly with him for a time. I used to go down to stay with him, generally accompanied by my wife, but on at least two occasions I stayed with him for ten days when he was alone in the house, after the death of Mrs Custance, with whom I was, on the whole, on quite good terms. On the occasions when I stayed alone with Colonel Custance we got on exceedingly well. It is pleasant to recall that at that time he was exceedingly kind to me. We shot and fished together, and our relations were almost affectionate.

The chief trouble between us arose because he would insist on trying to take my son away from me. He offered to pay for the boy's schooling, and of course I was only too glad to accept. In return I was pleased that the boy should go to his grandfather very frequently and for long periods at a time. But Custance was not content with this ; what he wanted to do was to get the boy altogether, and to induce me and his mother to relinquish our parental claims and rights. This I always declined to do. I was also very indignant with him because of what I considered to be his very odious treatment of and attitude towards his daughter. He was always what can only be described as " bullying " her, and she used to complain bitterly to me about him. This incensed me against him very much.

When I became a Catholic and made my son one the situation immediately became worse. Colonel Custance was very anti-Catholic, although (or perhaps, more correctly, just because) his only sister, Mrs Garnett, had married a Catholic and become one herself.   Although he " made a virtue of necessity " and declared that he had no intention of interfering with my son's religion, he was not perfectly honest about it.   He even threatened to leave money to my son on condition that he renounced Catholicism.   This threat he never carried out, but he made it, and the letter of remonstrance I wrote to him on the subject is still in the hands of his solicitors, Lewis & Lewis. Lewis & Lewis were never his solicitors until he started his libel suit against me.   The fact that he chose these solicitors, of all others, who were Ross's solicitors and acting for Ransome, added greatly to my feeling against him, for I felt that he was making common cause with my enemies, even though he declared that his choice of solicitors was quite uninfluenced by their connection with Ross and Ransome and was simply a " coincidence."

It may have been a coincidence, but, if so, it was a very unfortunate one.   To cut a long story short, after innumerable disputes about the boy, and after innumerable " rows " between us, caused by his behaviour to my wife, the climax was reached when a resettlement of his property was made on my son.   Olive was his heir, the property was tied up on her by her grandfather, Sir Hambledon Custance, Colonel Custance had no power to dispossess her.   But she voluntarily surrendered her rights and allowed the entail to be cut in consideration of his undertaking to give her the very modest income of £600 a year during his lifetime, and a life-interest of the whole property at his death, with remainder to her son.   The settlement was made, and signed by my wife, but Colonel Custance refused to sign any legal undertaking about the £600 a year, saying that his " word was good enough."   I strongly urged my wife not to sign the settlement without obtaining his signature to the undertaking to provide her with £600 a year.   However, she signed, being, as I consider, very badly advised and served by the solicitors who drew up the settlement and who ought never to have allowed her to sign without obtaining Colonel Custance's adherence to a binding legal agreement about the £600 a year.

No sooner was the settlement signed than Colonel Custance did exactly what I had warned my wife's solicitors that he would do. He wrote to my wife and said that unless the boy was handed over to him he would not pay her " allowance." My reply to this was immediately to remove the boy from the school where Custance had placed him, and to take him to my mother's house.

There can be no question about what Colonel Custance did. I have in my possession the letter he wrote to my wife, saying " the moment he takes the boy away all payments to you will cease." I wrote to him, pointing out that to stop payment of the income which was the " consideration " which had induced my wife to abandon her rights as heir in tail of the property was neither more nor less than fraudulent, and that if he carried out his threat he would in fact be committing a fraudulent, as well as a disgraceful and dishonourable, action.

Some time before this he had informed me that any letter I wrote to him would be " thrown unopened into the back of the fire." So, as I was now determined to force the issue, if necessary, into the courts, I wrote to him on a postcard, on which I said : " As you refuse to read my letters I am obliged to write to you on a postcard." I then went on as quoted above. People who profess to be horrified and scandalized at the " ungentlemanly " device of sending postcards containing private or controversial matter ignore the fact that if a man will not read your sealed letters the only possible way you can force him to read what you are determined that he should read is by sending him a postcard or a telegram. I did both. He thereupon went to Sir George Lewis, who was not only Ross's solicitor but one of his most intimate friends.

Lewis advised him to take criminal proceedings against me, and a summons was issued. I thus had the two cases on at the same time and my mind was much distracted between them. While the proceedings were pending, Custance and Lewis started other proceedings against me in the Chancery Court with a view to getting my son away from me. In the middle of all this my wife left my house and went to her father while I was away with my son in the country staying at a house called Hinton St Mary, with my mother and sister. When I got back to London she had gone.

I have already explained what happened, and how I allowed the Custance case to go against me practically by default, for I might as well have pleaded guilty once I was persuaded to refrain from putting in a plea of justification. Mr Comyns Carr, K.C., who was my counsel in the cases when I beat Ross and *The Evening News*, as well as in several other cases where I was successful, told me years later that I had an overwhelming justification for my libel on Custance, and that if I had pleaded justification I could not have failed to get a verdict. The production of Colonel Custance's letter, which I have quoted above, would have been alone sufficient to settle the case in my favour.

The fact of the matter is, and there is nothing to be gained by denying it, that I was " knocked out " by the loss of the Ransome case, the Chancery proceedings, and the defection of my wife. If I had been myself I would never have " climbed down " as I did, even though my then solicitor (whose name I will not mention, for he was a most charming man, and was perfectly loyal to me, as well as being most kind and considerate) wrongly advised me not to plead justification. That is, however, no excuse for me, for I have always made a habit in all my law cases of absolutely ignoring the advice of my solicitors whenever my own considered judgment differed from theirs. I have, therefore, nobody but myself to blame for what happened. I console myself by thinking that it was meant to happen. Providence does not " let down " anyone who is trusting in it, but it does not often allow that person to win great victories except at the cost of preliminary defeats and much tribulation.

After I had lost the Ransome case, and had been convicted and " bound over to come up for judgment if called on " at the Old Bailey in respect of my libel on Custance, my situation was fairly miserable. I was left alone in my dismantled and deserted home. I had been forced into bankruptcy, not directly for the costs in the Ransome case, which I was ordered to pay and which amounted to about £1500, but really in anticipation of that event. What actually happened was that I borrowed from moneylenders, and that they refused to give me time to pay, as I had often done before, and I was forced to allow a receiving order to be made against me. This was just before the Ransome case came on.

When I became bankrupt I was automatically compelled to relinquish membership of White's Club, to which I had belonged for more than twenty years. My sponsors at White's had been my uncle, Percy Wyndham, and the late Sir Reginald Graham of Norton Conyers. There is a rule of the club that anyone against whom a receiving order is made ceases, *de facto*, to be a member, but that he may be readmitted without ballot if he can show that no blame attaches to him financially, and that there is no suggestion of fraud or dishonesty. This precisely covers my case. I was told by the official who examined me in bankruptcy that no blame whatever attached to me, that my bankruptcy was a pure misfortune, and that I could get my discharge without the slightest difficulty. I was not even condemned as having been " unjustifiably extravagant." I have never made any move towards re-election at White's, chiefly because certain members of my family are on the committee of this club, the oldest club in London, which for many years was the personal property of my friend and cousin, the late Algie Bourke. My view was, and is, that if the persons who control the club had not sufficient good feeling to do something about it, I certainly did not intend to give them the opportunity of further indulgence in the favourite English sport of kicking a man when he is down. I have determined that I will never apply for my discharge in bankruptcy any more than I will ask my relatives in White's Club to put into force the spirit of the rules which govern their own select establishment.

Leaving out my beloved mother, the only person in my own sphere who showed me real kindness at this dismal moment of my life was George Wyndham. He went out of his way to be kind to me, and to associate himself with me publicly by asking me several times to stay at his country house, Clouds, and his death, which occurred shortly afterwards, deprived me of the only powerful friend I had.

It was at this period that I carried on for a short time (after refusing to succumb for many weeks) the *liaison* with the beautiful girl to whom I referred earlier in this book, who came and almost literally forced her way into my deserted house in Church Row the very day before I was due to go to the Old Bailey to be tried (and, as was a foregone conclusion, convicted) for libelling my father-in-law. Her name was D—— E——, and she arrived with a pearl necklace and other jewels, which she wanted me to take and sell to raise money for my defence and to carry me on. Needless to say I did not take what she offered, but I was inexpressibly touched and grateful. She came down to the court and welcomed me when I got safely out. Colonel Custance's advocate, Sir Richard Muir, acting on his client's instructions, implored the judge (the Recorder, Sir Forest Fulton) to send me to prison and to give me the "most severe sentence possible," but these amiable hopes on the part of the gallant Colonel were doomed to disappointment. The Recorder merely bound me over, and indeed, if I had but known it, I need not have been under any serious apprehension, for it is very unusual to send a man to prison for libel, and although I had not pleaded justification my defence (conducted by my old and loyal friend, Cecil Hayes) disclosed enough of the facts to give the recorder a pretty good idea that I was not quite the hardened ruffian which Colonel Custance, with the assistance of Lewis & Lewis and Muir, tried to make me out.

Referring to the way I was paralysed on this occasion I have noticed that the same principle is in action in the case of persons who play "systems" at Monte Carlo. There are a dozen systems which, if ruthlessly played out, with enough capital, will almost certainly beat the bank. The trouble is to find a man with a sufficiently iron nerve to play them. What almost invariably happens is, not that the system breaks down, but that the man who is playing it gets to a point in the game, after a big run against him, where he "throws up the sponge." I have known this to happen over and over again ; not in my own case, for the only time I ever played a system (at Ostend, in 1903) I went right through with it and won £350, starting with £50. The strain, however, was so great, especially as I had inadequate capital, that I have never done it again.

What beat me at the Custance libel prosecution at the Old Bailey was simply that my nerve went and that I was demoralized. My system (*le système Douglas*) was perfectly sound, and would have worked out almost automatically if I had allowed it to have a chance. But I "funked." Half the cases that are lost in the law courts fail for the same reason. Lawyers will always try to persuade a man to compromise. In fact, my experience is that, in order to win a case in the law courts, you have first of all to win a preliminary fight

R

with your solicitor and counsel. If you win that, you may then have a good chance to win the case itself. The one utterly fatal thing is to "leave yourself entirely in the hands of your legal advisers." This is just what I did when I threw away my chances in the Custance libel case.

CHAPTER XXXIX

I LOOK back with no satisfaction to what happened directly after my loss of the two cases referred to in the last chapter. I practically lived with D—— E—— for about three or four months. I saw her daily first for about a month, and went about with her in a perfectly innocent way ; I explained to her that, being a Catholic, I could not consent to lead an immoral life. In the end, however, I deeply regret to have to admit that I succumbed. I got hold of a certain amount of money by selling the books and letters of Wilde and in advance royalties on the book (English and American rights), *Oscar Wilde and Myself.* This enabled me to go on living at my partially furnished house in Church Row, Hampstead, to carry on the fight in Chancery about my son, and also to take D—— about all over the place in London to restaurants and similar resorts. I did this partly out of bravado and as a demonstration against my enemies, and against my wife, whom at that time I never expected to see or speak to again. I had burnt all her photographs and everything else in the house that might remind me of her. Her father and George Lewis had me followed continually by detectives. D—— and I used to see them waiting outside my house or her flat, and laugh at them. Colonel Custance and Lewis moved heaven and earth to induce Olive to start divorce proceedings against me. But this she absolutely refused to do, and when they tried to put pressure on her, her will power reasserted itself and she turned on them with such vehemence that she scared them right off their unholy projects.

Less than four months after our separation Olive rang me up

one day on the telephone. I answered, not knowing who it was. She begged me to come to see her. The sound of her voice on the telephone completely finished me, and I went straight off to see her and we " made it up." This of course caused a breach with D——, and my irregular life came to an end for ever. This was in 1913. Although my wife and I have never lived together again, we are the best of friends. I often go to stay with her and we keep up a constant correspondence. My reconciliation with Olive was a nasty knock for Custance, and also for George Lewis, who by this time had taken up the campaign against me in a personal and most vindictive way. This campaign he carried on for years. He had already appeared against me in the Ransome case and the Custance libel. In the years that followed he appeared against me again and again ; firstly on behalf of Ross, when he got an injunction from Mr Justice Astbury by which I was restrained from quoting in my book any of Wilde's letters or any part of the unpublished *De Profundis* in my own defence. Lewis also appeared, of course, as the solicitor for Custance on the numerous occasions when the case of the custody of my son came before Mr Justice Eve and afterwards Mr Justice Peterson in the Chancery Court (see *Eve and the Serpent*). He then, at the end of 1914, appeared against me at the Old Bailey when I prosecuted Ross, and again when I sued *The Evening News* in 1922. *The Evening News* case was his Waterloo as far as I was concerned. But the publication, in 1926, of my *Collected Satires*, which contained several scathing poems in which I mercilessly attacked him and held him up, in the legal phrase, " to contempt and ridicule," served to remind him that I was still alive and kicking. He died a few months ago, and poor Colonel Custance has been dead for two years. I regret very much that it was not possible for me to have a reconciliation with the latter. I long since ceased to have any ill-feeling against him, and when he was in his last illness I told my wife that I would like to be reconciled with him. However, he remained implacable, though from what he said just before he died I believe that he recognized that he had done wrong in the line of conduct he had followed in regard to my son, to whom he was devoted, but who, in the end, found out all the real truth about how I, his father, had been treated, and who, of his own accord, wrote to me and asked me to forgive him for what, as a child of fourteen, and poisoned by lies and misrepresentations about me, he had done himself. Needless to say I forgave him. I also wish to put it on record that I forgive George Lewis, and it is a fact that for at least twelve years I prayed for him and Colonel Custance by name as my greatest enemies, every day of my life.

I do not want to go in detail into all the struggle over my son. It would be impossible for me to tell the whole story without appearing to blame my wife, and that I decline to do. I will say, however, that I was never deprived of the custody of my son. The judge (Eve) made a point of this, and seemed to think that I ought to be very grateful for it. But as he ordered that I was to pay all the costs of the boy's schooling, and that during his holidays he was to spend two-fifths of the time with me and three-fifths of the time with his grandfather, and as moreover I had done nothing at all to make me unfit to have the complete custody of my own son (especially considering that all the time he was with me was invariably spent in my mother's house), I could not but think then, as I think now, that I was treated with the most monstrous cruelty and injustice.

In the end I got so exasperated by the odious necessity of having to send my son for the greater part of his holidays to Colonel Custance that I took him out of the jurisdiction, into Scotland, where I could defy the English Chancery Courts, being a Scotsman and the son of a Scottish peer. I went to Fort Augustus with the boy, took a house there, arranged with the Right Rev. Sir David Hunter Blair, Abbot of Fort Augustus, that my boy should be educated by the monks, and wrote to the judge informing him of what I had done, and that I had no intention of sending the boy again to Colonel Custance, and that I should remain with him in Scotland indefinitely. This of course was what is called " contempt of court." It was brought up against me, by the way, at the hearing of my libel action against *The Evening News* when I got £1000 damages.   The then Mr Douglas Hogg asked me in the witness-box whether I had not committed " gross contempt of court." I replied : " Yes, I committed contempt of court, just as all the apostles did. St Paul, for example, committed contempt of court over and over again."

Mr Hogg said : " You don't compare yourself with St Paul, do you ? " To which I replied : " Well, I don't see why I shouldn't." This reply was received with " loud laughter, in which the judge joined," but I went on to add : " We are told to imitate Christ, so I suppose we are at least equally entitled to imitate St Paul "—and Hogg had nothing more to say on that point.

The English Chancery Courts have (God be thanked !) no jurisdiction in Scotland.   As long as I remained in Scotland nobody could interfere with me in any legal way.   However, illegality has never been any bar to the late Sir George Lewis. Acting on the instructions of Colonel Custance he sent a private detective to the hotel in Fort Augustus where I was staying up till just before the date fixed for my removal into the house I had taken. This man got hold of my little boy while he was out fishing by himself, and carried him off in a car into England. When the boy disappeared we——that is to say, the monks at the Abbey and myself——were all in a state of the utmost consternation and anxiety, thinking that he had been drowned in the loch. For two days I was left in ignorance of what had happened.   It did not occur, apparently, to Lewis & Lewis or Custance that it would be only decent to let me know that the boy was safe and well. I heard nothing at all, and passed two days of agony before I got a telegram from my wife telling me that the boy was at Weston, her father's place in Norfolk.

Just before the kidnapping (a criminal offence in Scotland) took place my wife had agreed to come up to Scotland to join me and the boy. So if the kidnapping had been delayed only a few days we would all three—father, mother and child—have been living together again in the same house. I went to the police and applied for a warrant for Custance for kidnapping my son. I was referred to the Lord Advocate, who corresponds to the Public Prosecutor in England. After many weeks' delay, during which my mother joined me in Edinburgh, I was refused a warrant. The Lord Advocate at that time was Mr Munro-Ferguson, a friend of Mr Asquith.

Colonel Custance for his part, not content with having got my son away from me, went with Sir George Lewis to the Chancery Court and implored Mr Justice Eve to commit me to prison for contempt of court. This however Eve declined to do. He would not have looked very pretty if he had done it, and by this time he had had enough of me and my affairs, and discreetly retired from the case and handed it over to Mr Justice Peterson. Poor Custance somehow never had any luck in his attempts to get me locked up. He tried three times but never brought it off !

When I came up before Mr Justice Peterson he offered to give me back the boy on the same terms as before (two-fifths of his holidays with me and three-fifths with Custance), but as I now discovered that the boy had been privy to the " kidnapping," that he had been secretly corresponding with Custance, and that he had left me of his own accord, I told the judge that I would have nothing more to do with him and that I washed my hands of him. I did not see him again for nearly ten years.

In this attitude I was supported by my mother, who shared my indignation at the way I was treated. I was at that time intensely devoted to my son. His loss, and the horrible circumstances of it, completed my sense of the cruelty and injustice of the world. I gave up all idea of happiness in this life, and clung to Catholicism as my only consolation, in spite of the fact that I was very badly treated at that time by most of the Catholics with whom I had dealings, including the monks of the Ampleforth Benedictine School, where I had placed my son. The monks had supported me all through my fight for the custody of the boy, but when I definitely renounced the boy they made terms behind my back with Custance and Lewis. I wrote a sonnet about this which appears in my *Collected Poems*. The end of the whole story is what I have already related—namely, that my son, when he was of age and his own master, wrote and asked my forgiveness, which I of course gave him. Since then we have been on terms of the deepest affection. This action of my son was a bitter blow to Colonel Custance, and he did not long survive it.

CHAPTER XL

To go back to the period I had reached at the beginning of the last chapter, a few months after the Ransome action. My reconciliation with Olive was not really permanent or complete. After the first emotion of making friends with her again, I did not see much of her. I got rid of my Hampstead house and went to live with my mother, in the early part of 1914, at a small house she had taken for a few months in Chelsea. Previously to this, and right up to the time when, as I shall presently describe, I left England to avoid being "called up for judgment" for having (as was alleged) broken my recognizances by "repeating" my libel on Colonel Custance, I had been, with Crosland's assistance, doing all I could to bring Ross to book. Accidentally, and through a paragraph I saw in a Sunday paper, I got to hear of a sixteen-year-old boy, named Garret, who was then in prison, and who had at his trial called in his defence to speak for him a certain great friend and associate of Ross. I got permission from the Home Office to send a solicitor to see this boy in prison. The solicitor saw the boy, in the presence of a warder, and the boy made a statement more or less incriminating Ross, whom he declared he knew well. The boy declined to go into details, but said that if the solicitor would meet him, or send someone to meet him, at the prison gates on his release he would tell him everything.

This was done : the boy was met, and he made a statement incriminating Ross. I took the boy to Scotland Yard, and he repeated the statement (I not being present) to the police inspector, who took down what he said. The boy signed the statement. The police, however, after several days had elapsed, declined to take any action. I sent Crosland down to see the boy's mother in the country. In the end she came up and swore an information, and went, accompanied by my solicitor and with the boy, to apply before a magistrate for a warrant against Ross. The magistrate's clerk, however, told her to come again later in the day. She went away, and meanwhile the boy ran away and disappeared. I may say that this charge against Ross formed part of my plea of justification when I justified my charges against him later on in the same year.

Contemporaneously with this, and in pursuance of my determination to force Ross into the courts to prosecute me, and give me the opportunity of proving my charges against him, I wrote to various friends of his, including the then Prime Minister, Mr Asquith (Lord Oxford), making charges against him.

At the same time I wrote to Custance a letter in which I remonstrated with him on the attitude he had taken up towards my marriage, and the separation between my wife and myself, which I attributed to him. Custance took my letter to George Lewis, who immediately declared that by writing this letter I had broken my recognizances, and that an application should be made to the Recorder who had tried the case, and bound me over, to call me up " to show cause why I should not be committed to prison."

A summons was served on me. I saw in a flash the trap I was in. If the Recorder sent me to prison for six months, as I took it for granted (quite mistakenly) that he was certain to do, I was done for ever. For as soon as I was in prison Lewis would apply for a warrant against me for criminal libel on Ross, and, being in prison, it would be impossible for me to get the evidence required to defend myself and justify my charges. I accordingly took what looks on the face of it like the fatal step of clearing out of the country, and going to Boulogne.

Yet if I had not done this, so wonderful are the ways of Providence, I would never have settled Ross. If I had gone up before the Recorder it is extremely unlikely that he would have held that my letter to Custance constituted a breach of my recognizances. In fact, it did nothing of the kind, for it did not repeat the libel, or so much as refer to it, and had reference to something quite different. In any case, even if the Recorder had held that what I had done amounted to a breach of my recognizances, he certainly would not have sent me to prison, for he did not do so a few months later when I *had* repeated the " libel " on Custance, and added others. Supposing that I had gone up before the Recorder, nothing would have happened to me beyond, at the worst, a lecture and a warning to be careful. But (and this is the wonderful part of the story) if I had not run away, and gone to Boulogne, Ross would never have prosecuted me at the Old Bailey eight months later. As long as I was in the country he would never have dared to " go for " me. It was precisely because he thought that I had gone away and would never come back, or at any rate not for years, that he went with Lewis to a magistrate and applied for, and obtained, two warrants for my arrest, as I shall presently describe.

I fled from London on the 4th of March, the anniversary of my wedding day, and went to Boulogne, where I found Dick Luckman and his second wife and child staying at an hotel. I went to their hotel and remained in Boulogne till about two months after the war broke out.

While I was at Boulogne, Crosland came over to see me several times, and stayed as my guest at my hotel. One day dear little D—— E—— came with him, and spent two hours with me, and that was the last time I saw her, for immediately afterwards she went back to her native country, the United States (she came from San Francisco). She wrote to me from there about a year later, and begged me to come over to America. She told me she had now got " plenty of money." Fond as I was of her I was determined, for religious reasons, that nothing would induce me to see her any more. I thought it best not to answer her letter.

Crosland and I carried on the campaign against Ross and Custance from Boulogne. I had several hundred copies printed of two *Letters to my Father-in-law*, which I circulated in England. They both contained references to Ross, and were used as part of Ross's indictment of me later at the Old Bailey. Then one day Crosland went back to London, after spending a couple of days with me, and was arrested, and charged with " conspiring with Lord Alfred Douglas to bring a false charge " against Robert Ross in respect of the boy Garret.

The history of Crosland's trial, which lasted for eight days at the Old Bailey, belongs more properly to his biography than to mine. My old and valued friend, Mr Sorley Brown (who for years has fought my battles in his splendid paper *The Border Standard*), has just published a *Life of Crosland*, and I refer those who wish to read about this sensational case to that volume. Crosland was defended by Cecil Hayes, and the leading counsel against him was F. E. Smith, now Lord Birkenhead. The trial ended in the complete discomfiture of Ross and the triumphant acquittal of Crosland. As it was a case of conspiracy, I was also included in the charge, and if I had been in England I too would have been arrested and charged with Crosland.

As soon as I heard that Crosland had been arrested and released on bail (his surety being my cousin, Sholto Johnstone Douglas, the portrait painter, son of Arthur Johnstone Douglas of Comlongan Castle, Dumfriesshire, owner of " Old Joe," who won the Grand National in 1886, as I have already described in the first chapter of this book), I determined to return to England and stand my trial with Crosland. However, Crosland telegraphed to me not to come till he had seen me. He was out on bail, and asked the police if they had any objection to his going over to Boulogne to see me. The police raised no objection at all, which seems rather queer, but I think the explanation was that Ross and Sir George Lewis would have been only too pleased if Crosland had " skipped his bail," and allowed the case to go against him by default. Crosland came over to me and strongly urged me not to come back to England till his trial was over. We both felt perfectly confident that he must be acquitted, and that such acquittal would be a severe knock-out for Ross, and the enemy generally. The situation was that, if I came back, I would immediately be arrested on Ross's " Conspiracy " warrant, and would then, of course, be released on bail, but then, again, I would be rearrested on the Recorder's " Bench Warrant," which had been issued directly I left England. Then, supposing the Recorder sent me to prison (as I thought, quite mistakenly, that he was certain to do), I should be in a very awkward position with the other trial to face.

Consequently we agreed that it would be better policy to stay where I was and await the issue of Crosland's trial. We carried out this plan. Crosland came over to Boulogne and spent every week-end with me, and when his acquittal took place it of course carried mine with it. So there was the end of that.

At this time, before Crosland's acquittal, I actually had no less than three warrants out for my arrest in London! I knew of only two, the Recorder's " Bench Warrant " and Ross's warrant for " conspiring with Crosland to bring a false charge " against him (really, of course, the charge was perfectly true, as was subsequently established). But, in addition to these two warrants, Ross had also taken out a warrant against me for criminal libel. I knew nothing of this till I came back to England two or three months later.

Crosland was in great form in the witness-box in his case. I remember particularly one witty remark he made. In reply to a question from Mr F. E. Smith, he said something about the jury. Whereupon Mr Smith said : " Oh, never mind the jury, the jury can take care of themselves." Crosland replied : " Yes, but I want them to take care of me " ; which was received with great laughter. It is the healthiest thing in the world if you can get the judge and jury laughing at your replies in the witness-box, and nothing is so disconcerting to counsel opposed to you. Of course I don't mean that one should " try to be funny," nothing could be more fatal ; but if an answer comes out quickly and naturally, and happens to raise genuine laughter, it is a very good sign, especially in a criminal case ; juries don't laugh at a man's remarks if they are going to convict him. Crosland proved himself to be more than a match for the " deadly cross-examination " of F. E. Smith, and indeed he succeeded in making Smith look rather foolish several times. Smith endeavoured to " get his own back " by a very virulent closing speech to the jury, in which he attacked me in the most savage manner. I was not there to answer back, but I promptly replied by writing and getting a thousand copies printed and circulated of a lampoon called " The Rhyme of F. double E," which may be read in my *Collected Satires.*

During the time when Crosland was out on bail, and from the moment when he was arrested, my dear mother, at my request, supplied him with ample funds. Cecil Hayes defended him for nothing (or I suppose I ought to say for a nominal fee, for I believe he had five guineas marked on his brief, in contrast to F. E. Smith's five hundred guineas and " refreshers " which ran the whole amount up into thousands). Crosland also came over every week-end and stayed at my expense at Boulogne. I am obliged to mention all this because I afterwards discovered that Crosland (imitating the tactics of Oscar Wilde) went about telling everyone he met that neither I nor my family had given him sixpence at this time. My mother, as a matter of fact, gave him about £250, although at the time, with the war just starting, she was, like most other people, much embarrassed financially.

Just about this time my book, *Oscar Wilde and Myself*, which I had written with Crosland, giving him half the proceeds, came out. In the book there is next to nothing about Ross. The publishers prevented me from telling anything like the real truth about the part he had played, and in many other respects they interfered with the author in a way which was bound to injure the book. To " put the lid " on all this, the book actually appeared on the very day war was declared.

CHAPTER XLI

ABOUT two months after Crosland's acquittal (I think it was in October 1914) I returned to England. I saw that it was useless for me to stay any longer at Boulogne. When the war broke out I saw the Argyll and Sutherland Highlanders land at Boulogne. They were the first regiment to arrive. I was mad to go to the Front, and I wrote to Lord Kitchener, with whom I had a slight personal acquaintance (I had met him in Egypt when I was a boy staying with the Cromers, and again at lunch at Lady Henry Gordon-Lennox's, at Prince's Gate, when he had paid a lot of attention to me, and after lunch asked me to walk with him across the Park). I begged him to find something for me. I told him I spoke French like a Frenchman, and might be useful in that way. He replied at once, saying that he much regretted that he was unable to find anything for me at present. When you come to think of it, it was not very easy for him to give a commission to a man who had three warrants out for his arrest! But I was much disappointed. I saw our magnificent first army go off to the war, and alas! precious few came back as they went. I thought of joining the Foreign Legion, and wrote to my friend "Taffy Lewis." Colonel Lewis was a very distinguished soldier (at one time A.D.C. to King Edward) who used to review military books for me on *The Academy*, and who had been in Egypt for years, and just missed being Sirdar instead of Kitchener. Taffy wrote back enclosing me a letter of introduction to the Officer Commanding the Foreign Legion. He had been made an honorary member of their mess when he acted as war correspondent to *The Times* in Morocco. At the same time he strongly urged me not to join the Foreign Legion, and said it was a " mad idea," and that I would never stand the conditions. No doubt he was right, and anyhow, after a few days' war fever, I came to the conclusion that, as a preliminary to going to the war, I must first return to England and get rid of the Recorder's " Bench Warrant." I had no suspicion that Ross was going to prosecute me for criminal libel. After his crushing defeat at the hands of Crosland I thought he was finished, and I believe that no solicitor in the world, other than the late Sir George Lewis, would have advised him to take another chance at the Old Bailey.

If I had known that Ross was going to prosecute I would certainly have gone back just the same, for, obviously, I could not go on staying indefinitely in France, and I was longing for something to happen. In any case, I wrote to the Recorder, and told him I was coming back, and that I looked to him confidently to treat me fairly in view of the frightful provocation I had received from my father-in-law, who had smashed up my home and separated me from my wife. I also wrote to the police and told them that I would be on the boat arriving at Folkestone on the following day but one.

I must confess that my feelings on the boat, going across, were not very enviable. In fact they might be compared, greatly intensified, to those which animate the mind of a schoolboy who has been invited to step into the headmaster's study, with a view to assimilating what a young friend of mine the other day aptly described as " sixpennyworth of bend-over." I felt pretty sore (metaphorically, I mean) and very depressed. Crossing the Channel, as I had done a hundred times before, always with a certain amount of holiday feeling, seemed now a dismal business. If I had known what was in store for me I would have been even more gloomy. As it was I had a black feeling of impending trouble. I spent the whole time of my crossing saying my rosary. When the boat got in, the captain, who knew what was

s

to happen, politely asked me to go off first. A path was cleared for me, and I descended the landing stairs and was accosted by a nice-looking and smartly dressed detective in plain clothes. He carried my bag for me, and was most obliging. He said I could get my other luggage later on. I thought I was, of course, going on to London, but he said I was to go to the Folkestone Police Court to be charged. I did not in the least understand what he meant, as I thought I was being arrested on the Recorder's "Bench Warrant." But he told me I was arrested on a warrant granted on a sworn information to Robert Ross. Even then I did not understand. I thought that this was the old warrant for conspiring with Crosland to bring a "false charge," and that my arrest, as far as Ross was concerned, was a mere formality, and that I would perhaps be brought up before a judge and formally acquitted and discharged.

The detective drove me in a cab to the police station. I was locked in a cell, and told that I would be formally charged when the detective in charge of my case came down from London, which would not be before at least two or three hours. I was given some tea and bread-and-butter and a piece of cake, and left alone.

After two or three hours of waiting in the cell the door opened, and another Scotland Yard man came in. He said: " I will now read you the warrant, and must warn you that anything you say may be used against you." He then read the warrant, in which I was charged with " Falsely and maliciously publishing a defamatory libel on and about Robert Ross." I replied, when he had finished: " All right, I shall plead justification. Every word I have published about Ross is true, and will be proved up to the hilt."

I felt for the moment rather exhilarated, as I always do when the issue is definitely joined in any kind of fight. I found the detective quite friendly. He had already collected my luggage, and we went off in a cab to the station, where he bought two first-class tickets to London. He then offered me a whisky-and-soda, which I was very glad to get. He would not allow me to pay for anything. On the way up to London he opened my dispatch box and extracted a number of my letters, most of which had not the slightest bearing on the case at issue. I did not get these letters back till months afterwards, and after making an application in open court before a magistrate, asking for an order for their return.

When we got to London I was taken to the police station, I think it was the Marylebone Road, but am not quite sure—at any rate it was the police court at that time presided over by Mr Paul Taylor, before whom I appeared next morning. The police, as always, were exceedingly kind and friendly. They made me as comfortable as possible in the detention-room instead of locking me up in a cell. I was allowed to send out for dinner, and afterwards went to bed in the detention-room.

Next morning I was brought up before Mr Paul Taylor. I was represented by a solicitor whose name for the moment I forget. He appeared for me only on this occasion. He was very competent, and I think it was Crosland who had sent him along on my behalf. George Lewis appeared for Ross, and read out various extracts from my printed pamphlets and written letters, on which he asked the magistrate to commit me for trial. The magistrate asked me if I wished to say anything, and I said : " I plead justification." He said : " Very well ; of course you know that you cannot do that in this court, and I commit you for trial at the next sessions at the Central Criminal Court." I then applied for bail, and the magistrate said : " Oh, certainly, one surety in £500." My cousin Sholto was in court ready to go bail for me. At this point George Lewis rose and said to the magistrate : " You cannot let him out on bail, because there is a warrant against him from a superior court, issued by the Recorder, ordering him to come up for judgment in respect of charges of which he has been convicted in regard to another client of mine, for whom I also appear, Colonel Custance."

The magistrate then, with reluctance, and expressing his regret, declared that in that case it was not in his power to allow me out on bail, and I was sent off to Brixton Prison in a taxi. To this extent, therefore, Custance did at last succeed in getting me locked up, although it was only on remand, and for a few days.

When I got to the prison, and was shut up in a small cell on the ground floor, I must confess that my nerve failed. I suddenly realized for the first time that I really was right in the trap which George Lewis had laid for me. Here was I due to come up before the Recorder in a few days, certain, as I supposed, to be sent to prison by him, and thus placed in a position in which it would be utterly impossible to defend myself against Ross. So I took it that I was in for six months from the Recorder, and perhaps twelve or eighteen more on the top of that for libelling Ross. I realized, not for the first or last time, that it is very dangerous to tell the truth in England. I felt that I was " done," and the worst part of it all was that I would never be able to prove that I had told the truth about Ross, and he would be vindicated and whitewashed, and be able once more to pose as the pure, noble and disinterested friend of Oscar Wilde, in contrast to my depraved self !

I went through about two hours of mortal agony, during which I called on God, and reproached Him for deserting me.

Though it was a very cold evening, and my cell was far from warm, the sweat actually streamed down my face. At last I looked round in utter despair, and saw a New Testament, the only book in my cell. I snatched it up, and opened it and read these words :

" And when Herod would have brought him forth, the same night Peter was sleeping between two soldiers, bound with two chains : and the keepers before the door kept the prison.

" And, behold, the angel of the Lord came upon him, and a light shined in the prison : and he smote Peter on the side, and raised him up, saying, Arise up quickly. And his chains fell off from his hands," etc.

This struck me then, and strikes me now, as being a supernatural answer to my cry of despair and dereliction. Directly I read the words confidence returned to me. I did not see how I was going to get out of prison and defeat the frightful combination of deadly enemies in front of me, but I felt convinced that I would somehow be saved.

Just before my two hours' agony began I had seen the Catholic chaplain (not the one who is now at Brixton). I am glad to say that I have forgotten his name. He came to see me at my request, and asked me all sorts of vulgar and impertinent questions about my family ; why I had a title and so forth. I answered with what patience I could muster. He then asked me why I was in prison. I told him what had happened, and he said : " Can you prove what you have written about Ross ? " I said : " I do not know that I can, but I know that what I have said about him is true." He then said : " Well, in my opinion, you have acted simply out of spite, and you will deserve any punishment you get." To this I made no reply. I asked him if he would give me Holy Communion in the morning, and he said : " No, I cannot do that." He then went away. At the time I immediately recognized that this frightful experience was inevitable and complete. I said to myself, " Here begins my Passion," and then followed two hours when I was in a physical sweat of mental agony compared with which anything that I have suffered before or since was mere child's play.

Afterwards I remembered that during the last part of the

time I was in my half-empty home at Church Row I had one day bought, at some Catholic church, a little book called *The Holy Hour*. It described a form of devotion which consisted in offering oneself to suffer one hour with Christ in His agony and Passion. At the time I was very devout—as indeed I remained from that time on for many years—going to Mass and Holy Communion always every day, if it was possible to get to a church. The idea of this devotion fascinated and took hold of me, and I prayed hard that I might suffer with Christ, be betrayed by all my friends and those whom I loved (except my mother), and taste all the bitterness of His Passion.

This experience in Brixton Prison certainly was part of the answer to my prayer. After it was over I felt quite calm.

I stayed five days in Brixton, and was then taken first to the police court and then on to the Old Bailey. To my great joy and consolation, Olive turned up, and accompanied me to the Old Bailey. We drove across London holding hands, under the benevolent eye of a warder. Olive accompanied me to the corridor on the first floor, outside the courts, and while we were there together her father and Admiral Sir Reginald Custance suddenly appeared before us. When they saw her with me they were livid with rage, and Sir Reginald rated my wife in a loud voice and quite in the good old quarter-deck and grand old English gentleman (all of the olden time) style, bless him !

However, further bitter disappointments were in store for them, for the good old Recorder (may his soul rest in peace !) merely pretended to be very angry, snorted quite a lot in the most approved style, and spoke to me " with awful severity," exactly as if I were a little boy who had been caught stealing the jam. At the end of all this by-play, and after saying solemnly, " The question is now, what is to be done with you ? " he bound me over again with two sureties, to the disgust and indignation of the Custances and George Lewis.

I had already provided myself with two sureties, in anticipation of a possible miracle, my cousin Sholto and an Anglican parson, the Reverend James Mills, who came out of the void, evidently sent along by Providence, and offered in the kindest and most generous manner " to go bail for me to any amount." My counsel was Mr, now Sir Henry, Curtis Bennett, who did the apologizing to the Recorder and the court very gracefully, and, as it appears, evidently successfully. Thus the snare was broken and I was delivered quite as effectually as St Peter was delivered by the angel. Really, from this moment I " never looked back," except for one relapse which I shall presently describe. For although I was committed for trial, and had only about five weeks in which to get evidence against Ross, with the alternative of anything from six months' to two years' imprisonment, I felt perfectly confident.

Although I had been bound over with two sureties of £200 each, and although my two sureties were waiting to enter into their recognizances in court, I did not, after all, get out that night. Sir George Lewis somehow contrived that the police (that is to say, the detective in charge of the case) should refuse to accept my Anglican friend as a surety without " twenty-four hours' notice " for investigation. Mr Mills offered to take the police to his bank and show them that his balance there was more than five times as much as the sum for which he had gone surety, but the detective refused, and said he must make inquiries at his domicile next day.

The effect of this was, of course, as was intended, that instead of being let out at once, as was the Recorder's intention, I was kept in custody as a convicted prisoner. My sentence was " to be bound over with two sureties, or in default of producing sureties, six months' imprisonment." So at seven o'clock that evening, after I had been shut up in a cell for several hours, I was told that my sureties would not be available that night, and that in the meanwhile I was a convicted prisoner, with nominally six months to serve, and must go to Wormwood Scrubs. So off I went in the " Black Maria," with about a dozen other convicted prisoners, all of whom were handcuffed. I was exempted from this, in consideration of the fact that I was only " bound over," and due to go out next day. On the way to the prison we were allowed to smoke cigarettes and talk. We drove right down Piccadilly. It was a curious sensation to look out through the chinks of the cover of the sort of waggonette we occupied and see the clubs and restaurants and the people going out to dinner. This particular " Black Maria " was not a regular one, divided into cells, but I may say, with satisfaction, that I had then, and have since, been in a proper regulation " Black Maria."

When we got to Wormwood Scrubs the ceremony of " reception " took at least an hour and a half. All our clothes were taken away, and we were sent one by one into three or four bathrooms, which contained warm-water baths. When my turn came the reception officer, a delightful Irishman, full of jokes and good humour, and doing his best, in the most charitable way, to cheer everyone up, looked me over casually and said : " You needn't have a bath, you are quite clean." I was much upset, and said : " Oh, but please let me have a bath, I have been in Brixton for five days without one ! " The officer (in prison the warders are always called officers) said : " Well of course you can have one if you like." So I got my bath and enjoyed the hot water, and was lying luxuriously in it when a prisoner in prison clothes, who was helping in the " reception," looked in and said : " Get out quick, kid ; you are only allowed five minutes." He gave me a towel. After that I was inspected by the doctor. The same doctor was at the prison ten years later when I revisited the classic shades of Wormwood Scrubs— Dr Watson, kindest and most considerate of men, who always had a kind word for me and lent me books (with the approval of the Catholic chaplain) when I was in hospital.

All this took much longer than one would suppose. We were also given cocoa and bread (quite uneatable and as hard as a brick), and then conducted to our respective cells. I was put on the second and top floor of the sinister and forbidding-looking iron and steel house, smelling strongly of gas, with its rows and rows of numbered cells, to which I was destined. I was in the third or hard-labour division, and I must therefore, I imagine, have been in the same building where Oscar Wilde had been confined. I thought of him as I " went to bed " (a plank bed and no mattress), and said to myself : " Poor Oscar, however did he manage to stand this for two years ? " That was the first time I had had a comparatively soft thought about him since I read the " unpublished part " of *De Profundis.*

CHAPTER XLII

Ⅰ SLEPT like a log, in spite of plank bed and no mattress, being worn out, and was wakened by the ringing of the prison bell at five-thirty. I got up and dressed, putting on the ghastly prison clothes which had been served out to me the night before. I began to have a reaction and to feel frightened and wretched. What if there was some hitch about my sureties and I could not get out ? My imagination began to work fantastically, suggesting that the whole thing was a trap, and that once in this prison, a mere number without a name, I was done for, and would be kept indefinitely.

The door was unlocked and left open. I heard the clanking of tins and pails. Two prisoners came along with a sort of tank on wheels and told me to empty my slops. A warder looked in and said something which I did not understand. The door was shut and locked. Then there was a long pause. I remained apathetically sitting on the little backless stool which was all there was in the way of a chair. Uneatable and evil-smelling food was handed in. I looked at it with disgust and put it as far away from me as possible. It was nearly dark ; the only window, a small square, was so high up that I could reach it only by standing on my stool. I was faint with hunger, as I had had nothing to eat since breakfast the day before. I had been too agitated to eat my good lunch at the Old Bailey (cold chicken and bread), and owing to the fact that I had expected to get out before dinner-time I had not bothered about food. The bread and cocoa which had been offered me when I got into the " reception-room " I had not touched.

The door was again opened, and my untasted breakfast was

removed by a prisoner, who eagerly took possession of my bread
and stuffed it into his shirt. I sat on for some time in a dazed
condition, hearing the noise of walking and tramping outside.
Then a fierce-looking " officer " looked in and shouted angrily
at me : "What are you doing here ? Why haven't you made
your bed ? What do you think you are doing ? You ought to
be in the shed ! " I looked at him with wide eyes and then
burst into tears. I buried my face in my hands and sobbed. He
came up to me in the kindest way and put his arm round my
neck : " Here, sonny, this won't do—cheer up, no harm meant.
I know it must be very hard on you, first day and all. You
needn't go into the shed if you'd rather stay here."

His kindness made me cry all the more, and he tactfully went
away and came back ten minutes later, and asked me how I felt.
I said I felt all right now and would like to go to the shed,
though I had no idea what " the shed " was. He showed me
how to fold my blankets and lean my plank bed against the wall.
He got a wet towel and wiped my face and dried it, making
jokes all the time. May God reward him !

He then conducted me down two flights of iron stairs and out
of the dreadful hall into the open air, and so to the shed, a large
building, where about a hundred prisoners were working at
sewing sacks and picking oakum. I was given some oakum to
pick. Either before or after that, I forget which, I had an hour's
" exercise," walking round and round a yard, with a hundred
and fifty or so of other prisoners.

Then came more revolting food in my cell, the mere sight and
smell of it making me sick. Ten years later I starved on it for
seven weeks, losing nearly two stone of weight in the process.
But at this time I merely looked at it and hoped someone
would take it away soon. The editor of *The Tablet* (among
others) declares, in contradiction to me, that the food in prisons
is really excellent. Of course, never having been in prison, he

is bound to know more about it than I do ! Perhaps the editor of *The Tablet* likes lumps of stinking meat swimming in lukewarm kitchen grease. There is no accounting for taste. Personally, I do not fancy it, and when the time came I preferred, even starving as I was, not to eat it, and to live for seven weeks on crusts of bread and watery cocoa.

After " dinner " we went back to the " shed," and I picked more oakum. By this time I was in complete despair. I could not understand why my sureties had not come to take me out, and I made up my mind that something had gone wrong and that I was going to be kept in prison. Of course this was childish and unreasonable on my part ; but in prison, especially at first, one is not reasonable, and is liable to all sorts of panics and night-marish ideas. I sat in the shed for about two hours, and at last I heard my number called out—curiously, I forget the number. I jumped to my feet and went up to the officer who had just come into the shed and called my number. He said : " You are wanted by the Governor ; come along with me." I said : " Is it my sureties ? " He said : " I don't know anything about it. All I know is, you are to go to the Governor."

I followed him into one of the rooms leading into the recep-tion office, where I had been the night before. My heart leapt up, for there was the Governor talking affably to dear old Sholto and my clerical friend and benefactor, who both smiled and shook hands with me.

I was immediately taken into the reception-room and relieved of my prison clothes, my own clothes, watch and money being given back to me. The only thing I had been allowed to keep was my rosary, which I was wearing round my neck.

When I was " clothed and in my right mind " I went back into the other room, and the Governor shook hands and said : "Well, good-bye ; don't come back again " ; and I went off with my two sureties. Sholto had to rush off somewhere, but

Mr Mills carried me off to a restaurant and fed me sumptuously. Curiously enough, I could hardly eat anything. On my way home to my mother's—she was then staying at Cliveden Place—I thought to myself : " I cannot risk going back to that hellish place." I made up my mind that I would come to terms with Ross, which of course would have been easy enough to do provided I would " climb down " and withdraw my charges.

This state of mind, which had been produced by one night and day in a real convict prison (as distinct from Brixton, a remand prison, where you keep your own clothes and can order in any food that you like to pay for), was of course exactly the state of mind which Sir George Lewis, on behalf of Ross, had wanted to produce in me. If I had been let out the day before, as the Recorder fully intended I should be, I would not have been able to imagine how dreadful it is to be in prison as a convicted prisoner. I had thought it bad enough in Brixton, but Brixton was heaven compared with Wormwood Scrubs.

However, one night's good sleep in a real bed, in a comfortable bedroom, followed by bacon and eggs and toast and marmalade for breakfast, altered all my feelings. I swore to myself that I would spend the rest of my life in an underground dungeon before I climbed down an inch to Ross and Lewis. I spent a few days without profit with a solicitor who was not really fitted to cope with my case, and then good luck, or rather (for there is no such thing as luck) Providence, sent me to Carter & Bell— that is to say, Mr Edward Bell, for Carter is non-existent—and at last I had a solicitor who believed in me and approved of my methods. Mr Edward Bell is a Scotsman, and his great grand-father was hanged for being " out " in the '45 Jacobite Rising. He therefore has fighting blood and spirit of his own, and appreciation of the Douglas fighting blood and spirit in me. Leaving out the Chancery business, which had become hope-lessly compromised before he came on the scene at all, Mr Bell and I together never lost a case. We smashed Lewis & Lewis, with the able assistance of Mr Comyns Carr (now K.C., but then a junior), on two stricken fields, and even in my action against *The Morning Post*, where Mr Comyns Carr let me down rather badly, as I think, we won the case, though I did not get the damages to which I was entitled.

Then began the, at first apparently hopeless, task of trying to get evidence against Ross. I saw Mr Comyns Carr and made a statement to him. He said to me : " If you will undertake to go into the witness-box and say there what you have told me I will draw up a plea of justification ; but I tell you frankly that unless you can get quite a lot of real evidence, apart from your own, you will not have a chance."

I got most of the evidence myself at the very last moment, as I have already stated. I tried clue after clue, and came up against blanks and brick walls, and people who were " not going to be mixed up " in the affair. At last I got word, sent anonymously, that there was a certain Mr E., living at some number in a street near Campden Hill (I will not give his name, for obvious reasons), who was the respectable father of a young boy who had been a victim of Ross. When I got this information there were less than ten days to run before my trial was due to begin, and I had no evidence at all, although I had been to Guernsey in one fruitless quest, and to a dozen other places in vain. I went to the address given, and asked for Mr E. No such name was known there. My heart sank into my boots. I turned away and looked down the street of at least a hundred and fifty houses. What was I to do ? I prayed desperately to St Anthony of Padua, for whom I have always had a special cult. I walked a few yards with my eyes on the ground. A voice said : "What do you want ? Can I help you ? " I looked up and saw a beautiful little boy about ten years old, smiling at me. I said : " I was looking for someone at a number which was given me in this street, and now I am told there is no such name known there." He said : " Tell me the name and the number." I did so. He said : " All right, I know where it is. The numbers in the street have been changed."

He took my hand and led me right down to the other end of the street, stopped in front of a door and said : " You'll get what you want here." I let go his hand and went up to the door and rang the bell. I looked round and the little boy was gone. I looked down the street both ways and saw no sign of him. The door opened and I said : " Does Mr E. live here ? " " Yes, he does. Will you come in ? " was the reply.

With great difficulty I got from Mr E. confirmation of what I had been told. The difficulty was caused by the woman who had let me in, and who, I found, was his second wife, and step-mother of his two sons. She said : " Don't tell him anything. We don't want to have any scandal in the family." I appealed strongly to Mr E. I said : " If you don't help me I shall be sent to prison. For God's sake, tell me." He said : " Very well, I can't refuse. The boy himself is dead. After what happened when he left home he went to South Africa and died there. His elder brother, who is a private in the —— Regiment, now at Goring, will tell you the whole story." He gave me the name and military address of the brother and I went out.

This is the story to which I have referred as being what I believe to be a supernatural experience. It did not strike me till long afterwards, when I got the evidence which proved to be perhaps the most damning of all the evidence I got against Ross, that the whole thing was mysterious and wonderful. How should a little boy of ten years old know about the change of numbers, and where Mr E. lived ? Why should a child of that age go up to a man he had never seen before and say : "What do you want ? Can I help you ? " I firmly believe that the child was an angel, or, at any rate, that he was supernaturally moved to help me. He was a most beautiful little boy, and he had an angelic face and smile. And how did he disappear in the space of time, a few seconds, between when I let go of his hand and when I looked round again ? Perhaps Dr Barnes or Dean Inge will oblige with an explanation which will satisfy believers in the Darwinian hypothesis and the impossibility of miracles.

Even after this I had a desperate difficulty in getting the evidence. When I got to Goring I was told that the particular unit in which the man I wanted was serving had been transferred to a town in Norfolk. I went there, and went to the headquarters of the colonel of the regiment. It was a house belonging to a man I knew, Charlie Tracey, now Lord Sudeley, but he was not there himself. The colonel was odious. When he heard what I wanted he was insolent and rude, and declared that he would not let me see the man I wanted. I had to have a regular fight with him. In the presence of his adjutant and several other officers I told him that unless he produced the man, for whom I had a subpœna, I would apply to the judge for a " Bench Warrant," and that I would publicly expose him as a man who was trying to shield Ross and what he stood for. He grew red in the face and stormed out of the room, followed by his officers. The door was slammed and I was left alone.

After about five minutes a very charming young subaltern, very much a gentleman, which was not always the case in those days of " temporary gentlemen," came in and told me that the colonel had sent him to say that he had sent for the man, and that I might interview him in his (the subaltern's) presence. A few minutes later the young man arrived. The subaltern told him what I wanted, and said : " You are not obliged to answer Lord Alfred's questions unless you wish." The man was reluctant at first, but I appealed to him and said : " You don't want to shield the man who ruined your brother, and is, indirectly, responsible for his death, do you ? " I also told him that unless he told me the truth I would be sent to prison for denouncing Ross. He thereupon gave me the whole story, which was damning for Ross. I wrote down what he said, and he read it through and signed it, after being told by the subaltern that he need not do so unless he wished. I gave him a subpœna and three pounds, and told him he would have to be at the Old Bailey on the date fixed for my trial, early in December. This was a great triumph, and " bucked me up " considerably.

It never rains but it pours. After that, evidence began to flow in. I got the names of half-a-dozen people who could give me valuable information from a man I went to see at Yarmouth. In the end I had thirteen or fourteen witnesses. They were all respectable people. One was a clergyman of the Church of England, and I had not one single case of what is called " tainted evidence." The only one I had who was of that kind was the man I saw at Yarmouth, and he failed to turn up at the trial. When his name was called he did not answer. Subsequently my solicitor, Mr Edward Bell, traced him to one of the London hospitals, where he was informed that the man had been brought in " unconscious and suffering from a narcotic poison." Whoever was responsible for getting him in this condition did me a very good turn, for he was the only witness I had who might have been severely damaged in cross-examination by Sir Ernest Wild, Ross's counsel, now Recorder of London.

A dramatic scene occurred at the trial when the young soldier, whose evidence I had such difficulty in getting, gave his evidence. He told the story of how his brother, then a boy of sixteen, disappeared from home, and how he and his father obtained information that Ross was responsible. He described how he went to a bar in Copthall Avenue, which Ross frequented, and seeing Ross said to him : "What have you done with my brother ? " He said that Ross thereupon offered him money, which he refused, and then started blustering and threatened to

T

send for the police and give him in charge for " blackmail."
Finally, he said, he was frightened and went away. His brother
shortly afterwards went to South Africa, but he did not know
where he got the money to go. He died there. At this point the
poor fellow was overcome with emotion. Mr Comyns Carr said
to him : "Would you recognize the man you saw in the bar in
Copthall Avenue if you saw him ? " He replied : " I don't
know whether I would ; it is several years ago." " Well," said
Carr, " look round the court and see if you can see him." Amid
breathless silence the witness looked first of all up at the public
gallery, and then all round the body of the court. Finally he
cast his eyes down to the solicitors' table, where Ross sat next
to George Lewis, facing him. He said : " There is a gentleman
sitting at the table who bears a striking resemblance to the man
I saw in the bar in Copthall Avenue." " Will Mr Ross stand
up ? " said the judge, Mr Justice Coleridge. Ross stood up.
" That is the man," said the witness.

Will it be believed that this intensely dramatic scene was
absolutely unreported in all the papers ?

I have already described what happened after the trial, and
how the extraordinary testimonial to Ross was got up and signed
by three hundred and fifty prominent people, including the then
Prime Minister and his wife. I have never been able to arrive
at any satisfactory explanation of this astounding occurrence.
Perhaps Dr Barnes and Dean Inge, who presumably do not
believe in the devil, might be able to suggest a reasonable solution. I confess that it beats me entirely. One of the signatories
to the Ross testimonial was, by the way, Dr Barnes's predecessor
as Bishop of Birmingham, Dr Wakefield.

CHAPTER XLIII

AFTER I had finally disposed of Ross and established my
" Plea of Justification " against him, followed the long series of
appearances in the Chancery Court, culminating in the incident
I have already described, when I washed my hands of my son.
A period of two years then elapsed in which very little happened.
I was living with my mother in a charming house called Shelley's
Folly, three miles from Lewes, belonging to Lord Monkbretton.
I did nothing but read Catholic books—Lives of the Saints, St
Augustine, St Thomas Aquinas (I read the whole *Summa Theo-*
logica), St Teresa, St Catherine of Siena, and so forth. My
life on the whole was quite uneventful. I had made another
unsuccessful attempt to go to the war, directly after I defeated
Ross. I wrote to Kitchener again, pointing out that I had now
emerged from all my legal difficulties and that I had justified my
libels on Ross, and asking him now to give me a commission or
let me go as an interpreter. He replied, saying practically the
same as he had said before. I was in my forty-fourth year when
the war broke out, and as I had never been in the army, or
even in the militia or volunteers, I had of course no special
qualification. I am very glad now that I did not go to the war,
but at the time it was a grievance. Beyond a little snipe and
duck shooting up in Caithness-shire, which was the nearest I
could get during the war to the snipe bogs of the Orkney Islands,
where I have a standing invitation to go and shoot with my old
and valued friend, Mr Regan, I did nothing but read and take
long walks, with an occasional ride at Newmarket or elsewhere.
In this period I wrote and published *The Rossiad* and *Eve and*
the Serpent.

The only unusual incident that occurred was a visit to Mr Herbert Moore Pim, the Irish poet, who was then editing a paper called *The Irishman*. I went to stay as his guest at a charming cottage he had near Dunmurry, and remained several weeks. Mr Pim, who was afterwards my assistant editor on *Plain English*, which was, I suppose, more anti-Sinn Fein than any other paper in London in 1920-1921, was at that time an ardent Sinn Feiner, and ran *The Irishman* in that interest. In fact, he claims with Griffiths to have started the Sinn Fein movement. When the Sinn Feiners started murdering people, cutting off the noses of donkeys, and dragging the Catholic Church in the mire for political ends, Pim revolted and left them. He ended by being as violently " anti " as he had been before pro-Sinn Fein. At the time when, some years later, I telegraphed to him and asked him to come to London, and be my assistant editor in *Plain English*, he had been warned that he was going to be murdered, and the police had informed him that they were powerless to protect him. Pim, of course, is a Catholic, a convert, though he comes of Ulster Protestant stock, his uncle being Mr Justice Pim.

When I was at Pim's I read *The Jail Journal*, by John Mitchell. It greatly impressed me, and I became very sympathetic to the Irish Nationalist Movement. When I started *Plain English* I was still in sympathy with the movement, but, as a Catholic, I soon revolted against the campaign of murder and lying which was carried on by the Sinn Feiners, and as I got all my information on the Irish question from Pim I soon followed him in his change of views. But all this was three or four years after the time of which I am speaking, when I stayed with Pim and wrote in *The Irishman*. I greatly admired some of Pim's poetry written about this time. What he has written since seems to me to be nothing like so good. Just before this time I had first met my great friend Mr Sorley Brown, the editor of

The Border Standard, Crosland's biographer. He stayed as my mother's guest in a house at Hove, and we have since exchanged numerous visits in Galashiels and London. I can never sufficiently thank Mr Sorley Brown for all his chivalrous defence of me in that part of my native Scotland which is still sometimes called "The Douglas Country."

Then came the Pemberton Billing case, in which I was asked to give evidence for Mr Billing. I did so, and I helped to secure his acquittal at the Old Bailey, when he was tried on a charge of criminally libelling Miss Maud Allan—Maud Allan being, however, as I immediately realized, only a stalking horse for forces which I recognized as belonging to what I call the "Ross gang view of life."

This trial brought me into great prominence owing to the fight I had from the witness-box with Mr Justice Darling. After the Ransome case I had written to Mr Justice Darling telling him that the only reason I had not answered him as he deserved to be answered, when he attacked and bullied me in that case, was that I was bound by a promise, given on my word of honour, to my counsel, Mr Cecil Hayes, that I would "not attack the judge" however great the provocation. In this letter I said to Mr Justice Darling: "If ever I come before you again, as I pray God I may, you will see what will happen to you."

I have no intention of retailing all this business again in detail. It was fully reported in the papers. Mr Justice Darling tried to repeat the tactics with me which he had used in the Ransome case. But on this occasion I was not bound by any promise, and I was free not only to defend myself but to carry the war into the enemy's camp. My methods were entirely successful, for after a duel lasting about five minutes, during which Mr Justice Darling threatened to have me removed from the court, he gave up the struggle, and left me to give my evidence exactly as I chose to give it. Later he made certain remarks about me in his summing up, and I rose to my feet in the body of the court and called him "a damned liar," a remark which was received with a perfect tornado of cheers and hand-clapping, lasting for several minutes ; under cover of which I discreetly retired.

(It has often been wondered why Mr Justice Darling did not commit me to prison for contempt of court on this occasion. Well, I called him "a damned liar," and if he had committed me for contempt the question must ultimately have arisen of exactly what were the words he had used which I had stigmatized as lying words. The shorthand report of his summing-up speech would have shown exactly what he said, and the question would have arisen as to whether it was true or not. Well, it was not true, and Mr Justice Darling knew it was not true. So that explains why Mr Justice Darling was not taking any more risks with me.)

When I left the court after the verdict in this case I was loudly cheered by a crowd of several thousand people outside the Old Bailey.

Several years later, when my case against *The Evening News* was in the list, I was informed by my solicitor that it was coming on, on a certain day "next week," and that it was to be tried by Mr Justice Darling. I immediately took a cab to the Law Courts, sent in my card to the "Associate" (the official who settles the order of cases and arranges what judge shall take what case), and asked if I might see him. He came out to see me in the corridor of the courts, and asked me stiffly what I wanted. I told him that I had been informed that Mr Justice Darling was to take my case against *The Evening News*. He said : "Yes, that is so." I said : "Well, I refuse to have my case tried by Mr Justice Darling, and if he attempts to try it I will make such a row as has never been heard before in the Law Courts." He said : "What is your objection to Mr Justice Darling ? " I then said that I did not wish to say a word against Mr Justice Darling, and that no doubt his intention would be to give the case a fair trial, but, I said, " in view of what happened in the Billing case is it conceivable that he will not be prejudiced against me? And, in any case, surely he would not wish to try a case in which I am concerned, if he knows that I strongly object and want the case to be tried by some other judge. Why," I went on, " should this one judge of all others be selected to try this particular case?" This was so reasonable that the Associate was bound to admit the force of what I said. His reply was: " There are only three judges on the rota at present, and Mr Justice Darling happened to be the one selected for your case, but, in view of what you say, we will give you Mr Justice Bray instead." I said : "No, thanks ; I won't have Bray either." This tickled the Associate so much that he began to laugh. He said : "Why, what is the matter with Mr Justice Bray?" I then explained that he had tried the case in which Crosland was non-suited when he sued Ross for malicious prosecution, and that in the course of his remarks he had attacked me most unjustifiably when I was not there to defend myself, and that I had written and circulated all over the Bench and Bar a sonnet about him, the last line of which was :

" And down the ages bray and bray and bray."

(The sonnet appears in my *Collected Satires*, published by the Fortune Press in 1926.)

The smiling Associate said : "Well, you know, Lord Alfred, litigants are not supposed to come here and choose their own judges, but may I ask what judge *would* suit you." I replied : " Oh, I don't mind the Lord Chief Justice " (he was the third judge on the rota). " Very well, then," said the Associate, " we will give you the Lord Chief Justice." I thanked him and withdrew, but next week my case was taken out of the list and put on right after the Long Vacation, when it ultimately came before Mr Justice Horridge, and I won it easily, as I have already related.

In 1919 my *Collected Poems* was published by Mr Martin Secker. The volume is now out of print, and a new *Collected Poems*, which include *In Excelsis* and other poems, will be shortly brought out. The sale of my poetry, which has been the re-printing again and again of stuff I wrote thirty or more years ago, with a few additions from time to time, has now run into a good many thousand volumes. In addition to that, my poems have been extensively pirated in America, and a thousand copies were sold in France of the original volume *Poems*, with a French prose translation. My new Collected Edition will contain my light comic and nonsense verses, which have also gone on steadily selling for the last twenty or thirty years.[1]

Nothing more which would be of any general interest occurred during the five years when I was at Shelley's Folly until I became the editor of a new paper called *Plain English*, in 1920.

---

[1] Since this was written my *Complete Poems* has duly appeared.

CHAPTER XLIV

JUST before *Plain English* was started my brother Percy married for the second time, the lady who survives him as Mary, Marchioness of Queensberry. He wrote to me unexpectedly and told me of his marriage, and that his wife wanted to give him a horse as a wedding present which should revive the old family colours, salmon, green sleeves and cap, which had been my father's colours and Arthur Douglas's (" Old Joe ") and mine in France. The idea was, he said, to buy a three-year-old which was entered in the Derby. I wrote back and said in effect : "What's the use of buying a three-year-old to run in the Derby, when it is quite impossible, even for a great deal more than your wife would be likely to give, to buy one that would have the slightest chance of winning ? Why not buy a horse to win a big handicap at the beginning of the year ? " I went on to tell him that I knew that Bob Sievier had a horse, called " Royal Bucks," which he told me was sure to win the Lincolnshire Handicap, and that I thought he would probably be willing to sell, as he had not enough money at present to back the horse in the sort of way he liked to bet.

My connection with Sievier was brought about in a curious and unexpected way. During the time I had *The Academy* he was, I considered, one of my greatest enemies. He had published coarse and offensive paragraphs and " jokes " about me in his paper, *The Winning Post*. I had retaliated by " roasting " him whenever I got the chance in *The Academy*. His dislike of me was entirely founded on a misapprehension of my attitude towards Oscar Wilde, who was his *bête noire*. He chose to imagine that, having been mixed up with Wilde as a boy, I was still more or less concerned in that sort of thing, which, as a matter of fact, he might have known from public events I had long utterly repudiated and reacted against. During the years that succeeded my editorship of *The Academy* he still kept up this attitude towards me, and although I had never spoken to him, or he to me, he had glared at me, and I had glared back, on several occasions when we had seen each other at race meetings. I was therefore, as may be imagined, greatly surprised to get from a Press-cutting agency, one day, a cutting from *The Winning Post* about the Pemberton Billing case in which, while having nothing very pleasant to say about Billing, Sievier had gone out of his way to speak of me in a very kind and generous way, with a reference to the part I had played in the case and the " courageous attitude " I had adopted in giving evidence. He wrote in his paper that he wished " entirely to withdraw " anything he had ever said or written against me.

I wrote to him and said I was glad to read what he said, and that I had never understood why he should attack me as he did, and that I accepted his expressions of regret for what he had done and written, in the spirit in which they were offered. He wrote back reaffirming what he had said in his paper, and again expressing his genuine sorrow for having misjudged and calumniated me. He asked me to go to stay with him at his home, Fitzroy House, Newmarket. Life in those days at Shelley's Folly was somewhat dull and uneventful. The prospect of getting a ride or two was blissful to me. (I had not been on a horse's back for several years except on one or two occasions when my very good friend, Dale the trainer, who then lived near me, had let me ride one of his horses in Lord Monkbretton's park.)

I accepted Sievier's invitation, and had a very pleasant visit, which included among its attractions early morning rides on Bath and Tweedledum. I also later, during another visit, induced Sievier to publish in *The Winning Post* a slashing article about Ross and a certain friend of his. The article was entitled "O.H.M.S.," and created considerable stir in the clubs, and also in the Foreign Office, producing, indeed, exactly the effect which I had designed it to have. No one but Sievier would have published it. This article was in the nature of a counterblast to the attempt which was then being made by the Asquiths and others to rehabilitate and whitewash Ross at my expense. While I was with Bob Sievier he told me all about Royal Bucks, whom I saw doing his work daily at exercise, and I knew for a fact that he had great confidence about winning the Lincoln Handicap.

My brother wrote back and said that he and his wife would take my advice, and would I ask Sievier if he would sell the horse, and how much he wanted. I wrote to Sievier, and he wired : "Bring your brother and Lady Queensberry along to stay a few days." So we all went to Fitzroy House, and Royal Bucks was sold over the dinner-table the night we arrived, for £3000—a jolly good bargain, considering that within a few months he won the Lincoln Handicap and the City and Suburban in his first two appearances in the Douglas colours. The colours, by the way, were altered, as the horse ran in my sister-in-law's name. My brother ought to have won at least £20,000 over these two superlative *coups*, but he made a sad hash of things, and insisted, against the combined advice of Sievier and myself, in going off on a wild goose chase to America in search of certain properties there which he had formerly marked down as valuable.

Doubtless these properties had value, but the usual fate over-took poor Percy about them. He did no good, and came back cleaned out. The whole thing ended in tragedy, for when he came back from America he was very indignant because Royal Bucks had not been run in his name, and " the hell of a row " took place all round, in which I, as his brother, of course took his part. The result was a quarrel between Sievier and myself. I am glad to say, however, that this is now quite at an end, and that I am convinced that he acted with perfect loyalty towards my dear brother, whose death about a year later was a frightful blow to me. The same applies to my sister-in-law, Mary Queensberry, with whom I was also embroiled at this time, but who is now, I am glad to say, on terms of sisterly affection with me, and who has proved herself a true and loyal friend. Unfortunately at the time of Royal Bucks' victories I had no money to back him with, being at that time almost literally penniless. However, Sievier sent me £100 when he won the Lincoln and the same when he won the City and Suburban, while my sister-in-law put me a " pony " each way on him for the second race. (After all, I had done them both a very good turn.) I forget the price he started at, but I won a few hundreds. It ought to have been thousands of course, but hard up as I was then, even my small win was exceedingly useful. Sievier kept the horse in his stable and trained him for both races, and anyone who knows him will have no difficulty in guessing that most of the £3000 he got for the horse went on him at a long price when he won the Lincoln, and that he followed up his winnings over the second victory.

Just before Percy went to South Africa he had been staying with some friends of mine and his, the Conchies, who had a house in Great Cumberland Place and a castle and grouse moor in Perthshire. To my amazement, one day, Percy told me that Mr Conchie had asked him why " a clever fellow like your brother does nothing." Percy replied : " It's all very fine. What can he do ? All the papers boycott him. He can't get an article printed anywhere. His only chance would be a paper of his own."

" Very well," said Conchie, " I'll start a paper for him."

I may say that for two or three years before this happened I had prayed to Saint Anthony of Padua every day for a paper, but I did not see the slightest earthly chance of getting it.

So I got a paper of my own again, which I held for only about sixteen months. I called it *Plain English,* and it was a sixpenny weekly. For the sake of old association, Conchie, at my request, paid £100 for the title *The Academy,* which had been kept alive by someone who had brought out sufficient "dummies" to preserve the title. So our paper was called *Plain English, with which is incorporated The Academy.* Mr Conchie gave me an absolutely free hand and £50 a month salary, and I must say that, as a proprietor to work for, he was a very pleasing contrast to Eddie Tennant in the first days of *The Academy.* Not only did he never dream of interfering with my editorial functions, but he frequently sent me letters and telegrams of congratulation when a particularly good number came out. I got Pim over from Ireland to act as my assistant editor, and between us we produced a very lively sheet. Of the first number brought out only about three hundred and fifty copies were sold, but by the time I left the editorship the circulation was nearly three thousand, and going up every week.

The paper was a "Diehard" Conservative (indeed I claim to have invented the Diehard party), Catholic—although seventy-five per cent. of my readers were non-Catholics—and very anti-Lloyd-George-and-Coalition. We also put up a strenuous fight (far stronger than that made by any other paper) against the iniquitous surrender to Sinn Fein, and the betrayal of the Irish Loyalists, which will ever remain the darkest blot on the history of the Neo-Georgian period of English history. It is a fact that the Ulster Defence Council came to us after having been, in vain, to every other paper in London, including *The Morning Post,* and asked us to give details of the Sinn Fein outrages which were going on, unreported in the craven London Press, week by week. I saw the President, and agreed to print

anything they liked to send in, and we went on printing details
of outrages every week in spite of the fact that I was threatened
with "reprisals," and warned anonymously that I would be
shot. It is rather remarkable that *Plain English*, for which
I claim that it was the only secular Catholic paper published in
England since the Reformation, should have been the one paper
in London to fight the battle of Ulster and the Irish Loyalists.

It was thanks to Pim's extensive knowledge of the whole
history of Ireland that I was able to point out that nearly all
the Irish revolutionary leaders in the past had been Protestants
and not Catholics, and that therefore the attempt that was being
made in certain quarters to identify the Catholic Church with
Sinn Fein was a perversion of the truth. As a matter of fact,
a great deal more than half the Irish men and women who
were murdered or reduced to beggary by the Sinn Feiners were
Catholics, just as the vast majority of those Irishmen who fought
and died for Great Britain in the war were Catholics.

Our policy on *Plain English* was also strongly anti-Semitic.
No other paper, with the exception of *The Morning Post*, did so
much as *Plain English* to open the eyes of the public to what
the Jews were doing. It is, yet, the incredible fact that, some
two or three years after the death of *Plain English*, *The Morning
Post* deliberately published a libel on me, written by a Jew, to
the effect that I had "made it a paying proposition to publish
vile slanders about the Jews." I sued *The Morning Post* for
libel and it pleaded "justification." The case was fought
entirely on the question of my allegations about Winston
Churchill and the report issued by the Admiralty on the battle
of Jutland. Apart from this question, my attacks on the Jews
were scarcely touched on in the trial of the action. *The Morning
Post* called Winston Churchill as a witness, and my counsel,
Mr Comyns Carr, in the middle of the case, suddenly announced,
just before Mr Churchill was called into the box, that he would

not cross-examine him, and a pendant to this was (why I have never been able to begin to understand) that the evidence and cross-examination by Comyns Carr of Lord Balfour, which had been taken " on commission " and was in court in official printed page form, was also suppressed.   I was so indignant at this that I left the court, after making a protest.   In the result I got a very unexpected verdict, but only a farthing's damages. After my counsel's virtual throwing up of the case I had no expectation of getting a verdict.   In this case I was cross-examined by Sir Patrick Hastings, and I may say without fear of contradiction that I " wiped the floor with him " almost as effectually as I did in the case of Marshall Hall.

The conduct of *The Morning Post* on this occasion (it has since changed hands, so that what I am saying does not apply to the paper as it now is) seemed to me so revealing of the sort of thing that commends itself to " Patriotic Britons " that in the end it almost revolutionized my feelings about the Jews.

I feel now that it is ridiculous to make accusations against the Jews, attributing to them qualities and methods which are really much more typically English than Jewish.   No Jew that ever drew the breath of life would have rounded on another Jew in the way *The Morning Post* rounded on me ; for it is a fact that more than half of the " vile slanders " which I published in *Plain English* on the Jews were taken bodily out of the columns of *The Morning Post*, and moreover my policy on the Irish Question, and every other political question, was identical with that of *The Morning Post*.

In fact, it would be easy for me to show that if I borrowed some of *The Morning Post's* facts and figures about the Jews, they made no scruple to borrow in a wholesale manner, and reproduce in their leading articles, the ideas and arguments of *Plain English*.   I was far from objecting to this.   The more the ideas and arguments of *Plain English* were disseminated the more I was pleased ; but that *The Morning Post* should help itself, as it did, to all my thunder and then join hands with my enemies to squash me, seemed to me a clear case of out-Heroding Herod.

My present view about the Jews is that if the English (as they apparently do) like to be " bossed " by the Jews, and get very angry with anyone who tells them about it, there is no sense in blaming the Jews for taking advantage of the situation. If a Nation or a Party or any body of persons chooses to lie down on its face and invite the Jews to come and trample on it, why blame the Jews for accepting the invitation ? I used to get very excited about these questions, and about politics generally, when I had *Plain English.* I was desperately sincere, and quite ready to die or go to prison for my convictions. But the way I was treated on this occasion by *The Morning Post*, and by others who professed to share all my views, and the subsequent prosecution and imprisonment I underwent in return for my efforts to help my country, completely cured me of any desire to meddle further in English politics or " patriotic " movements.

Leaving out all questions of my accusations against Mr Churchill for which I was convicted, and on which I do not desire to add a word, his reception into the bosom of the Conservative Party, after he had spent twenty-five years of his life in abusing and attacking and trying (most successfully) to keep that party out of power, convinced me that there was no place for me in English politics. I have no polite name for that sort of business.

CHAPTER XLV

I RAN *Plain English* for sixteen months, at the end of which period the editorship was taken away from me as the result of an ignoble intrigue, which did very little credit to the intelligence of those who engineered it. These people were apparently fatuous enough to imagine that *Plain English*, which was my creation and largely written, as well as closely edited and supervised, by me, could be more successfully carried on with another editor. " *Plain English* is a splendid paper," said these silly persons, " but we would prefer that it should have another editor." This was just as if they had said : "We like Lord Alfred Douglas's poems very much, but we would rather have them written by someone else ! "

I, in the meanwhile, started another paper of my own, called *Plain Speech*, which I ran for several months entirely on subscriptions obtained by appealing to the public. When I was pushed out of the editorship of *Plain English* I brought out a number of *Plain Speech*, in which I appealed for funds, and I said plainly that unless I obtained them the first number of *Plain Speech* would also be the last. When I left *Plain English* I took with me my assistant editor, Herbert Moore Pim, and all the best contributors. I also almost immediately drew over nearly all the subscribers and circulation. At the end of three months my new paper had a circulation of over two thousand. Money came in in a wonderful way. In response to my first appeal I got about £250 in free gifts. After that Mr Ernest Brown, a patriotic merchant in the City, with the greatest generosity sent me £50 a week regularly, right up to the time when I closed down the paper. It cost about £75 a week to run the paper, and the balance required I got easily enough.

What stopped the paper in the end was simply that my health broke down, and, after a very severe attack of influenza, I was brought almost to death's door, and was incapable of doing another stroke of work for many months. This followed on all the strain of the long fight which was what the editorship of *Plain English* and *Plain Speech* entailed. The strain culminated in the trial of my action for damages against *The Evening News*, which had published a false report of my death, placarded it all over London (I had the curious experience of seeing the placard announcing my death and buying the paper), and, under cover of an " obituary notice," grossly libelled me. The trial came on just before *Plain Speech* expired. I lasted out through the trial and two days in the witness-box, and then, a few days after the verdict, I collapsed. I was very ill for several weeks.

My wife helped to win this case for me by coming to court and sitting with me all through the trial. Her presence, and the moral support she gave me, to a large extent paralysed the attack on me in reference to her father, which was one of the chief features of the brief prepared by Lewis & Lewis for Douglas Hogg, who was the leader for *The Evening News*. My answers in cross-examination on this point were of course greatly strengthened by the fact that my wife was supporting me and that, if necessary, I might have put her into the witness-box to prove the truth of what I said about the way her father had treated me.

Mr Justice Horridge was distinctly hostile to me when the case began. My counsel, Mr Comyns Carr, made what very nearly proved the fatal mistake of not putting me into the box directly after he opened his case. I told him over and over again in consultation that I would never win the case unless I went into the witness-box, but he and Mr Bell between them persuaded me, very reluctantly, to let him do the case in his own way. The result was, of course, that Hogg got in a deadly attack on me, painting me as blackly as possible to the jury, and reading out my stolen letters to Wilde and others, while I had to sit and listen to him without replying.

At last I told Carr that I could stand it no longer, and that if I did not go into the witness-box we might as well throw up the case. By this time he saw what a frightful mistake he had made, and he asked leave of the judge to let me go into the box " in rebuttal." Hogg, of course, strongly opposed this. The judge hesitated, or appeared to hesitate, and I was in agonies, but he finally said : " It is entirely in my discretion whether or not I allow him to go into the box now, but on the whole I think that the jury would like to hear him, so I rule that he may go into the box." I was saved. If I had not gone into the box I was finished for ever, for if I had lost this case (and most people thought that I had not a hundred-to-one chance of winning it) I could never have got over it.

Directly Carr had finished my examination-in-chief, and Hogg started to cross-examine me, I got in some very strong remarks about George Lewis. The judge said to Hogg : " I am not stopping this witness because I imagine that you would not wish me to do so "—as much as to say : " He is cutting his own throat, and it is no business of mine to stop him." I took no notice, and went straight on, and my case began to develop. By the end of the day, when the case was adjourned, I had begun to produce an effect with the jury, and the judge was beginning to " sit up and take notice."

Carr said to me in an agonized voice as I left the court : " For God's sake, be careful." I said : " Don't worry, I have got the jury already, and the judge is beginning to come round."

Next day my cross-examination went on all day. Half way through my cross-examination the judge came right round to my side, and I had got the jury ever since the first half-hour. Thereafter Mr Justice Horridge helped me as much as he could. He tried on one occasion to stop Hogg asking me a very awkward question, but before he had time to overrule the question I whipped out a devastating reply. "Well, you are answered," said the judge to Mr Hogg, with a smile.

Hogg made a bad slip by referring to my book, *Oscar Wilde and Myself*, and in a minute the judge had the book produced, and told me to read any passages I liked to the jury. "You put it in, you know," he said to the discomfited Hogg. I read several passages with deadly effect. The question of a date arose, and I said : "Well, I can't tell you the exact date, but if you look at *Eve and the Serpent* that will settle it. Immediately the judge was on to it. "What is *Eve and the Serpent*?" he demanded. I told him it was a poem I had published, and Hogg produced it, describing it as "a disgraceful and scurrilous attack on one of the Chancery judges." The judge meanwhile was reading it with evident relish. I tried to soften it down by saying : "It was not exactly meant for Mr Justice Eve, it was just a punning skit on the Chancery Courts, based on the fact that one of the judges is called Eve." "Come, come, Lord Alfred," said the judge, "do yourself justice ; you know you meant it for Mr Justice Eve." "Well, I suppose I did," I replied, nothing loth.

Then followed the summing up, entirely in my favour. Verdict for plaintiff, damages £1000, the jury adding a rider about the scandal of my stolen letters being brought up against me again and again in lawsuits, and expressing an opinion that these letters ought now to be returned to me or destroyed. Then, of course, the inevitable "Notice of Appeal." The judge expressed a strong opinion that there were no grounds of appeal, but allowed the appeal to be entered, adding, however, that it must be on condition that the damages were paid into court by next day.

I shook hands with Carr and thanked him for what he had done. He said, very generously and modestly : " It was nothing to do with me. You won the case yourself in the witness-box." Then followed the reports in the papers, with most of the stuff favourable to me hacked out as usual. But even the unfairness of the Press could not spoil my triumph. The appeal was dropped, and I cashed in my £1000. *The Evening News* of course had to pay all the costs, which must have run to a big amount. It relieved its feelings by " sacking " Machen, the author of the obituary notice !

I ought also to say that I was greatly helped in this action by the kind and generous support I got from the late Doctor Byres Moir, my family doctor, and from the late Monsignor Bickerstaffe Drew and the Catholic Bishop of Clifton, who all voluntarily came and gave evidence for me as to my character. No doubt their evidence produced a great effect on the jury. Also owing to the kindness and charity of Sister Mary Vincent, of the Convent of Mercy at Hull, I not only had the prayers of her community but those of two thousand schoolchildren every day for many weeks right up to and during the trial.

CHAPTER XLVI

I HAVE already said all I want to say about my trial and conviction at the Old Bailey for libelling Winston Churchill. I was sentenced to six months in the Second Division. The Second Division confers no privileges, except in the matter of writing and receiving letters and visits. (One a month is the allowance in each case.) Apart from that, a prisoner in the Second Division might just as well be sentenced to simple "imprisonment" or "imprisonment with hard labour." The labour is the same in every case. When I was in prison I was put to work, for the first ten days, in the "Shed" to sew mail bags. After that I was transferred to the garden. There were about fifteen of us "gardeners." Some were Second Division and others were hard labour. We all did exactly the same work. So if the hard-labour people were doing hard labour so was I. Part of the work we did was filling carts with coal and then dragging the carts. This "swinging a shovel" is fairly hard work, and I did my share of it, although the officer who looked after the gardeners, a charming and kindly fellow, named Belcher, told me that I need not do it if it overtired me. My natural desire was to do the same as everyone else did, and, if I had had enough to eat, my work in the garden, which conferred the privileges of being in the open air for five or six hours a day, without a hat in all weathers (this was in December and January), would have done me no harm at all. But unfortunately, starved as I was and weak for want of food, it caused internal injuries from which I have never recovered.

I have already described my reception at Wormwood Scrubs in 1914. When I went again in 1923 (on 13th December) everything was just the same. I was worn out and sick when I reached the prison. I think I ought to have been sent straight to hospital. However, I did not say anything about how ill I felt, and the doctor did not notice it, and I spent seven weeks, during which I was nearly starving, in the ordinary prison, getting weaker and weaker, because I could not eat the food. For the first two weeks I ate nothing but the crusts of the bread and drank the half-pint of weak cocoa in the evening. The last meal was at four o'clock, nothing more after that till next day's "breakfast." I believe I would have died if the Deputy Governor, who was always very kind and pleasant to me, had not happened to pass close to me one day in the garden. He stopped and said : "You are looking frightfully ill. You must report to the doctor." I said : "Oh, I don't know, I don't feel any worse than usual." He went away, and next day the doctor sent for me and had me weighed. Evidently I had lost a lot of weight, because he asked me about the food. I asked how much weight I had lost, but they would not tell me. I had by this time gone on the "vegetarian diet," because it was slightly less nauseating than the other, but except for a tiny piece of cheese (very nasty, but eatable) and a sort of pudding which came three times a week and had a slight suspicion of sweetness about it, there was scarcely anything I could eat.

The doctor doubled my allowance of cheese and cocoa and pudding. Then I was weighed again in a few days, but my weight was still going down rapidly. He said : "You must go into the hospital. I can't give you any more to eat outside the hospital because I am tied by the regulations. But if you go to hospital you will get good food, and plenty of it." I was only too glad to go, and by that time I was so weak that the officer who took me across had to put his arm round me to hold me up.

It shows what a state of collapse I was in that I remember being filled with horror and apprehension because, when I got to the hospital, there was a cat standing at the door with a mouse in its mouth. I dislike mice very much, and I had never seen a sign of one in my cell in Hall B (No. 69), to my great relief. So when I saw the cat I remembered that someone had told me that there were swarms of mice in the hospital. I said to the officer : "Will there be mice in my ward ? " He said : "Well, there *might* be, but you needn't mind them, they won't hurt you." (People never can understand that one's dislike to mice is not connected with any apprehension that they may be liable to bite one !) I was frozen with horror. I thought to myself : " If the place is going to be full of mice it will just about finish me." When I was left alone I prayed desperately to St Anthony of Padua to keep mice away from me. It is the extraordinary fact that I never saw one again, or heard the slightest sound of one, the whole time I was in the hospital, though other prisoners told me that the place was full of them.

The hospital has two floors. There are wards with beds in them just like ordinary hospital wards, and there are also rows of separate cells. The wards are airy and cheerful, and the cells are much less forbidding than the cells in the ordinary prison. They have much larger windows, which you can look out of without standing on a chair, and the hospital itself is pleasantly situated in the garden of the prison. When I got into a private cell, with its green walls and a little cot (actually with real sheets and a pillow), I began to feel better. The food seemed too delicious to be real. It was just ordinary roast beef or roast mutton and rice-pudding, but, starving as I was, it seemed like ambrosia. I also got half-a-pint of milk a day and some *real* bread. There was no butter, only margarine, which I never would eat. So I preferred my bread dry.

I was horrified, after I had been in hospital about three weeks, to gather from something the doctor said on one of his visits that when my weight got back to normal I would have to go back to Hall B. I was so much less wretched in my cell in the hospital that the idea of going back to starvation gave me cold shivers. I again had recourse to St Anthony, and though I was weighed every week, and though I really was " fed up " and had plenty of good food, I never anywhere near got back my weight, and I stayed in the hospital right to the day of my release.

For the last six weeks in prison I used to play the American organ in the Catholic chapel at Mass and Benediction. This was a treat, as it gave me a little variation from the deadly monotony. We used to have " choir practices," which were rather amusing. The " choir " chiefly consisted of a few Borstal boys and a sprinkling of Sinn Feiners. I was very friendly with the Sinn Feiners. Although I had been so anti-Sinn Féin, I felt very sorry for them and sympathetic, as they were Catholics, gentlemen and political offenders. I thought it very unjust that they should be treated as ordinary prisoners. Some of them had frightful sentences—as long as twelve or eighteen months. One of them, McGrath, a very nice fellow, looked terribly ill when I went out. I told them just before I left to cheer up, as I was *going to get them out.*

When I got out I wrote to the Home Secretary about them. It was while the Labour Government were in power, so logically (as I told the Home Secretary) they had no right whatever to object to Sinn Feiners. It was, I dare say, a mere coincidence that, directly after that, they were transferred to Brixton as political offenders and put in the First Division, which compared with the Second Division is simply luxury, as you can have your own clothes and food. A few weeks later they were let out altogether. So, even if I had no part in securing their release, I certainly brought them luck.

I was very friendly with Art O'Brien, one of the Sinn Feiners, and when I went out I smuggled a letter from him to his sister.

Father Musgrave, the Catholic chaplain, was very kind to me, and it was, of course, he who made me "organist" as soon as the other prisoner who played the organ finished his sentence and went out. There was one extraordinary old chap in the choir who had been in prison altogether, on and off, for twenty-nine years. He fancied himself as a solo singer, and sang the solo part in *Regina Lætare* at Easter. He also had his own ideas as to how the hymns ought to be sung, which frequently differed from the way they were scored in my hymn-book. I played them as they were written, but he said I was wrong, and Father Musgrave said : " Never mind, play it his way, it's a tradition of the prison." However, one day Father Musgrave himself remonstrated with him, and said he was wrong ; whereupon he replied : " Excuse me, Father, I've been twenty-nine years in prison, and if I don't know how to sing these hymns I don't know who should."

While Father Musgrave was away for a time, owing to illness, his place was taken by a Carmelite, from Church Street, Kensington, Father Forti, who also showed me the greatest possible kindness. A friend of mine, Mr Rose, bullyragged the Home Secretary into giving me permission to have writing materials, on the ground that I was a distinguished poet, and that it was outrageous to deprive me of the means of exercising my art. Accordingly I was given a school copy-book, as supplied to Borstal boys, and a pencil. I felt that it was "up to me" to write something, as my friend had been to so much trouble. So I wrote a sonnet, with considerable difficulty. I had no intention of writing any more. But one day I had another shot and produced another sonnet, and then again a third. Quite accidentally they hung together, and I conceived the idea of writing a long poem all in sonnets. I worked hard at it, invoking St Anthony and St Thomas Aquinas whenever I got "stuck," and produced the seventeen sonnets which make up my poem *In Excelsis,* which appeared in *The London Mercury* and was afterwards published by Martin Secker.

A week before I came out of prison I started saying it to myself every night in bed so as to get it by heart. It was fortunate that I did this, as the Home Office, for reasons best known to itself, confiscated my copy-book two days before I left prison, and have refused to give it back to me, though I have twice asked them to reconsider their decision.

Prison is terrible beyond belief. It makes me indignant to read letters and articles from people who talk about " coddling " prisoners. I would like to give such people (and also most of the judges on the Bench) just what I had in the Second Division —six months, which, with remission marks, is really only five months. It is unrelieved misery all the time. I was better off in the hospital, because I had enough to eat, and was allowed as many books as I wanted. But, on the other hand, I was soon ill from want of air and exercises. You are not obliged to do any work in hospital, but many do it to kill time. It is awful to be locked up for twenty-two hours (sometimes twenty-three hours) out of every twenty-four in a tiny cell. Each day is like a month. Time passed much quicker before I went to the hospital. If I could have had the food I had in hospital, combined with the fresh air and exercise I got in the garden, I would not have complained. But it was a choice between starving on the one hand and claustration in a kennel on the other. (In a ward you may be worse off than in a cell.)

Just before I left prison, during the last week in fact, I had a return of the unreasoning panic I had had nine years before in Wormwood Scrubs. I thought they would not let me out. I was " bound over " in addition to my imprisonment, and up to the last minute the Governor received no word from the Home Office about the acceptance of my surety (Sholto Douglas again). I could see that the Governor was worried about it on my

behalf, and this terrified me.   Finally the Governor said :
" You had better write to the Home Office yourself."   I did.
I implored them not to torture me further, and to send word
that I was to be released on the day my sentence expired.
This produced the desired result, but I was in agonies to the
last day.

It took me two years to get over the effects of my imprisonment.   Soon after I got out I went abroad, first to Bruges and
then to Brussels.   I was very ill at both places, and suffered from
a kind of blood poisoning, which was due to starvation and other
things.   I am nearly well now, apart from the internal injury.

There is really nothing more to tell of my life, which at present
appears to have settled into a placid groove.   When I had somewhat recovered from the effects of my imprisonment I went
abroad a second time, with my son Raymond, who was for a
short time in the Scots Guards.   We had a very pleasant time in
Monte Carlo, and various places in France.

About this time I began to·notice, more particularly, that the
attitude of " Society," speaking generally, had changed towards
me.   All of a sudden everyone I met, wherever I went, began
to be kind and amiable.   This was entirely due to the sympathy
which my imprisonment and sufferings aroused.   The English are
like that.   They have very little imagination, and they will go
on behaving in a perfectly brutal way for years to a man, not
out of ill-nature, for really they are the most good-hearted and
kindly people *au fond*, but simply, as I say, from want of imagination and because they have never taken the trouble to find out
the facts about the man in question for themselves, but have been
hypnotized by parrot cries and mass suggestion.   Then one day
insensibly the scale tips in the other direction, probably as the
result of a long process whose details are hidden in obscurity.

I suppose the two main reasons why I have been so unkindly and harshly treated in England are that I am a Scotsman and that I am a poet. The English do not understand the Scots. They call them "mean," which is the most ludicrous libel, for the Scots, man for man, are far more generous and more hospitable, and more inclined to stick up for the under dog, and to fight for "lost causes" (supreme test of generosity) than the English. Their attitude towards the Stuarts shows this. They went on being Jacobites, and fighting and dying for the Stuarts, long after the English had got to the stage of denouncing as "traitors," and hanging, and otherwise persecuting, anyone who continued to uphold the claims of his lawful sovereign. My own direct ancestor, Sir John Douglas, was the only Douglas who was out on the right side in the '45 Jacobite Rising, and was imprisoned for two years in the Tower, and narrowly escaped being hanged.

Also the English hate poets, as long as they are alive (I mean real poets, of course ; they love sham poets and persons who recite "little things of their own" in drawing-rooms), but when real poets die the English begin to appreciate them and to get sentimental about them. This sometimes happens even while the poet is still alive. After abusing and persecuting a poet for the greater part of his lifetime they sometimes end by being quite "nice" (to use the universal English word) to him and about him. I rather hope they will go on being "nice" to me, for I admit that I am a little weary of my "thirty years' war," and I am not disinclined to take a rest and to bid farewell to the arena. The only thing that would get me "out" again would be another paper of my own, and that seems quite beyond the reach of probability.

APPENDIX

WHILE this book was actually in the press, and at the time when I was just getting the proofs, a sale by Messrs Dulau, of Old Bond Street, of a quantity of Oscar Wilde's letters was announced, and Messrs Dulau sent me a copy of the (limited to 105) special edition of their catalogue containing copious extracts from the letters. Some weeks earlier they had approached me, through my friend Mr A. J. A. Symons, and had asked and obtained from me my permission to include in their sale numerous letters of Wilde's containing references (many of them abusive and scandalous) to myself.

This permission I gave, only making the condition that Messrs Dulau's catalogue should be prefaced by the following note, which duly appears on page v of the catalogue :

" We have submitted the letters in this catalogue for examination to Lord Alfred Douglas. Lord Alfred raises no objection to their dispersal in view of their historical and self-revealing interest, and considers that his consent is sufficiently indicative of the attitude he takes up towards the references to himself which they contain."

That attitude, of course, can only be described as one of contemptuous indifference. I could have prevented the sale of these letters, with their lies and libels, and, above all, perfidious suppressions of the truth about myself, but I did not attempt to do so.

It was perhaps fortunate that I had finished writing this book, in which throughout I have endeavoured to be as kind and as generous as possible to the memory of Wilde, before I read the letters to Robert Ross written from Paris by him during the last year of his life. The perfidy and meanness of his references to myself in these letters are rather hard to forgive.

Here is an extract from one dated only " 1900 " but written evidently about the month of March :

" Frank Harris is here also Bosie. I asked Bosie what you

suggested without mentioning any sum at all—after dinner—he had just won £400 at the races—and £800 a few days before—so he was in high spirits. When I spoke to him he went into paroxysms of rage, followed by satirical laughter—and said it was the most monstrous suggestion he had ever heard—that he would do nothing of the kind—that he was astounded at my suggesting such a thing."

Not a word in the letter to hint that at the time when he made the suggestion I had already given him large sums of money and had expressed my intention of going on giving him financial assistance as long as I had any money to give him.

On the occasion to which he refers (alluded to in the course of this book) he had asked me for £2000, and I had told him that as up to that time I had received only £8000 from my father's estate, and could not expect to get more than another £6000 as my whole inheritance, and that this was all the money which I had any expectation of getting for the rest of my life, I could not possibly give him such a large sum all at once.

Before he asked me for the modest sum of £2000 I had already given him, a few moments before, two thousand francs (£80). In fact it was my gift to him of this sum which started his begging, or rather demanding, more money. What he said in effect was : "I am much obliged for this two thousand francs, but does it not occur to you that now that you have come into all this money you ought to do something substantial for me ? I think you ought to give me at least a couple of thousand pounds."

I was taken aback by his impudence, and I told him frankly that I thought his suggestion was outrageous, that I did not see any reason why he had a right, as he seemed to think he had, to look to me for financial support, but that I was, all the same, ready, as his friend, to help him, in reason, whenever I could, as I had already done.

At the time when this incident occurred I had already given him at least £200 that year.

In the letters which follow this letter of Wilde's in Dulau's catalogue right down to the time of his death there are constant references to money and constant references (often unflattering) to me.

But not once does Wilde mention that I had given him money, and was giving him money at regular intervals, as I did from the moment I inherited my small fortune right up to the day of his death.

At the time of the action for libel which I brought against Mr Arthur Ransome, in 1913, I obtained from the Piccadilly Branch of the National Provincial Bank, who were my bankers during the last year of Wilde's life, a certified copy of my passbook. It contained numerous entries relating to cheques payable to Wilde under the name, which he then went by, of Sebastian Melmoth. Altogether the amount I sent to Wilde that year in cheques (including £20 given to Ross two days after Wilde's death to pay for the funeral) amounted to £390. The entries in my passbook were put to me one by one by my counsel, and naturally counsel on the other side could make no attempt to dispute them. The first of the cheques I drew to Wilde under the name of Melmoth was in February 1900, the last was in November of the same year, a few days before his death. These cheques represented only the money I sent to him by post in ten months. In addition to this I gave him a large quantity of ready money.

During that year I was living most of the time at Chantilly, where I had my racing stable, but I was constantly coming up to Paris for a night or two, and on these occasions I invariably asked Wilde to dine with me, and as invariably gave him money. The least I ever gave him in ready money on these occasions was five hundred francs (£20), but more often it was one thousand or two thousand francs.

It is exceedingly fortunate that I happened to be living at Chantilly, and not at Paris, during this period, and that as a consequence a good deal of the money I gave to Wilde was sent to him in cheques. But for this there would be no record of my having given him anything at all, and his lies and perfidious suppressions of the truth in his letters to Ross could not have been exposed.

Ross was sitting in court during the trial of the Ransome libel action, and so was Mr More Adey, who was in close touch with his successor as literary executor to Wilde. Yet these letters of Wilde's to Ross containing his abuse of me and his mean and odious suppressions of the truth about my generosity are given to the world and to posterity without a word to annotate or correct their false witness.

Unfortunately, after the Ransome case I lost the certified copy of my bank-book, and though the dates and amounts of my cheques in favour of Wilde could be substantiated by reference to the official shorthand notes of the trial, I once more went to the bank, a few days ago, and asked the manager if he could look up the old ledgers and find for me the record of all cheques drawn to Melmoth. I was just in time, for the manager informed me that the ledgers are kept for thirty years and then destroyed, and he sent me the following list of the cheques and their dates. The variation in the name, as Melmott, Melmoth and Melnotte, is simply the result of carelessness in the clerk who copied the entries into the ledger. It will be observed that the amounts added together come to £332, and not £390. I feel pretty certain that this is simply because one cheque of £50 and another of £8 have been overlooked by the clerk who went through the old ledger, because at the time when I wrote my book, *Oscar Wilde and Myself* (in 1914), with the late T. W. H. Crosland, we both made the amount £390, and it so appears in that book. But in any case this is not a matter of great importance, the point being merely that I was continually sending cheques to Wilde, in addition to giving him considerably more in ready money, and that in all his letters to Ross he not only makes no reference whatever to this fact, but complains of my " meanness," and leaves it to be inferred (as has been inferred by all his biographers, including Frank Harris, Ross, Sherard, Davray, André Gide, and others) that I never gave him so much as a five-pound note after he came out of prison.

I append the letter I received from the manager of the National Provincial Bank and the list of the cheques drawn in Wilde's favour :

208 and 209 PICCADILLY, LONDON, W.1.
30th November 1928.

DEAR SIR,—Referring to your call on the 28th inst., we beg to hand you herewith a list of the payments made in favour of Melmott,

Melmoth or Melnotte from the 12th February 1900 to the 15th
November of the same year inclusive.

We have also traced that on the 30th April 1901 there was a
payment according to your account in favour of Ross for £20.

We trust that this is the information you require. Yours faithfully,

GEO. W. SADLER,
Deputy Manager.

LORD ALFRED BRUCE DOUGLAS

*Payments to Melmott, Melmoth or Melnotte, between February
and November* 1900

		1900		
To Melmott or Melmoth		Feb.	12	£20
,,	,,	,,	19	£125
,,	,,	,,	27	£12
,,	,,	Mch.	16	£25
Melnotte		May	10	£25
Melmott or Melmoth		June	30	£25
,,	,,	July	17	£50
,,	,,	,,		£25
,,	,,	Aug.	16	- £15
Melnotte		Nov.	15	£10
Also		1901		
Ross		Apl.	30	£20

Included in Messrs Dulau's sale is also Wilde's disgraceful letter
to Ross, written after I left him at Naples, in which, referring to
me, he says : "As soon as there was no money he left me." At
the Ransome trial Mr More Adey (Ross's most intimate friend)
gave evidence of the fact that when I was forced, against my will,
to leave Wilde at Naples, I gave him £200, which sum was paid to
More Adey on my behalf in two cheques of £100 each, drawn by
my mother and sent by Mr Adey to Wilde. Here, again, the letter
is offered for sale without a word to correct the wickedly false witness
which it bears against me.

Finally, the inspection of the letters offered for sale by Messrs Dulau has revealed a most startling and dramatic confirmation of the view expressed by me in this book that Ross played false over the MS. of the unpublished part of *De Profundis*, which is a letter to me beginning "Dear Bosie" and signed "Your affectionate friend Oscar Wilde." Here are two extracts from a letter written to Ross on 1st April 1897 from Reading Gaol containing Wilde's instructions to Ross about the disposal of this MS., which Ross has kindly "presented to the British Museum," although obviously it was never his property, and he had no right to give and the British Museum no right to receive it, because quite clearly it is my property :

"The copy done and verified from the MS. the original should be despatched to A. D. by More, and another copy done by the type-writer so that you should have a copy as well as myself."

"There is no need to tell A. D. that a copy has been taken, unless he should write and complain of injustice in the letter or misrepresentation ; then he should be told that a copy exists."

Ross kept the original manuscript for himself, and did not even send me a copy. I saw the letter for the first time in the year 1912, when it was exhibited to me at the office of Messrs Lewis & Lewis as part of the documents relating to the "Plea of Justification" put in by Ransome as his reply to my action for libel. At the same time a copy of it was sent to me by Lewis & Lewis. Up till then I had no knowledge of its existence, though no doubt Wilde imagined that I had duly received it. As is explained in this book, this complete misapprehension, due to Ross's villainy, led to our being at cross-purposes during the whole of the rest of his life after he came out of prison. Obviously he must have taken it for granted that I had received the letter, and it must have been a matter of perpetual amazement to him that my anticipated complaints about the "injustice" and "misrepresentation" in his abominable letter did not materialize. If I had received the letter, the whole course of subsequent history might have been altered. My indignation at Wilde's grotesque lies and misrepresentations, and his abuse and insults, would perhaps have cured me once for all of my infatuation for him, which still survived so strongly in those days. Again, on the other hand, it is possible, and indeed probable, that I would have forgiven him.

In any case the MS. now reposing in the British Museum quite plainly belongs to me, and I shall expect that the custodians will now hand it over to me. It would be an insult to them to suppose that they would ever have accepted it as a gift from Ross (after he had used it against me in the Ransome action) if they had known that Ross had neither a legal nor a moral right to have it in his possession at all.

INDEX

327

Y

Wilde, Lady, 113

Wilde, Mrs Oscar, 59, 60, 64, 86, 104, 159

Wilde, Oscar, 21, 24, 25, 28, 30, 33-35, 37-44, 47, 51, 56-65, 67-70, 72, 74-92, 95-124, 126-129, 132-167, 169, 180-184, 190, 192, 193, 203, 204, 209-211, 215, 234, 237, 242, 248, 249, 259, 260, 276, 281, 297, 307, 319-325

Wilde, William, 113

Wills, Mr Justice, 116

Winchester, 2, 8, 9, 17, 18, 21, 24-26, 28, 48, 49, 51, 56, 57, 193, 245

Winning Post, The, 297, 298

Wixenford, private school, 14-16

Woman of No Importance, A, 40, 86

Woodhouse, George, trainer, 168, 171-173, 178, 180, 181

Wormwood Scrubs Prison, 21, 280-285, 310-316

Worthing, 40, 86

Wyndham, Rt. Hon. George, 18, 19, 65, 68, 69, 106, 224, 237

Wyndham, Hon. Percy, 19, 20, 54, 188, 207, 255, 256

Wyndham, Madeline, Hon. Mrs Percy, 19, 48, 54

Wyndham, Percy, son of Sir Hugh, 188, 190, 191

YARMOUTH, 289

York, 54

Young, Dal, 161

PRINTED IN GREAT BRITAIN BY
LOWE AND BRYDONE (PRINTERS) LTD., LONDON.